WHERE THE MEANINGS ARE

WHERE THE MEANINGS ARE

CATHARINE R. STIMPSON

ROUTLEDGE • New York and London

First published in 1984 by Methuen, Inc.

Reprinted in 1990 by Routledge, an imprint of
Routledge, Chapman and Hall, Inc.
29 West 35th Street, New York, NY 10001
Published in Great Britain by Routledge
11 New Fetter Lane, London EC4P 4EE

Typeset in Great Britain by Nene Phototypesetters
Ltd. and printed in the United States of America

Library of Congress Cataloging in Publication Data

Main entry under title: Black literature and literary
theory. Includes index.

1. American fiction – Afro-American authors – History
and criticism – Addresses, essays, lectures.
2. African fiction (English) – Black authors – History
and criticism – Addresses, essays, lectures.
3. Caribbean fiction (English) – Black authors –
History and criticism – Addresses, essays, lectures.
4. Literature – History and criticism – Theory, etc. –
Addresses, essays, lectures.   I. Gates, Henry Louis.
PS153.N5B555   1984   813'.009'896073   84–6636

ISBN 0–416–37230–9
ISBN 0–415–90334–3 Pbk

British Library Cataloguing in Publication Data

Black literature and literary theory.
1.   English literature – Black authors – History and
criticism   2. English literature – 20th century –
History and criticism
I. Gates, Henry Louis
820.9'896   PR478.B5

ISBN 0–416–37230–9
ISBN 0–415–90334–3 Pbk

For my mother, Catharine C. Stimpson

Contents

ACKNOWLEDGMENTS   *ix*

INTRODUCTION   *xi*

1   BLACK CULTURE/WHITE TEACHER (1970)   *1*

2   "THY NEIGHBOR'S WIFE, THY NEIGHBOR'S SERVANTS":
    WOMEN'S LIBERATION AND BLACK CIVIL RIGHTS (1971)   *11*

3   WHAT MATTER MIND: A THEORY ABOUT THE PRACTICE OF
    WOMEN'S STUDIES (1973)   *38*

4   THE ANDROGYNE AND THE HOMOSEXUAL (1974)   *54*

5   ON WORK (1977)   *62*

6   TILLIE OLSEN: WITNESS AS SERVANT (1977)   *67*

7   SHAKESPEARE AND THE SOIL OF RAPE (1980)   *77*

8   AD/D FEMINAM: WOMEN, LITERATURE, AND SOCIETY
    (1980)   *84*

9   ZERO DEGREE DEVIANCY:
    THE LESBIAN NOVEL IN ENGLISH (1981)   *97*

10   THE COMPANY OF CHILDREN (1982)   *111*

11   FEMINISM AND FEMINIST CRITICISM (1983)   *116*

12   THE FEMALE SOCIOGRAPH: THE THEATER OF VIRGINIA
    WOOLF'S LETTERS (1984)   *130*

13   ADRIENNE RICH AND LESBIAN/FEMINIST POETRY (1985)   *140*

14   FEMALE INSUBORDINATION AND THE TEXT (1986)   *155*

15   A WELCOME TREATY: THE HUMANITIES IN
    EVERYDAY LIFE(1986)   *165*

16 NANCY REAGAN WEARS A HAT: FEMINISM AND ITS CULTURAL
CONSENSUS (1987)   *179*

NOTES   *197*

INDEX   *224*

ACKNOWLEDGMENTS

1. "Black Culture/White Teacher" appeared in *Change in Higher Education Magazine*, 2, 3 (1970), 35–40. Reprinted with permission of the Helen Dwight Reid Educational Foundation. Published by Heldref Publications, 400 Albemarle St., N.W., Washington, D.C. 20016. Copyright @ 1970.

2. "'Thy Neighbor's Wife, Thy Neighbor's Servants': Women's Liberation and Black Civil Rights" is from *Woman in Sexist Society: Studies in Power and Powerlessness*, edited by Vivian Gornick and Barbara K. Moran. Copyright @ 1971 by Basic Books, Inc. Reprinted by permission of the publisher.

3. "What Matter Mind: A Theory About the Practice of Women's Studies," was in *Women's Studies*, 1, 3 (1973), 293–314; "The Androgyne and the Homosexual" in *Women's Studies*, 2, 2, (1974), 237–47. Both reprinted with the permission of Gorden and Breach Science Publishers Ltd.

4. "On Work" is reprinted with the permission of its publishers from *Working It Out*, edited by Sara Ruddick and Pamela Daniels (New York: Pantheon Books, a Division of Random House, Inc., 1977), pp. 71–76.

5. "Tillie Olsen: Witness as Servant" was first in *Polit*, 1, 1 (1977), 1–12. Reprinted with permission.

6. "Shakespeare and the Soil of Rape," originally published in *The Women's Part: Feminist Criticism of Shakespeare*, edited by Carolyn Lenz, Gayle Greene, and Carol Neely (Urbana and Chicago: University of Illinois Press, 1980), pp. 56–64, is reprinted with the permission of the Press.

8. Johns Hopkins University has given permission to reprint "Ad/d Feminam: Women, Literature, and Society," from *Literature and Society: Selected Papers from the English Institute*, edited by Edward W. Said (Baltimore: Johns Hopkins University Press, 1980), pp. 174– 92.

9. The University of Chicago Press has given permission to reprint "Zero Degree Deviancy: The Lesbian Novel in English," which appeared in *Critical Inquiry*, 8, 2 (1981), 363–79; and "Nancy Reagan Wears A Hat: Feminism and Its Cultural Consensus," from *Critical Inquiry*, 14, 2 (Winter 1987), 00–00.

10. "The Company of Children" was first published in *Ms.*, 11, 1/2 (1982), 125–29. Copyright held by author.

11. "Feminism and Feminist Criticism" appeared in *Massachusetts Review*, 24, 2 (1983), 272–88. Reprinted with permission of the journal.

12. "The Female Sociograph: The Theater of Virginia Woolf's Letters," first appeared in *The Female Autograph*, edited by Domna C. Stanton (New York: New York Literary Forum, 1984), pp. 193–203. Permission to reprint given.

13. "Female Insubordination and the Text" was first published in English in *Women in Culture and Poltiics*, edited by Judith Friedlander, Blanche Wiesen Cook, Alice Kessler-Harris, and Carroll Smith-Rosenberg (Bloomington, Indiana: Indiana University Press, 1986), pp. 164–76. Reprinted with permission of publisher. Translation rights retained by Éditions Tierce, Paris.

14. The author has copyright for "Adrienne Rich and Lesbian/Feminist Poetry," which was first published in *Parnassus: Poetry in Review*, 12/13, 2/1 (Spring/Summer/Fall/Winter 1985), 249–68.

14. The Council of Chief State School Officers has granted permission for the reprint of "A Welcome Treaty: The Humanities in Everyday Life," which first appeared in *The Humanities and Civic Responsibility*, edited by Hilda Smith (Washington, D.C.: Council of Chief State School Officers, 1986), 33–47.

INTRODUCTION

Around 1861, Emily Dickinson looked at a dying day and wrote:

> "There's a certain Slant of light,
> Winter Afternoons—
> That oppresses, like the Heft
> Of Cathedral Tunes—"[1]

The shaft inflicts a "Heavenly Hurt," an awareness of despair, a glimpse of the face of death. This laser beam leaves no physical scar, but:

> " . . internal difference,
> Where the Meanings, are—"

Over a century later, another writer, Maurice Sendak, imagined a little boy named Max and a country where "the wild things are." Max is sweet, but he can scowl as well as smile. He can speak vengefully as if he were a predator and his mother Little Red Riding Hood. His name signals his divided nature. The roots of "Max" hang in the Latin word for "greatest." "Max" is also the lead-off syllable for "maxims," rules, laws, and truisms. Yet, the name has whiffs of violence. For a maxim is a machine gun and "maximite" a smokeless gun powder. One evening, Max " . . . wore his wolf suit and made mischief of one kind / and another / his mother called him 'WILD THING!' / and Max said 'I'LL EAT YOU UP!' / so he was sent to bed without eating anything."[2]

Then transformations bust up Max's bedroom. His temporary punishment cell becomes a forest, an ocean. Wolf-boy becomes the captain of a private boat. He sails to the place where the wild things are. He magically tames these terrible creatures with their claws, horns, yellow eyes, and large, scaly bodies. He has power over the powerful and freedom to do as he pleases. So blessed, in bliss, Max plays with the wild things, bays at the moon, swings from trees, lashes his tail. However, the wild things are inhuman. Max is lonely. He gives up being the king of the beasts in order to return to being a mother's beloved son. He sails home. In his room, he pulls off the hood of his wolf-suit and reclaims his nurturing regularities: a hot supper, a slice of cake, a glass of milk, the moon gazing at him through his window.

An image of a slant of cold sunlight in a poem that a childless woman of genius wrote; an image of the gleams of warm moonlight in a man's fantastic story about mothers and sons; a reminder of the interior spaces where the meanings are; a journey to a jungle where the wild things are—all these are but a few of the elements in the varied, contradictory, seemingly out-of-control collage that contemporary cultures create from past and present; but two illuminated spaces in their mixed-up mixed-use zones. In 1857, Matthew Arnold, Dickinson's English contemporary, gave "On the Modern Element in Literature," his inaugural lecture as the Professor of Poetry at Oxford. As if he were confronting an even worse collage, a country without heft but with crowds of wild things, he calls out for "intellectual deliverance" from "the spectacle of a vast multitude of facts awaiting and inviting . . . comprehension."[3]

I write now as the self-named step-daughter, and perhaps out-of-step daughter, of Arnold. That ambivalent sense of legacy, at once uncorked and bottled-up, appears in invisible ink in the essay "A Welcome Treaty: The Humanities in Everyday Life." Like Arnold, I seek "intellectual deliverance," a way in which to read collages and mottled geographies, a vision of coherence, or, at the very least, a coherent vision. I, too, am grateful for a "critical spirit" that might help us to become conscious of the frames cultures use to block out, and block, consciousness. However, Virginia Woolf and other students of ideology have warned me about such seductively lofty and appealing Arnoldian terms as "critical spirit," "human nature," and "immortal work." For these words are about illusions. They promise phenomena they cannot deliver. Each phrase points to the presence of something that does not exist, that is, a universal human or aesthetic quality that pre-dates, transcends, and will live beyond specific human histories and cultures.

So questing, so questioning, I have found feminism a space where meanings are. Here, Emily Dickinson, Virginia Woolf, and other women of language become richer, deeper, at once more enigmatic and more clear. Some naive notions of intergalactic space have described it as empty, blank, a cleaned-out vacuum. However, sharper scrutinies see forms and matter in the void. Similarly, some naive notions for our intra-global cultures project women as silent beings. If they speak, they babble. (Arnold writes only of the "man of genius.") However, feminism provides a hearing room and a reading room in which to realize how energetic women's engagements with language have been; how inventively women have strung language along. Here, too, in the space of feminism, myths about mothers and daughters spring up beside those about mothers and sons. Myths about wolves in costume lose their innocence and glamor. Here, I, as glossator, hear wild things speak—exuberantly, passionately—as women. In little Max's kingdom, wild things are at once asexual and masculine, hardly women.

Since the 1960s, feminism has split again and again until it has become feminisms, a set of groups, each with its own ideology, identity, and agenda. No matter how much they might upset each other, no matter how much they might pull apart, they can still link together, as if they were the fingers of two hands, one right, one left, both active. A feminist regard of, and sometimes regard for, cultures can display that interplay of division and unity. This book attempts to do so. Indeed, several of its articles, like "Nancy Reagan Wears A Hat," concern feminism's disagreements about culture and some handy reconciliations.

A thread of thought, with three reinforcing filaments, has sewn feminisms together and now loops through this book. Men have helped to spin this thread out, but most of the labor has been that of women, more often in far-flung groups than alone. My own work would have been lesser, and less fun, if I had not had my colleagues in the United States and elsewhere, in *ad hoc* groups and institutions.[4] A sense of group purpose has sustained us, as the Atlantic Ocean did dolphins before waste and sewage polluted it. The first filament suspiciously pokes at the common place of women in culture and commonplaces about them. The skeptical analysis of women in culture is vital because the notions of what a "woman" is, like the notions of what a "man" is, are the off-springs of culture. Neither Nature the Mother nor God the Father parents our gender systems, our posses and roundups of femininity and masculinity. Human beings, as social beings, do. As a result, the words "man" and "woman" have, not a monolithic and rock-solid meaning, but many interpretations.

This first filament of thought lights up when it touches the restrictions against women as agents of culture—in pulpits, for example, or at podiums. Why could Matthew Arnold, and not George Eliot, another formidable contemporary, be a Professor of Poetry at Oxford? It shows the absence of women from formal texts and the lack of sense about women when they do appear. Why must the Cumaean Sibyl, that prophetic voice, be so lame-brained? Why, when the god Apollo asked her what she wanted, did she request long life and then forget to ask for youth as well? Lingering on for a millenium, shrivelling to a palmful of dust in a bottle, crying for death, the Cumaean Sibyl may be a parable about the vanity of all desire. She may also be a bleak warning about the myopia of female insight.

Though this filament of thought reacts positively to logic, reason, poise, and fact, it scorns a vapid pose of neutrality. It burns bright and hot with anger because of the pain, the beatings, the rapes it documents. *Where The Meanings Are* prizes rhetorical control, the taut compression of a Dickinson line. However, controlling anger is no synonym for denying it. I sometimes describe this book as a "fencing text." First, its narrator likes to sit on the fences that demarcate fields of perception and inquiry. This position permits her to watch several of them grow, or decay, at once. It is also compatible with finding one field more fertile than another. Next, its narrator enjoys the sport of fencing. The wrestler walks naked into the ring. The fencer does not. S/he dresses defensively in padded vest, gauntlets, mask, equivalents of irony and footnotes. The wrestler struggles with another sweaty human body. The well-costumed fencer flicks out with a foil. S/he must be fast, deft, disguise strength in precision's grace. The fencer should love the choreography of the game, but that foil has its targets.

In her poem, "The Phenomenology of Anger," Adrienne Rich dramatizes anger as a necessity. This feeling is like a middle passage between suffering and healing; between passivity and activity; between fear and forgiveness. Rage and outrage inspire movements. Indeed, feminism's second filament of thought probes women's resistance to violence, injustice, and inequity, no matter how rude and inchoate that resistance might seem, no matter how hidden or trivial its sources might be. It meant something to me, as a child, that I had several card games among which to choose. One was an ordinary deck, with kings, queens, jacks, and jokers, good for rummy and baby forms of poker. Another was Old Maid, which warned me against becoming a spinster with thick eyeglasses and thin hair. However, the third game unwittingly prepared me for my later vocations. For it asked me to shuffle and deal a pack about women authors. The winner assembled the most sets, not of treys and deuces, but of the novels of Willa Cather or Louisa May Alcott.

The third filament carries the reconstruction of culture. In part, this entails changing arts, letters, and sciences to include the subjects of women and gender. This book reflects my engagements with women's studies, a transdisciplinary effort to alter all education in theory and practice; the new scholarship about women, a narrower attempt to change research and thinking; and feminist criticism, a perspective on art, literature, film, and the media.[5] Since 1969, change has happened. The number of women's studies courses in American higher education alone has grown from 16 to over 30,000. In 1973, my essay "What Matter Mind" proposed that women's studies practitioners act to get a national organization together. Within a decade, two groups (the National Women's Studies Association, the National Council for Research on Women) had formed.

In part, the reconstruction of culture demands new laws and customs; finer judgments; more spacious values; new, finer, and more spacious actions. Perhaps even more than I risk the name of blasphemer, I risk charges of Utopianism. Secular societies are more apt to scoff at soft Utopians than they are at blasphemers. Nevertheless, unabashed advocacies and longings haunt this book. They year for wilder, more palpable meanings for splendid words that we now sentimentalize, ignore, and debase. Perhaps the very challenge of the splendor of these words provokes escapes into sentimentalization, evasion, and debasement. My advocacies and longings call for faith in both a rigorous culture and democracy. They see and seek a partnering of freedom and community; independence and social justice; self-reliance and a love that commingles self-abandonment and charity.

Defining love, I print two pieces about families. In 1977, "On Work" told of a woman who likes her profession and who has rejected women's traditional tasks, those of mothering. In 1982, "The Company of Children" presents the same woman. She still likes her profession, but she now lives with another woman and helps to raise her four children. Demographic trends, the growth of "alternative families," for one, dwell at home.

Though feminist, *Where The Meanings Are* begins with a piece about black literature that never mentions feminism. Like other histories and autobiographies, this shows the temporal ordering of movements for justice in the United States. Those concerning race have preceded and influenced those concerning gender. "Black Culture/White Teacher" is about a young, white, female, non-tenured English professor in the late 1960s in a college class about black literature. Finally, for good reasons, she refuses to teach the class again. "Black Culture/White Teacher" makes grievous, ironic errors. Using the generic he, I write as if all black writers are male. This pronominial reductiveness erases black women writers and their daunting, renewing texts. One example: "The black writer, himself active, writes books about acts which call for more action."[6] Living amidst the struggle between hegemonic white and marginal black cultures, I also seem to imply that this is the only violent cultural tension in the United States.

Yet, "Black Culture/White Teacher" is a linguistic gamete, a germ cell mature enough to fuse with another gamete to form new life. Its "chromosomes" include four rough themes, at once moral convictions and critical theories, that were to help in my study of women and gender. First, the study of literature and of texts, no matter how captivating, is perverse unless outrage at the pain we inflict on each other attends that study. Next, we must celebrate, and marvel at, the ways in which people, in spite of pain, in part to spite pain, create culture. Next we may think of the literary text as "autonomous," rather as we may think of one flower as "autonomous" after we have picked it. However, no text exists in isolation. "Black Culture/White Teacher" is ignorant of the words "ideology" and "sign system," but it places a text within a context of writers and readers who ascribe and assign meaning. Finally, a complex society, like the United States in the late twentieth century, will resound with a number of voices, with diversity and variety, with dialogues and polylogues. There may be no aesthetically logical relationship, only a politically logical one, between the vitality of a voice and the judgments passed upon it.

Obviously, "Black Culture/White Teacher" is concerned with racial differences in which those differences signify, justify, and ratify one race's domination of the other, here white of black. In turn, the processes of domination themselves intensify and harden a belief in the naturalness and rightness of a system of difference in which some have power and others do not. United States culture has a number of metaphors, which this book may deploy, that picture the relationship of the powerful to the powerless. Among the more polite are those of the ladder, in which the powerful are on the top rungs, the powerless on the bottom; the circle, in which the powerful are in the centre and the powerless either on the perimeter or beyond the charmed figure altogether; or the car, in which the powerful are in the driver's seat and the powerless, at best, are passengers.

Primarily, feminism responds to sex and gender differences in which those differences signify, justify, and ratify one sex's domination of the other: male over female, men over women, masculine values over feminine. No feminist likes domination: rote, rotten, and brute authority. For a feminist, space is a location in which to roam, play, plant, and settle; not in which to bluster and bully, or, in response, to cower and huddle. However, *Where The Meanings Are* reflects and refracts a feminist argument about sexual differences that matters for both theory and practice. A "minimalist" position declares that men and women are pretty much the same. They need and deserve similar rights, opportunities, responsibilities, and joys. A "maximalist" position declares that men and women may demand similar rights and opportunities, but they are not pretty much the same. Women may have special values, a culture, and even vulnerabilities, that all of us must respect.

In law, the argument about sexual difference has appeared in the struggles about "protective legislation." In arts and letters, it emerges when critics think about the possibility of a "female language" or "female brush-stroke" or "female eye" or "female sense of space." A minimalist, like me, will suggest that it means something that Virginia Woolf, as she dashed off a letter, was a woman. However, exactly what it means depends on her time, place, languages, and circumstance. On the other hand, a maximalist might read in Woolf's syntax, rhythms, and alphabets a "femaleness," a nature, that unifies women in all their times, places, languages, and circumstance.

Sophisticated though the arguments about sex and gender difference can be, they edge towards an error in which failures of logic, perception, and behavior can compound together. This error is clinging to binary oppositions. At their most benign, binary oppositions over-simplify categorizing as the missionary position does sex. At their most malign, translated into an active belief in "Good Us, Bad Them, Praise Us, Get Them," binary oppositions damage the interests of survival itself.

Obviously, binary oppositions have structured much of Western thought. They usefully exist in some processes of consciousness and, perhaps, occasionally, in "nature." However, the bind of binary oppositions can blind us to complexities. Indeed, that can be their purpose during an anguished search for certainties. Think of a poet who has haunted me since I first read him, Gerard Manley Hopkins. In "Spelt from Sibyl's Leaves," he cries for life to wind "Off her once skeined stained veined variety . . . " and to wind around but two spools, to pack " . . . her all in two flocks, two folds— black, white; right / wrong; reckon . . . mind / But these two . . . "[7] Part of the importance to feminist thinking of Simone de Beauvoir's *The Second Sex* is how thoroughly she investigates the patterned ways in which men have traditionally bred the meanings of "man" through setting up a bipolar distinction between "man" and "woman" and then insisting that man is what woman is not: sun to her moon, wildness to her domesticity, etc., etc.

As obviously, people often confront a choice between one of two alternatives. Either a legislator votes for parental leave, or s/he does not. Either a tennis-player serves an ace to win a tie-breaker, or s/he does not. However, to assume too frequently that we must choose between one of two ways of acting erases social and psychological possibilities. Marring contemporary debates about the humanities is a rigid insistence that transmitting the humanities can *either* reflect the principle of "excellence" (a word that misuse has so inflated that it lacks the currency of meaning) *or* the principle of "equity" (a word that misuse has so deflated that it lacks the meaning of currency), but never both principles.

Reconstituting the patterns de Beauvoir exposes, reductive feminist thinking describes the world too exclusively as a binary opposition between female/male, man/woman. Shuttling between the spools of the two sexes limits our movements among the skeins and veins of the countless differences among women that race, class, age, tribe and nation, age, and creed produce. "Tillie Olsen: Witness as Servant" gazes at the gap between rich and poor. A persistent theme of *Where The Meanings Are* is the literature of differences (Adrienne Rich poems, lesbian novels) that sexual preference, that confluence of eros and power, creates. Too often, as we know, the differences among women are the result of great, invidious divisions among groups. Many women suffer from these killing discriminations, but other women sustain them. The differences between an anti-Semitic Christian woman and a Jewish woman can be far more murderous than those between a Christian man and woman; the differences between a racist white woman and a woman of color can be far more murderous than those between a white woman and white man.

One inoculation against these moral, social and cultural viruses is to think the differences among women through seriously, to respect some, to reject and fight against others. In *Where The Meanings Are*, this remedy increasingly becomes part of a larger hope: that understanding the differences among women (which I name, without much syllabic lightness, "herterogeneity") will become a laboratory of care in which we can understand socially-constructed differences in general. Such a hertero-geneous laboratory demands a receptive consciousness, akin to the negative capability that Keats demanded of the poet. This mind must be wary as well as open, for it must avoid an error of proud Western empathy that fuses voyeurism, emotional greed, and appropriation: to pal around with others as if they were the Exotic Other and to presume warm, loving feelings between Self and this delicious, sensational Not-Self.

Social differences among groups are the cause, consequence, co-existent, and co-inefficient of other sorts of difference. *Where The Meanings Are* is often about literature and the contrasting, shifting states of mind and feeling that literature presumably figures out. For Dickinson, the price of the "internal difference" between not-knowing and knowing, between oblivion and consciousness of oblivion, is pain. For other women writers, such an "internal difference" is a prelude to action. The abolition of ignorance tears up quack prescriptions for quaaludes of the will. For still other writers, psychoanalysis graphs the internal differences that create meaning among ego, superego, and id; between our "conscious life" and our unconscious being and its doings.

In the last pages of *Where the Meanings Are*, the definition of "internal difference" takes a linguistic as well as a psychological turn. I am no philosopher of language, nor a skilled technician of the text. I am, instead, a humming, drumming writer, critic, and organizer who wants her material and moral world to be different than it is. Yet, like everyone else, I have had my crude notions of what language is and does. My notions mutter that languages are well-regulated, but arbitrary, systems that are less the "revelation" or "expression" of reality and more the producer-directors of realities. In part, these systems do their job, to give us our daily meaning, through combining, recombining, and dealing with their internally different elements. Similarly, the spirals of DNA are a structured arena within which four chemicals— those siblings of adenine, cytosine, thymine, and guanine— play with and against each other's differences to assemble life's prolific forms. Of course, culture/language names our genetic endowment, not the other way around. DNA and ACT and G may be the letter of the current law of molecular biology, but they are letters first.

A question without the closure of a certain answer opens up the last pages of *Where The Meanings Are*. How are we to write on the space of an interleaf between two pre-existing pages? One, the more powerful, the better read, tells of a feminism that uses language to change the moral and material world and to empower women as human agents. The second page, now being inked in, tells of a theory that, like feminism, believes in the potency of language and ideology, of discourse. Our languages may, or may not, be the course of Dis, the god of the underworld. However, unlike feminists, this theory is agnostic, even atheistic, about language's referential powers and about a human agent's control of those powers. How, on such an interleaf, are we to parse this: "Women are the subjects of the sentence of their lives." How are we to publish both a political program and a deconstruction of the word "program"?

The mere presence of this question places *Where The Meanings Are* within the boundaries of post-modernism, a word that the historian Arnold Toynbee may have invented. For some, "post-modernism" is but modish jargon; for others, a catch word, even a catch-as-catch-can word, with which to name the late twentieth century in the West. I am more sympathetic with the latter entry. For me, "post-modern," which replaces "post-structuralism" in *Where The Meanings Are*, is a tent of a word. We gather beneath the canvas to rehearse and perform acts that partake of both the circus and a survival course: coming to terms with "our time."

The post-modernism of *Where The Meanings Are* assumes that "the modern world" and "modernism" have taken place in many societies. The blast furnaces of industrialism have been built. Indeed, their fires are going out. Post-modernism watches capital float across national boundaries, and labor crawl from industrial to service jobs, which admit women as skimpily rewarded members of the public labor force. Culturally, Picasso and Matisse are sales for auction houses, blockbusters for museums, and booty for thieves. Joyce is a professional scholar's stock-in-trade. Post-modernism distrusts the hierarchical; the authoritarian; fixed codes (at once stable and rigged) that race, class, gender impose upon behavior; and the theory that language's own fixed code represents reality. Post-modernism submits two schemata to cognitive therapy: those old binary oppositions and the more modern focus, at once political and scientific, on the apparently isolated object. Post-modernism prefers to sense patterns, connections, relationships. It responds to ironies, ambiguities, open ends, multiple perspectives. The post-modernist can see, simultaneously, on a split screen, pictures of the same piece of New York State territory on the Richter Scale, in a Hudson River Valley School painting, on a TV program about riverine pollution, and in a Sally Ride photograph taken from a space shuttle. The post-modernist also realizes that this paragraph is but one image of post-modernism.

Where The Meanings Are tells, then, of some of the arguments within feminism during the re-designing and designing of cultural spaces. No matter how icy or salty those quarrels can be, they are often sweet reason itself in comparison to some of the opposition that the new thinking about women and gender has stimulated. Some of the negative voices that

Where The Meanings Are records are fearful of any cultural and educational change. Their owners hold the silver cross of tradition before the werewolf of new syllabi. Other voices, unknowingly demonstrating the truth of a feminist analysis, argue that the subjects of women and gender are too trivial for grown-up consideration. Still other voices declare that feminism and thought are natural enemies. As saturated in ideology as any speaker, these voices nevertheless find feminist thinkers, those old nags, neigh-saying on the bias.

After the election of Ronald Reagan in 1980, two more sets of voices have even more vigorously pitched and blended in. One, fundamentalist theology, swears its allegiance to a sacred text, for Christians the Holy Bible. For such theologicians and believers, feminism *is* blasphemy. Indeed, only a revisionary theology can reconcile feminist thinking and our hegemonic monotheisms. The second set of voices, neo-conservative, finds feminist analyses both wrong in themselves and symptomatic of the wrongs of liberalism. Putatively entrenched in higher education and the media, liberalism has wreaked havoc. Educators prefer shreds and patches of culture to "great books" and "eternal values." We have, not cultural literacy, but cultural litteracy.

I have been lucky. Sticky words, telling silences, and bureaucratic maneuverings have been the chief weapons that people have used against the narrative voice of *Where The Meanings Are*. I have been the child of a century of violence. I have seen the broken teeth of battered women whom I love. I have known survivors from regions beyond imagination's reach. Yet, despite my differences and deviancies, I have been physically secure. Class, race, and the education my family offered me have protected me. Although written from that security, *Where The Meanings Are* is a plea against the violence and scarcities, the cruel wildness and afflictions, the "seal of despair," of its century. It is a plea, too, for such pleas to mean enough to work, here, in the space of this world.

Each part of *Where The Meanings Are* has had audiences, readers, provokers, and supporters, whom I thank and whom I cherish. Each part has taken oxygen from the environments of the new scholarship about women. I am especially grateful for consistency of counsel from Arlyn Diamond, Lee Edwards, Judith Friedlander, William Germano, Carolyn Heilbrun, Elizabeth Janeway, Myra Jehlen, Herbert Leibowitz, Nancy K. Miller, Marysa Navarro, Martha Nelson, Marjorie Perloff, Jean Sacks, Domna C. Stanton, Ruth Sullivan, and Marilyn B. Young. I have been happily at home with Elizabeth Wood and with Kirsten, Kate, Sarah, and Sandy. Finally, Ms. Scheinberg and Ms. Johnston were impeccable in their assistance in preparing *Where The Meanings Are* for press.

1   BLACK CULTURE/WHITE TEACHER
(1970)

Most white people misread black literature, if they read it at all. Their critical twistings are still another symptom of the dominant attitude toward black people and black culture in America. The white ego insists upon control. Not only do white readers demand that black literature satisfy their needs and notions, but they literally read it according to them. They have trouble, to paraphrase James Baldwin, getting off its back.

Some readers use black literature politically—to condemn Western history and white racism, and to earn credit from a would-be revolutionary future. An Eldridge Cleaver becomes their surrogate rebel leader: bombastic, schematic, vicious to homosexuals, unfair to white women, but a rhetorical broom for change. Exploiting black writers, such readers evade responsibility: applauding an outraged minority takes the place of dealing with a disagreeable silent majority.

Other white readers, even the most sophisticated of them, use black literature emotionally—for kicks, for a "primitive" energy lost or missing from their own lives. In Ralph Ellison's words, they "seem to feel that they can air with impunity their most private Freudian fantasies as long as [the fantasies] are given the slightest camouflage of intellectuality and projected as 'Negro.' They have made of the no-man's-land created by segregation a territory for infantile self-expression and intellectual anarchy." Unfortunately, these readers go on to dismiss their black savants of the nitty-gritty at their whim. They make one race both sage and scapegoat. The brief history of white affection for black writers during the Harlem Renaissance in the 1920s is a paradigm of such behavior.

Still other readers use black literature for intellectual capital. Some, for example, read it as evidence that an alien culture supports the ideas and values of the dominant culture. To these people, the black writer may be a rengade and prophet, but the vision he forges in the smithy of his soul is a familiar one. Such readers, though, find the new black voices confusing. Others use black writing to dig out information about an alien culture. They recognize that some black writers, like Ellison, work with symbols, but usually they think of black artists as naturalists, and they look to them for reports about a scene they could themselves never view. Yet their sense of naturalism does not coincide with true black naturalism—the kind, for instance, of Ed Bullins, the playwright; white commentators, like Walter Kerr, call them rhetorical, overblown, or inaccurate.

Some readers, of course, have more than one of these tendencies. When Robert Bone says, "Like any other artist, the Negro novelist must achieve universality through a sensitive interpretation of his own culture," he is insisting that black literature be a document which conforms to Bone's own critical ideology.[1] The white readers of black literature have a good deal in common. The pressure of the past, fear, and vanity make them like protest fiction, which, no matter how grim or didactic, appeals to them. It says that to be black is to be miserable: being black is worse than being white. Protest fiction massages guilt. *If I read Native Son, I must be all Right.* It titillates a sense of justice. *If I read Native Son, my moral faculties are alert.* It offers an underworld tour. *If I read Native Son, I'm really getting data about tenements and rats.* Protest themes, like those of "passing" or of the tragic mulatto, also flatter whites. Black murderer Bigger Thomas may be the putative protagonist of *Native Son*, and murderous white capitalism the villain, but the hero is Max: a lawyer, a white.

My ideas about black literature were put together in an urban college classroom the color of a stale yellow legal pad. I was teaching a course called "Books and the Black Experience in America." There were twenty-five students, all girls, mostly middle class, nineteen of them white, six black, all of them sitting tensely together. History has made geniality improbable.

I would prefer not to teach that class again. White people at the moment have neither the intellectual skill nor the emotional clarity nor the moral authority to lead the pursuit of black studies. Race, to the dismay of many, to the relief of others, has become a proper test for deciding who is best at certain intellectual, as well as political, activities, and teaching black literature is one of them.

I want to keep reading black literature, though. What matters is reading it accurately. And doing that demands a new, practical, literary theory for white people.

White readers cling to mutually contradictory stereotypes: the Black as Militant; the Black as Struggling, Suffering Sacrifice; the Black as Sambo; the Black as Beast; the Black as White (Almost); the Black as the Hot Time in the Old Bed Tonight. This confusion marks not simply the ordinary jumble of the human mind but an oppressive mode of reading based on contempt. It reveals white ignorance about the idiosyncrasies, the idioms, the intricacy, and the integrity of the black experience. Whites, trying to dispel their ignorance, often become patronizing or politically desperate.

One day a black student came to my office. "I can't take that girl any longer," she said, naming an earnest but naïve and bossy white student.

"I'm tired of being asked how I do my Afro and how I dance."

"Come on," I said, *"she doesn't really say those things, does she?"*

She did.

In class the next day a white student asked the black students, "How does it feel to be black?" An attractive and highly intelligent black senior replied, "I'm here to learn, not to educate you."

The white students were angered. They had assumed the privilege of instant understanding. "How can we learn if you don't tell us?"

'Try reading the books," they were told.

White witlessness about the black oral tradition is a particular source of misreading. Whites tend to ignore, despise or steal from rich, figurative black speech. Or they call it the language of the ghetto, the deprived, the folk. Yet black literature uses it in addition to the more conventional American public speech. Black language seems neither esoteric, like the mumbo-jumbo of a cult; nor heavy, like interoffice memoranda; nor jargonish, like faculty chitchat. Rather, it seems subtle, precise, vibrant. Its speaker, as much leader or performer as speaker, possesses both formal oratorical power as spontaneous wit. Often the word is part of a stylized game, like the dozens, or of a dramatic pattern, like the call-and-response. Perhaps the deep structure of black language is African. Certainly its texture reflects the slave experience in America:

> When black people were brought to America [Mike Thelwell, the black writer, says] they were deprived of their language and of the underpinnings in cultural experience out of which a language comes. It is clear that they developed two languages, one for themselves and another for the white masters. . . . The only vestiges we can find of the real language of the slaves are in the few spirituals which have come down to us. . . . It is a language produced by oppression, but one whose central impulse is survival and resistance. . . . It depends on what linguists call para-language; that is, gesture, physical expression and modulation of all cadences and intonation which serve to change the meaning—in incredibly subtle ways—of the same collection of words. It is intensely poetic and expressive.[2]

Nor are white readers blind and deaf only to the linguistic complexity of black literature. Their ignorance of the realities of American history is equally troublesome. They know George Washington, George Wallace, and precious little in between. Free falling in the intellectual emptiness are some myths, called history, and some illusions, called myth. Such American ahistoricity is a paradox. Americans tend to be possessive; they like to get, to keep, and get more of things; possessive people are usually conservative; conservative people usually study history—they feel they are clutching time itself. The American distaste for even an informal knowledge of the past may be defensive. Certainly it protects most white readers from grasping the bloodier experiences which black literature reflects, the daily effort it has made to preserve and to transform itself, the many ironic strategies it successfully deploys, and the intensity of the moral passion it so frequently emits.

My class was reading Frederick Douglass's Narrative of his life to 1845. Most of the white students had a strange notion of slavery. Many still seemed to believe in Tara. "Where were you all those years you were going to school?" a black student finally asked. "When you saw those pictures of the cotton fields, who'd you think all those people were out there in those handkerchiefs?"

Another day we were reading Booker T. Washington's autobiography, Up from Slavery which includes his famous address to the Atlanta Exposition in 1895. There the ambiguous, proud, wily leader praised white strength and black labor. To white cheers and black silence he promised law, order and social segregation. We called Booker T. a disaster, an Uncle Tom. But a black student contradicted us. "Booker T. knew what he was doing," she said. "He was speaking in Atlanta. He was running a school in the Black Belt just after Reconstruction. He was doing what he had to do to keep his people alive."

One of the more romantic modern myths makes the artist a prophet. He lightens our dark corners, bears witness to suffering, and rebukes vulgarity and evil. But most whites who write about blacks betray the myth: far too often they are accomplices of racism. Some white writers, to be sure, are more honorable than others. Lillian Smith is more compassionate than the repellent Margaret Mitchell, Harriet Beecher Stowe more righteous than Thomas Dixon, a P.R. man for the Ku Klux Klan. However, even the best of black characters created by white writers function within white contexts. They objectify white notions, values, ambitions, theatricalities, anxieties, and besetting fears. William Styron's Nat Turner—Dark Hued Screw-Up, Vengeful then Repentant Onanist, Lusting after White Flesh—dramatizes not black rebellion but Styron's quasi-Freudian, quasi-existential vision of history. As white writers bear down upon their black characters, they seem to impose a weight that is heavier and more masterful than the one they commonly impose. Further, they betray a liberal function of art: to take into strict account the otherness of others.

White ideas about black literature are more than private fancies. They are also embedded in public institutions which, if more open today than they once were, are still relatively closed to black people. (The *American Literary Anthology*, to take one example, which has government support, publishes some black writers, but it has neither black editors nor black judges.) For moral, psychological, political, aesthetic and practical reasons, many blacks have written to influence or to please those institutions. They have made much of their work conform to white expectations. White audiences have been able to let their errors about black people harden into habit. Black audiences have often been alienated. This is, in part, what Arna Bontemps means when he says, ". . . the Negro reader has little taste for any art in which the racial attitudes of the past are condoned or taken for granted. . . . This is what he has come to expect in the fiction in which he sees himself."

Paul Laurence Dunbar, born in 1872, died a tubercular drunk in 1906. The first professional black writer in America, he was economically dependent on a white audience. He wrote two kinds of poetry: traditional formal verse, which he liked, and Negro dialect verse, which he sold. He used white culture to describe his own black experience, and black culture to describe a white notion of black experience. Skilfully, if unhappily, he mirrored for his audience their deluded fantasies of an old South in which the masters were benevolent and the happy, happy darkies wished Mistah Lincum would "tek his freedom back." Dunbar's white patron, William Dean Howells, reveals how whites treat black writers. In an introduction for Dunbar, Howells dismisses the traditional verse, but he praises the dialect poems:

> . . . divinations and reports of what passes in the hearts and minds of a lowly people whose poetry has hitherto been inarticulately expressed in music, but now finds, for the first time in our tongue, literary interpretation of a very artistic completeness.

Many of Howells's phrases, such as "our tongue," are beguiling: Big Massa will bless Emerging Talent, if the price is right. Howells was perhaps the first to make a black writer a "vogue," to borrow a term from Langston Hughes. Ironically, some of the most insidious harm white readers have done to black literature has been through excessive praise of one person. Nearly every decade has had one (and rarely more than one) house nigger in the library of art. To him all praises flow. *Look*, white readers say, *that boy sure can write.*

Obviously, not every black writer writes for the white audience. Many new, brilliant black writers, like some of their ancestors of the Harlem Renaissance, work for blacks. They ignore the whites, whose needs and pleasures they find irrelevant at best. The whites then feel rejected. (It is unlikely that whites, no matter how much they read, will ever really share the new black consciousness.) Other black writers, like many whites, shrug off the separation of readers into racial camps. Some think it contrary to the spirit of art; others think it contrary to the spirit of integration. Still others believe that education, geography, taste and class divide readers more accurately than color. Still others say the whole question is of only momentary urgency. In a while, they claim, asking for whom Chester Himes wrote *Pinktoes* will have the same urgency as asking for whom Shakespeare wrote *Macbeth*— King James or the boys down at the Globe.

Yet the black writer's conception of his audience influences his writing as pressure does mercury. (I suspect that black literature falls into two categories: books written mostly for blacks and books written mostly for whites—which must often include explanatory detail about black customs.) When the writer takes his audience seriously, he assumes his work will *do* something, not as a crystal ball hanging in the void, but as a force for better or worse which has been someplace and is going somewhere. White readers generally overlook this purposeful quality of black literature. Yet breaking the back of colonialism and liberating a people call for a literature of content, and literary questions become more than exercises. Answering them means resolving political, racial and ethical problems. For the black writer today it also means being accountable to the black community. As Eldridge Cleaver has said, "The next group we [the Panthers] are going to have to move against . . . are these black writers. . . . Before it wasn't important what they wrote because black people weren't reading what they said anyhow. But now black people are reading and it's important what is being written."

One morning I extravagantly praised Black Boy *as a narrative of rebellion, exile and flight. "I can't accept what you say," a black student said. "Richard Wright debases black people. He has no sense of the community. How can you fall all over* Black Boy *when it has passages like this: '. . . after the habit of reflection had been born in me, I used to mull over the strange absence of real kindness in Negroes, how unstable was our tenderness, how lacking in genuine passion we were, how void of great hope, how timid our joy, how bare our traditions, how hollow our memories, how lacking we were in those intangible sentiments that bind man to man, and how shallow was even our despair'?"*

How indeed should we judge a book? Because of its "art" or because of its attitude toward black people? Is a book a thing or a gesture, a "being" or a "doing"? Are the laws of literature those of craft or of ideology? Can some alchemy of the intellect reconcile the two? What is the best source of black literature—Western and American civilization, of which black culture is a part, or African civilization, from which black culture has been ripped? What matters more—free sensibility for an elite, or sensible freedom for a race?

The best questions for white readers to ask themselves about black literature are those of fact. They must call a moratorium on their normative judgments. Biases, like rodents on the ropes between ship and pier, run up and down their statements about value. They should also end all but the most tentative kind of descriptive criticism. The ignorance, the failures that make normative criticism arrogant make descriptive criticism inaccurate. The white reader who assumes that he can usefully say whether a black writer is "good" or "bad" is likely to be enough out of touch with present realities to make his analysis of that writer suspect.

Too many white readers, whether they claim to be experts or not, persist in applying the old vocabulary of art to the new forces of black literature. The pricklier writers, like LeRoi Jones, are particularly abused. Only a few critics look directly at Jones, his work, and his concept of black revolutionary cultural nationalism. More people, hiding behind literary traditions, label his work shapeless, chaotic, too mean and too dirty to make sense, or to make his sense acceptable. (One puzzling thing about black literature, of course, is not its homicidal rage, but the lack of it.) Such criticism is actually personal (*Jones scares me but I can't admit that*), political (*Jones is revolutionary and I can't stand for that*), or social (*Jones is unmannerly and I won't stand for that*). The tools of literary criticism thereby become weapons of reprisal, and art itself the victim.

American speech fails to describe our racial agony. Not only is speech untrustworthy because people and institutions have misused it in the past, but its grammatical structure is inadequate. We lack, for example, a pronoun to portray our false collectivity, and *we* to summarize a phony *we-ness*. No vocabulary exists to describe black literature.

Nor do we possess a body of theory, one which is neither adventitious nor malign, that might give order to its contradictions and subtleties and flux. The neglected black critics provided only the beginnings. Black artists are now carrying on with the job. Only blacks can create such a theory. A white attempt to do so, no matter how earnest, will be morally unacceptable. The odds are that it would also be impractical. Besides, a black aesthetic will doubtless explore the relationship between writing and revolutionary politics. Since a common principle of black revolutionary politics is the need for black self-determination, it would be obviously inconsistent for a white person to make critical, authoritative comments.

In the meantime, white Americans should read black literature. They can work to put black writers on reading lists and in libraries. They can support magazines, publishing houses, and theaters which blacks control. Plenty of informed black opinion exists to help white people make intelligent guesses about which black groups serve elements in the black community. White readers must also accept black authority of interpretation. If they speak about black literature, they should speak as informally, as personally, as possible. We have already had enough formal, impersonal white authorities on black literature. And if some of us must teach it (and for deplorable reasons we will probably have to help teach it for a while), the best teaching might well be unorthodox teaching: talk to white students about why they may not always understand, let black students work together if they choose, and never assume that teaching black literature is the road either to salvation or happiness.

For white readers to *like* black writers who threaten them with violence is pathological. Either such readers are masochists who enjoy death warrants; or disbelievers who assume that black writers are simply playing around; or fools who think that the menacing black gesture will never touch them. Yet white readers will find much they might legitimately like. Nearly all black literature emanates an unusual energy. While speaking of murderous times, it proclaims existence. It works with expansive themes: escape, endurance, conflict, the need for dignity, the nature of power. Indeed, it offers white readers the best analysis of white power. Refusing to kowtow to the sacred cows, it dissects the diseases of the American body politic.

Notions of identity are particularly complex in black literature. They are bound up with concepts of freedom: seeking one demands seeking the other; having one means having the other. Much of the writing concerns the agony between the life white people impose upon blacks and a black's private self. Many black characters struggle until the fight consumes them, and they are sacrificed. Many white writers, to be sure, also dramatize the quest for self; but their characters often repudiate the family. For black characters the question of blood is more difficult. Are they black or partly white? If blood is mixed, how should one respond? Like the child of a master class? Like the whelp of rape? Or with indifference? No black character can ignore the family. Many of the best affirm it. So doing, they make family and community, blood and race, near synonyms of speech and feeling. The poet Nikki Giovanni writes, "Black love/is Black Wealth."

Autobiography is a suspect genre. Not only does its subjectivity cast doubt on objectivity (even if desirable) about the self and others, but the form itself blurs distinctions between the two: the subject may claim for himself the experience of others. Nor can specific autobiographies be trusted. Some, like those of Booker T. Washington, are crafted to advance public goals: to impress blacks, to please whites, to exemplify black progress, to pledge allegiance to white safety. Yet black autobiographies, including the slave narratives, are unique statements about identity. They appeal because they so little conceal. The black writers, I suspect, are more conscious of their origins and their lives than white writers. As they describe their own lives they also describe a territory and time of history.

Black writing, despite its seriousness, is more than a Literature of Solemnity. Much of it has what Clarence Major calls "radiance." Fantasies, excursions into inner space, are bold and ingenious. Explorations of the supernatural, excursions into cosmic space, are rich and convincing. Wit, both defensive and offensive, is acid and flamboyant. Comedy efficiently exposes individuals and society. A boy, publishing in the journal *What's Happening* and signing himself "Clorox," is on to himself, and others as well.

Black poetry offers complex drama, and intricate new rhythms, syntax and diction. This is Don L. Lee's, "We Walk the Way of the New World":

> we run the dangercourse.
> the way of the stocking caps & murray's grease.
> if (u is modern u used duke greaseless hair pomade)
> jo jo was modern/ an international nigger
>   born: jan. 1, 1863 in new york, mississippi.
> his momma was mo militant than he was/is
> jo jo bes no instant negro
> his development took all of 106 years
> & he was the first to be stamped "made in USA"
> where he arrived bow-legged a curve ahead of the
>   20th century's new
> weapon: television.
> which invented, "how to win and influence people"
> and gave jo jo his how/ever look; however u
>   want me.
>
> we discovered that with the right brand of cigarettes
> that one, with his best girl,
> cd skip thru grassy fields in living color
> & in slow-motion: Caution: niggers, cigarettes
>   smoking
>   will kill u & yr/health.
> & that the breakfast of champions is: blackeye peas
>   & rice.
>
> & that God is dead & jesus is black and last seen
>   on 63rd street
>   in a gold & black dashiki, sitting in a pink hog
>   speaking swahili with a pig-latin accent.
> & that integration and coalition are synonymous,
> & that the only thing that really mattered was:
>   who could get the highest on the least or
>   how to expand & break one's mind.
>
> in the coming world
> new prizes are
> to be given
>
> we *ran* the dangercourse.
> now, it's a silent walk/ a careful eye
> jo jo is there

to his mother he is unknown
(she accepted with a newlook: what wd u do if
   someone loved u?)
jo jo is back
& he will catch all the new jo jo's as they wander
   in & out
and with a fan-like whisper say: you ain't no
                    tourist
                    and Harlem ain't for
                    sight-seeing, brother.[3]

Black plays demand a vital relationship between actors and audience, which is also participant and chorus. Black novels promise acute characterization. (In contrast, twentieth-century white novels tend to cultivate a single sensibility, to lavish imaginative energy upon the ego in solitude.) Creating characters means not only focusing the imagination upon others, but also detecting psychological fraud, sniffing out the gap between illusion and reality, between word and deed: these gifts exist in abundance in black literature. White American writers often reduce strong women characters to bitches or big-booted, big-boobed, loutish Tugboat Annies. Black writers, if they avoid the temptation to assign outworn sex roles within a rigid nuclear family, give their women characters respect.

Flexible yet structured, like a blues performance, black literature organizes human experience for the sake of experience, vitality and consolation. It reflects a sense of ritual which is both sacred, for addressing the gods, and profane, for addressing the people. In contrast, the official rituals of white America seem metallic. Either they celebrate death (the medal ceremonies in the Rose Garden) or technology (the rocket launchings).

The black writer, himself active, writes books about acts which call for more action; when he does, he is the model of the man of letters. White people, if they read black literature properly, must eventually rebel against their own world, the world which the books reveal: to do nothing but read is to be evasive, to do nothing but speak is to be unspeakable. The end of theory is the call to practice.

2

"THY NEIGHBOR'S WIFE, THY NEIGHBOR'S SERVANTS": WOMEN'S LIBERATION AND BLACK CIVIL RIGHTS 1971

> Thou shalt not covet thy neighor's house, thou shalt not covet thy neighbor's wife, nor his manservant, nor his maidservant, nor his ox, nor his ass, nor anything that is thy neighbor's.
>
> Tenth Commandment

The optimism of politics before a revolution is exceeded only by the pessimism of politics after one. One current optimistic theory sees all the oppressed classes of America joining together to storm the citadel of their oppressor. Black liberation and women's liberation as movements, blacks and white women as people, will fight together. I respect black liberation, and I work for women's liberation, but the more I think about it, the less hope I have for a close alliance of those who pledge allegiance to the sex and those who pledge allegiance to the skin. History, as well as experience, has bred my skepticism.

That blacks and women should have a common enemy, white men and their culture, without making common cause is grievous, perhaps. They even have more in common than an enemy. In America they share the unhappy lot of being cast together as lesser beings. It is hardly coincidence that the most aggressively racist regions are those most rigidly insistent upon keeping women in their place, even if that place is that of ornament, toy, or statue. Of the ten states that refused to ratify the Nineteenth Amendment, giving women the vote, nine were southern. The tenth was Delaware. Gunnar Myrdal, in a brief appendix to *An American Dilemma*, his massive study of American blacks, tersely analyzed this peculiar national habit. Both blacks and women are highly visible; they cannot hide, even if they want to. A patriarchal ideology assigns them several virtues; blacks are tough; women fragile. However, the same patriarchal ideology judges them *naturally* inferior in those respects that carry "prestige, power, and advantages in society."[1] As Thomas Jefferson said, even if America were a pure democracy, its inhabitants should keep women, slaves, and babies away from deliberations. The less education women and blacks get, the better; manual education is the most they can have. The only right they possess is the right, which criminals, lunatics, and idiots share, to love their divine subordination within the *pater familias* and to obey the paterfamilias himself.

The development of an industrial economy, as Myrdal points out, has not brought about the integration of women and blacks into the adult male culture. Women have not found a satisfactory way both to bear children and to work. Blacks have not destroyed the hard doctrine of their unassimilability. What the economy gives both women and blacks are menial labor, low pay, and few promotions. White male workers hate both groups, for their competition threatens wages and their possible job equality, let alone superiority, threatens nothing less than the very nature of things. The tasks of women and blacks are usually grueling, repetitive, slogging, and dirty. After all, people have servants, not simply for status, but for doing what every sensible person knows is unappetizing.

Blacks and women also live in the wasteland of American sexuality, a world which, according to W. E. B. DuBois, one of the few black men to work for women's emancipation, "tries to worship both virgins and mothers and in the end despises motherhood and despoils virgins."[2] White men, convinced of the holy primacy of sperm, yet guilty about using it, angry at the loss of the cozy sanctuary of the womb and the privilege of childhood, have made their sex a claim to power and then used their power to claim control of sex. In fact and fantasy, they have violently segregated black men and white women. The most notorious fantasy claims that the black man is sexually evil, low, subhuman; the white women sexually pure, elevated, superhuman. Together they dramatize the polarities of excrement and disembodied spirituality. Blacks and women have been sexual victims, often cruelly so: the black man castrated, the woman raped and often treated to a psychic clitoridectomy.

These similarities in the condition of blacks and women add up to a remarkable consistency of attitude and action on the part of the powerful toward the less powerful. Yet for a white woman to say, "I've been niggerized, I'm just a nigger, all women are niggers," is vulgar and offensive. Woman must not usurp the vocabulary of the black struggle. They must forge their own idiom by showing how they are, for instance, "castrated" by a language and a tradition that makes manhood, as well as white skin, a requisite for full humanity.

Women's protest has followed black protest, which surged up under the more intense and brutal pressure. Antislavery movements preceded the first coherent woman's rights movement, black male suffrage, woman's suffrage, the civil rights movement, the new feminism. For the most part, white women have organized, not after working *with* blacks, but after working *on behalf* of them. Feminism has received much of its impetus from the translation of lofty, middle-class altruism into the more realistic, emotionally rugged salvation of the self.

The relationship between black rights and woman's rights offers an important cautionary tale, revealing to us the tangle of sex, race, and politics in America. It shows the paradox of any politics of change: we cannot escape the past we seek to alter, any more than the body can escape enzymes, molecules, and genes. As drama, the story is fascinating. Blacks and white women begin generous collaborations, only to find themselves in bitter misalliance. At crucial moments, the faith of one in the other changes into doubt. High principles become bones of contention and strategies violate high principles. The movements use each other, betray each other, and provoke from each other abstract love and visceral hostility. The leaders are heroic—men and women of great bravery, resilience, intellectual power, eloquence, and sheer human worth whose energy is that of the Christians and the lions together. And the women of the nineteenth century, except for their evangelical Christianity, sexual reticence, and obsequious devotion to marriage, the family, home, or at least to heterosexuality, worked out every analysis the new feminism is rediscovering.

Unhappily, whenever white radical men control the agencies of black liberation, their feelings about women are unwittingly first-class tools in making feminists out of their wives, sisters, and lovers. Henry B. Stanton, Elizabeth Cady Stanton's husband, warned her that he would stay out of town if she took part in the 1848 Seneca Falls meeting (where American women first came together to organized against their oppression). She did take part; he did leave town. Ironically, Stanton, an agent for antislavery societies, wrote his business letters on paper embossed with the figure of a kneeling, manacled black female slave. That Stanton might be unsympathetic to feminism had been apparent for some time. Eight years earlier, Angelina Grimké Weld, the prominent white antislavery agitator from Charleston, South Carolina, had written: "We were very much pleased with Elizabeth Stanton who spent several days with us, and I could not help wishing that Henry were better calculated to mould such a mind."[3]

The editors of *The History of Woman Suffrage* summarized the trouble women radicals had. The most liberal of men, they said tartly, find it almost impossible "to understand what liberty means for woman. Those who eloquently advocate equality for a southern plantation cannot tolerate it at their own fireside."[4] To be fair, such failures of the masculine imagination, such needs of the masculine ego, were not present in several of the most notable male radicals. Nor were they limited to white men. In 1833 black students joined their white colleagues in an attempt to keep women out of Oberlin College. Nor were men the women's only opponents. Women themselves, even activists, denounced militant women, even before they were militant feminists. Catharine A. Beecher, an educator, exemplifies such failures of the feminine imagination, such weaknesses of the feminine ego. In 1837 she published *An Essay on Slavery and Abolitionism, with Reference to the Duty of American Females*. This prim, stiff little tract tells an anonymous male friend why he should refuse to join an abolitionist society and a clearly labeled Angelina Grimké why she should refuse to urge women to join one. I loathe slavery, Miss Beecher sniffed, but those exasperating, divisive abolitionists simply refuse to recognize the necessity of *gradual* emancipation of the slaves. Women may work against slavery, but only if they appeal to kindly, generous, peaceful, benevolent principles. Their soft pleas must never go beyond domestic and social circles. After all, Miss Beecher said:

> Heaven has appointed to one sex the superior and to the other the subordinate station. . . . It is therefore as much for the dignity as it is for the interest of females, in all respects to conform to the duties of the relation.[5]

Miss Beecher, a rubber stamp of her age, never doubted her station. Only eccentric women did.

Antislavery work of women, even outside domestic and social circles, was magnificent. Obvious as organizers, fundraisers, and agitators, they were also an imperceptible moral force. The now misunderstood *Uncle Tom's Cabin* was written by a woman. In the last of his autobiographies, Frederick Douglass, the fugitive slave who became the most famous black leader of the nineteenth century and who had his own troubles with white male abolitionists, said:

> When the true history of the antislavery cause shall be written, women will occupy a large space in its pages, for the cause of the slave has been peculiarly woman's cause. Her heart and her conscience have supplied in large degree its motive and mainspring. Her skill, industry, and patience, and perseverance have been wonderfully manifest in every trial hour. Not only did her feet run on "willing errands," and her fingers do the work which in large degree supplied the sinews of war, but her deep moral convictions, and her tender human sensibilities, found convincing and persuasive expression by her pen and voice.[6]

The women had to be durable. During one national convention of the

American Anti-Slavery Women in Philadelphia, they were physically attacked. They continued to speak as stones flew through the windows. That night a mob, maddened by the idea of the abolition of slavery and by the sight of women meeting, especially with black men, burned the meeting hall.

The reasons why women who later became America's great feminists were first active in antislavery work must have been complex, various, and deeply personal. Many of them, for example, came from slavery-hating families, and the antislavery movement was already there for them to enter. However, I think one overriding motive drove women into such work, making, in Douglass' words, "the cause of the slave . . . peculiarly women's cause." In 1884 Frederick Engels decreed: "The modern individual family is founded on the open or concealed domestic slavery of the wife, and modern society is a mass composed of these individual families as its molecules."[7] Decades before that American women felt themselves to be slaves. Their society, unlike modern society, had forcefully reduced them to that social, legal, economic, and psychological state. Not only did women feel that they had always been slaves, but they clearly identified themselves with the American black slave. Recognizing the severe oppression of the black, they saw, perhaps for the first time, an image of themselves. The horrible biblical injunction, "Servants, obey your masters," became synonymous with "Wives, be in subjection to your own husbands."

The identification white women made with black slaves was pervasive. The wife of a southern planter described herself to Harriet Martineau, the traveling English intellectual, as "the chief slave of the harem."[8] The call for a woman's rights convention, the ante-bellum ancestor of teach-ins and consciousness-raising sessions, to be held on Worcester, Massachusetts, proclaimed:

> In the relation of marriage (woman) has been ideally annihilated and actually enslaved in all that concerns her personal and pecuniary rights, and even in widowed and single life, she is oppressed with such limitation and degradation of labor and avocation, as clearly and cruelly mark the condition of a disabled caste.[9]

Elizabeth Cady Stanton, speaking before the New York State Legislature in 1860, hammered home the point:

> The Negro has no name. He is Cuffy Douglas of Cuffy Brooks, just whose Cuffy he may chance to be. The Woman has no name. She is Mrs. Richard Roe or Mrs. John Doe, just whose Mrs. she may chance to be. Cuffy has no right to his earnings; he can not buy or sell, or lay up. Mrs. Roe has no right to her earnings; she can neither buy nor sell, make contracts, nor lay up anything that she can call her own. Cuffy has no right to his children; they

can be sold from him at any time. Mrs. Roe has no right to her children; they may be bound out to cancel a father's debt of honor. The unborn child, even by the last will of the father, may be placed under the guardianship of a stranger and a foreigner. Cuffy has no legal existence; he is subject to restraint and moderate chastisement. Mrs. Roe has no legal existence; she has not the best right to her own person. The husband has the power to restrain and administer moderate chastisement.

Witty, passionate, Stanton went on:

> The prejudice against color, of which we hear so much, is no stronger than that against sex. It is produced by the same cause, and manifested very much in the same way. The Negro's skin and the woman's sex are both *prima facie* evidence that they were intended to be in subjection to the white Saxon man. The few social privileges which the man gives the woman, he makes up to the (free) Negro in civil rights.[10]

The feminists saved their keenest empathy for black women. They showed an intuitive respect, a warmth, often missing in the white male radicals of the period. Angelina Grimké first rebelled against slavery when, a child, she saw a woman slave being mercilessly beaten. Perhaps the white women also felt some guilty relief at not being black, an impulse leading to moral action as well as to the more naive gestures of philanthropy. An anecdote about Elizabeth Cady Stanton is suggestive. One of Stanton's cousins, who ran a station on the Underground Railway, took her and some other young girls to visit a quadroon woman hiding on his third floor. The fugitive slave told her story. Somewhat pedagogically, Stanton asked if she did not find a similarity between being a woman and being a slave. "Yes," the fugitive allegedly answered. ". . . but I am both. I am doubly damned in sex and color. Yes, in class too, for I am poor and ignorant; none of you can ever touch the depth of misery where I stand today."[11]

It is a measure of the deep sense of identification between women and black slaves that even the opponents of woman's rights used the analogy between the two. Their tone, of course, was one of self-righteous approval, not of righteous outrage. The *New York Herald* decreed in an 1852 editorial:

> How did woman first become subject to man as she now is all over the world? By her nature, her sex, just as the Negro is and always will be, to the end of time, inferior to the white race, and therefore, doomed to subjection; but happier than she would be in any other condition, just because it is the law of her nature.[12]

The ever-reliable Catharine Beecher had earlier given the game away. Asking the North to understand the South, she had written: "the Southerner feels (as irritated by the) interference of strangers to regulate his domestic duty to his servants as . . . a Northern man would . . . in regard to his wife and children."[13]

The more mature the feminist movement became, the more deftly it compared chattel slaves and white women for strategic gain. Once Susan B. Anthony, the unyielding mistress of civil disobedience, heard that a white man had incarcerated his wife and child in an insane asylum. Such locking up of rebellious wives, sisters, and daughters was not, it seems, an uncommon agent of repression. The woman, despite her family's testimony to her sanity, had been in the asylum for eighteen months. Anthony helped the woman and child to escape and to hide. Defending herself, Anthony drew upon public support for fugitive women. She reasoned: "In both cases an unjust law was violated; in both cases the supposed owners of the victims were defied, hence in point of law and morals, the act was the same for both cases"[14] Less dramatically, Lucretia Mott utilized the slaveholder to clarify the behavior of all men. She did not expect men, unlike women, to see how they robbed women. After all, slaveholders "did not see that they were oppressors, but slaves did."[15]

Inseparable from the psychological identification feminists had with slaves and the political use they made of it was a profound moral faith. All persons—men, women, whites, blacks—have certain inalienable rights; self-determination is one. In the Declaration of Independence and even in the Constitution, America organizes itself around those rights. When they protest, women and blacks are only seeking the simple human rights that they ought naturally to possess, but of which they have been unnaturally deprived. Moreover, any good person who fights for the freedom of one enslaved class must fight for the freedom of another. Liberation groups are all alike because all groups should be liberated. Loving the right for its own sake means loving the right everywhere.

The editors of the *History of Woman Suffrage* say flatly that the antislavery struggle was the single most important factor in creating the woman's rights movement in America— even more important than the material demands of an underdeveloped country and the spiritual support of a still-lively revolutionary tradition.[16] Certainly the antislavery struggle gave feminism its energetic, triumphant, articulate morality. In the company of "some of the most eloquent orators, the ablest logicians, men and women of the purest moral character and best minds in the nation," women learned the "a.b.c. of human rights," including their own. Angelina Grimké asserted:

The investigation of the rights of the slave has led me to a better

> understanding of my own. I have found the Anti-Slavery causes to be the
> high school of morals in our land—the school in which *human rights* are
> more fully investigated, and better understood, than in any other.[17]

The antislavery movement taught women the austere disciplines of organizing for an unpopular cause, especially the need for patience in any long social struggle.

More important, women broke the near-psychotic taboo against their participation in public life. At first, the American Anti-Slavery Society would permit Angelina Grimké to speak only before small private groups of women. Then men began to sneak in surreptitiously to hear the lady abolitionist from the South. The Anti-Slavery Society saw it had a good thing going and scheduled Miss Grimké for large public meetings. Predictably, the churches were horrified. Theodore Dwight Weld, the abolitionist who was passionately in love with her, and whom she married in 1838, wrote that: ". . . folks talk about women's preaching as tho' it was next to highway robbery—eyes astare and mouth agape."[18] However, after hearing Miss Grimké, Sojourner Truth (called the "Lybian Sybil"), Lucretia Mott, Abby Kelley Foster, Mrs. Maria W. Stewart, and others, the "folks" became a more silent majority. In general, working against slavery made women stronger, more confident, and more responsible. Such qualities made their lack of rights even more implausible.

Ironically, the antislavery movement probably helped feminism most by treating women so shabbily. It imposed independence upon them. Women had been part of the movement from the beginning. A Lydia Gillingham had been an officer of the first Anti-Slavery Society in America. Women were in Philadelphia on December 4, 1833, when a national convention of abolitionists formed the American Anti-Slavery Society. To its shame, the convention refused to seat women delegates. To their glory, the women, black and white, met together five days later in a schoolroom to found a separate Female Anti-Slavery Society. Rejection bred an unpredictable rebellion. Or, as the editors of the *History of Woman Suffrage* report grimly: ". . . through continued persecution was woman's self-assertion and self-respect sufficiently developed to prompt her at last to demand justice, liberty, and equality for herself."[19]

Feminists in the antislavery movement had two groups of enemies. The first were their friends. Sympathetic to woman's rights, they still asked antislavery women not to preach feminism for a while. In effect, the women were asked, as they are today, to sacrifice themselves in order to help others stop still others from sacrificing still others. Angelina Grimké and her intelligent sister Sarah, the second of the Grimké family's exiled and alien daughters, were early subjected to such pleas. Let your lives symbolize feminism, Theodore Weld told them at length, not your actual speeches. You are damaging the cause of the slave; you are losing your value as agitators. John Greenleaf Whittier, the radical poet, accused the sisters of splitting the left. His rhetoric should be hauntingly familiar to those who, for example, wish to work both against the Vietnamese war and for justice for the Panthers. "Is it necessary," he asked

> . . . for you to enter the lists as controversial writers on this question (of woman's rights)? Does it not *look*, dear sisters, like abandoning in some degree the cause of the poor and miserable slave. . . . Is it not forgetting the great and dreadful wrongs of the slave in a selfish crusade against some paltry grievance of your own?[20]

The Grimkés listened, consulted their consciences, and replied: "The *time* to assert a right is the *time* when that right is denied." If men were to reject them as antislavery agitators simply because they were women, then they had to defend themselves as women before they could be effective antislavery agitators. Appealing to his political self-interest, they asked Weld if he could not see that a woman "could do, and *would* do a hundred times more for the slave if she were not fettered?"[21] Angelina, defending Sarah, the more ardent feminist of the two, said:

> I am still glad of sister's letters (about woman's equality), and believe they are doing great good. Some noble-minded women cheer her on, and she feels encouraged to persevere, the brethren notwithstanding. I tell them that this is a *part* of the great doctrine of Human Rights, and can no more be separated from emancipation than the light from the heat of the sun; the rights of the slave and of woman blend like the colors of the rainbow. However, I rarely introduce this topic into my addresses, except to urge my sisters up to duty. Our *brethren* are dreadfully afraid of this kind of amalgamation.[22]

A second group of enemies of feminism among "the brethren" was nakedly hostile. They loathed woman's rights, either because they loathed woman or because they had a notion of her place in life that failed to include an antislavery movement. Their chauvinism helped to split the abolitionist movement in 1840. One group, led by William Lloyd Garrison, welcomed women, even letting them hold office; the other group excluded them. In that same year, in London, at the World Anti-Slavery Convention, male chauvinism enjoyed international triumph. Some American women asked to be seated as delegates. Yelped the Reverend Eben Galusha of New York: "I have no objection to woman's being the neck to turn the head aright, but do not wish to see her assume the place of the head." Intoned the Reverend A. Harvey of Glasgow: "if I were to give a vote in favor of females, sitting and deliberating in such an assembly as this, . . . I should be acting in opposition to the plain teaching of the Word of God."

The convention, after hours of debate, overwhelmingly voted to keep ladies out.[23]

Wendell Phillips, an American, assured the women that they could follow the convention with as much interest from their seats behind a curtain as they could from the floor. Would you say that, the women snapped back, to Frederick Douglass or to any other black man? That night Lucretia Mott, the Quaker moralist, who saw authority in truth, not truth in authority, walked down Great Queen Street with Elizabeth Cady Stanton. They decided to hold a woman's rights convention in America as soon as they got back. The men to whom they had just listened were obviously in need of some education on the subject. Eight years later, in the Wesleyan Chapel of Seneca Falls, New York, the convention was finally held. Mott and Stanton, women of several causes, were to bring their greatest zeal to woman's rights. For the first time, their view of wrong was subjective, their vision a part of their own flesh.

The erratic bonds between women's rights and black liberation finally ruptured after the Civil War on the rough edges of the suffrage issue. Before the Civil War nearly all feminists were fierce abolitionists; during the Civil War they willingly stopped their arduous work on their own behalf. The last woman's rights convention was held in February 1861. There the invincible giants of early feminism—Mott, Anthony, Stanton—spoke for emancipation of the slaves, though crowds, as they often did, gave the women a hard time. Conventional war-relief tasks soon bored Anthony and Stanton, and the indifference to the war and to the principles of freedom on the part of many northern women appalled them. The women of America, Anthony said, "have been a party in complicity with slavery."[24] To stamp out that complicity, she and Stanton organized the Loyal League.

The Loyal League was to gather 400,000 signatures on petitions demanding emancipation for every slave. It was to turn the feminists into tough, efficient organizers. Yet its first meeting in New York in May 1863 foreshadowed the conflict between militant feminists, who said that justice for woman was a more important step in national safety than freedom or franchise for any race of men, and other women, who said several things. The New York gathering was more or less serene. However, a resolution linking the rights of women and those of blacks came up for a floor vote. It read, "There can never be a true peace in this Republic until the civil and political rights of all citizens of African descent and all women are practically established." Mrs. Hoyt of Wisconsin thought the resolution inexpedient. Bringing feminism into war work would frighten away war workers; the Loyal League should not involve itself "in any purely political matter, or any ism obnoxious to the people"[25] Sarah M. Halleck thought the resolution unfair to blacks. Their rights, she said, echoing prewar and postwar debate, have priority over women's rights. "The negroes have suffered more than the women, and the women, perhaps, can afford to give them the preference. . . . It may possibly be woman's place to suffer. At any rate, let her suffer, if by that means, *man*-kind may suffer less."[26] Halleck suggested that the words "all women" be deleted. From the audience came an anonymous cry, "You are too self-sacrificing." The older warriors supported the resolution. The orator Ernestine L. Rose, a Polish exile, declared that women must not be thrown out of the race for freedom. However, she asked rhetorically, can man be free if woman is not? Besides, she went on, women have been the equivalent of slaves. To support freedom for some slaves, and not for others, would be a foolish inconsistency. Then Angelina Grimké Weld spoke:

> I feel that we have been with the (Negro). . . . True, we have not felt the slaveholder's lash; true, we have not had our hands manacled, but our *hearts* have been crushed. . . . I want to be identified with the Negro; until he gets his rights, we never shall have ours.[27]

Eventually the resolution, which had a terrible prophetic truth, passed. The militants had taken the first, brief, parliamentary battle.

When the Civil War ended, many women had toiled to the point of exhaustion. Josephine Sophie Griffing, for example, had done relief work of an extremely systematic sort for freed slaves and she had also helped to found the ill-fated Freedman's Bureau. Feminists were legitimately convinced that their devotion to the Union, to blacks, and to the Republican party merited a reward. Their strategy was to act out the 1863 Loyal League resolution, to make black rights and woman's rights dependent upon each other. The next five years were to make paper boats of their hopes, mired in the mud of party politics and prejudice, luffing before the irresistible power of black claims.

The feminists also had to confront the fact that during war, when only Susan B. Anthony had kept up even part of a guard, some legal rights for women, won at such expense of body and spirit, had been lost. The New York State Legislature, for example, had weakened a law of 1860 giving women the right to equal guardianship of her children. The amended law simply forbade a father to bind out or will away a child without the mother's written consent.

The immediate question was who in the great mass of the disenfranchised should obtain the ballot. The arena was a series of amendments to the Constitution. The Fourteenth Amendment provided that if the right to vote were denied to any "male inhabitants" of a state (excluding Indians not taxed), who were law-abiding citizens over twenty-one, that state's basis for representation in Congress would be proportionately reduced. Its purpose was to give the vote to black men. The militant feminists, led by Stanton and Anthony, furious that the word "male" should be put in the Constitution for the first time, sought to have it struck out. They would then claim the right to vote under the altered amendment.[28] According to the Fifteenth Amendment, the right to vote could not be abridged because of "race, color, or previous condition of servitude." Its purpose was to insure the vote for black men. The militant feminists wanted to add the word "sex." All else failing, the women decided to press for a Sixteenth Amendment, specifically giving them the ballot.

Suffrage, a symbol of citizenship, is also a source of power and self-protection. Having it often seems irrelevant, but not having it is degrading. For women, who had to pay taxes, the vote meant that the old revolutionary American war whoop, "No taxation without representation," would finally have some substance. Perhaps the militant feminists would not have freely chosen suffrage as their do-or-die issue at this time, but suffrage as an issue was there. The women had to respond to the pull of the gravity of the black civil rights movement. The cannier strategists also figured that unless women took advantage of the current national concern about suffrage, they would have to spend years making the country interested in the question again.

Their demands were just. Freedom and civil rights were the natural property of everyone, not one sex. It was politically illogical and bitterly unfair to put two million black men into the polling places and to keep fifteen million black and white women out. Susan B. Anthony spoke out sharply against the oligarchy of sex that made men household sovereigns and women subjects and slaves. Arguments given in support of black male citizenship in debate and court were mimicked to support woman's full citizenship. In 1867 the great black woman Sojourner Truth put it all together:

> There is a great stir about colored men getting their rights, but not a word about the colored women; and if colored men get their rights, and not colored women theirs, you see the colored men will be masters over the women, and it will be just as bad as it was before. So I am for keeping the thing going while things are stirring; because if we wait till it is still, it will take a great while to get it going again. . . . I am above eighty years old. . . . I have been forty years a slave and forty years free, and would be here forty years more to have equal rights for all.[29]

As morally impeccable as the militant feminists, position was, its support was negligible. Facing the enmity of old friends and of time itself, for it was the Negro's hour, they were lonelier, more beleaguered than they had ever been before and they were ever to be again. The Republican party opposed them. Its more honorable members thought that black men, for whom they had fought the Civil War, deserved the vote; more cynical politicians figured that freed slaves would gratefully feel that the Grand Old Party deserved their vote. Democratic party manuevers added to Republican distrust. Democrats, including a notorious bigot, George Francis Train, used the question of woman suffrage to embarrass the Republicans. Why not give women the vote, they taunted, if your concern about civil rights is so pure that you wish to give it to black men? (Their cute ploys foreshadowed those of southern Democrats in 1964, who put women under the protection of the Civil Rights Act. Their concern for women was patently false, but their hope that taking care of women would prevent people from taking care of blacks was patently sincere.) Accepting the loud public support of Train, the militant feminists damaged their reputations and their cause among blacks and whites.

Nearly all the white male abolitionists, even those sympathetic to women, opposed woman's suffrage at this time. They saw black male suffrage as the fitting triumph of their decades of antislavery toil. They sensed that the turbulent American political climate favored them at last. They felt that the same climate did not favor women, since too many people still irrationally believed that votes for "strong-minded women" were simply the folly of "weakminded men." Fusing woman suffrage to black suffrage would lead to anger, confusion, and defeat. Many feminists agreed with them, perceiving themselves not as suicidally self-abnegating, but as shrewd and ethical. They reasoned that the advance of black men out of the pit of disenfranchisement would speed their own.

Necessarily, most black leaders also opposed the militant feminists. Among them was Frederick Douglass, who had long supported woman's rights. In Rochester, New York, he had founded an active Female Anti-Slavery Society, whose members included Elizabeth Cady Stanton, Susan B. Anthony, and Sojourner Truth. Arguing with Douglass from 1842 on, Stanton had swept away his arguments against woman's rights, until he came to believe that women had precisely the same right to participate in civil government as men and beautifully analyzed the reasons why women might not recognize their own unique oppression. His Rochester newspaper had supported woman's rights conventions; indeed, at Seneca Falls, he had been almost alone in supporting Elizabeth Cady Stanton's call for the vote for women, then thought, if not blasphemous or wildly daring, at the very least counterproductive. He had also insisted that meetings of black free men be opened to women. Now he was as surprised by the militant feminist refusal to support suffrage for blacks before suffrage for women as they were angered by his refusal to make suffrage for women a condition for suffrage for blacks.

Douglass eloquently, repeatedly, stated his powerful case. The black man needed the vote more than the white woman, because the black man lacked the thousand ways a woman had "to attach herself to the governing power of the land." Woman might be "the victim of abuses . . . but it cannot be pretended . . . that her cause is as urgent as that of ours." In 1868 he wrote to Josephine Griffing in Washington to decline an invitation to speak for woman's suffrage. "The right of woman to vote is as sacred in my judgment as that of man," said he. However, for the moment, his loyalties were to his race:

> to a cause not more sacred, certainly more urgent, because it is life and death to the long-enslaved people of this country. . . . While the Negro is mobbed, beaten, shot, stabbed, hanged, burnt, and is the target of all that is malignant in the North and all that is murderous in the South his claims may be preferred by me without exposing in any wise myself to the imputation of narrowness or meanness towards the cause of women.[30]

The brief history of the American Equal Rights Association typifies the tension between the few who put woman's suffrage first and the many who put black suffrage first. The Eleventh National Woman's Rights Convention had bred the Equal Rights Association in May 1866. Its goal was nothing less than the reconstruction of the national sense of right; its hope was to "bury" the concepts of the black man and of the woman in the grander concept of the citizen. It worked vigorously for universal suffrage for a year. However, the Association nearly broke apart during its first national convention, held in the Church of the Puritans, New York, in May 1867. The fissure appeared in a floor fight over another of the resolutions irrevocably linking black suffrage to woman's suffrage. Elizabeth Cady Stanton and her faction supported it, those opposing it argued that anything that delayed getting the vote for black men was immoral and that black suffrage did not necessarily imply that the fight for woman's suffrage would be harder. The quarrel then degenerated into an odious squabble about whether blacks were more oppressed than women. Lucy Stone had written that black men, having legal and social rights women lacked, were better off. Nonsense, Abby Kelly Foster answered "(The negro is) without wages, without family rights, whipped and beaten by thousands, given up to the most horrible outrages, without that protection which his value as property formerly gave him."[31] Behind the competition for the unpleasant title of Most Oppressed Class in America lay a serious moral and political question. If history, which is so miserly about justice, is to help only one of several suffering groups, what standards can we possibly use to choose that group?

The resolution did pass. However, that autumn the citizens of Kansas generously voted *not* to amend their state constitution to permit either women or blacks to vote. The militant supporters of woman's suffrage, who had also campaigned for black suffrage, working nearly a year, traveling from twenty to forty miles a day under frontier conditions, facing down the hostility of liberal whites, suspicious blacks, and local Republicans, were blamed for the defeat of black male suffrage. The 1868 annual convention of the Equal Rights Association was bitter, and the 1869 annual convention decisive. The Association broke apart over the question of endorsing a woman's suffrage amendment. Frederick Douglass said:

> When women, because they are women, are hunted down through the cities of New York and New Orleans; when they are dragged from their houses and hung upon lamp-posts . . . then they will have an urgency to obtain the ballot equal to our own.

A voice shouted, "Is that not all true about black woman?" Douglass, who loved human rights for all, put race before sex. "Yes, yes, yes," he answered, "it is true of the black woman, but not because she is a woman, but because she is black."[32] A black woman, Mrs. Francis Harper, a powerful orator, abolitionist, and feminist, concurred. Forced to choose between race and sex, she must let "the lesser question of sex go. Being black is more precarious and demanding than being a woman; being black means that every white, including every white working-class woman, can discriminate against you." Harper argued bitterly: "the white women all go for sex, letting race occupy a minor position."[33]

On May 14 friends of woman's suffrage, including delegates to the Equal Rights Convention, met separately in the Brooklyn Academy of Music. A few days later, they founded the National Woman Suffrage Association; a few months later, some of its members, motivated by personal animosities and a lesser devotion to militancy, created the more decorous American Woman Suffrage Association. The feminist movement, schismatic itself, was formally separated from the antislavery and black suffrage movement.

On March 30, 1870, Douglass celebrated the adoption of the Fifteenth Amendment. Using the considerable grace and power at his command, he immediately called for a campaign for woman's suffrage. He and his friends among the feminists resumed their old, warm ties. Perhaps American culture had exposed itself when it granted the vote to black men fifty years before it granted it to any woman. However, black men were soon virtually to lose the vote in the South. American culture also exposed itself in the fact that women never lost what they were eventually so laboriously to win.

On their own, the feminists still compared themselves to black slaves. One of the most intriguing, grotesque uses of the metaphor occurred at the Louisana Constitutional Convention in 1879. Mrs. Caroline E. Merrick, an able woman, was lobbying for either full or limited suffrage for her sex and the Convention asked her to address it. Her son encouraged her to speak, and her husband, the Chief Justice of the Louisiana Supreme Court before the Civil War, permitted her to do so. Perhaps, Mrs. Merrick suggested, men might find women's demands for their rights as surprising as a procession of slaves approaching "the lordly mansion of their master with several spokesmen chosen from their ranks, for the avowed purpose of asking for their freedom." Still, men must not refuse to give women the vote simply because they have never asked for it. Remember, Mrs. Merrick said:

> In old times most of our slaves were happy and contented. Under the rule of good and humane masters, they gave themselves no trouble to grasp after a freedom which was beyond their reach. So it is with us to-day. We are happy and kindly treated (as witness our reception here to-night) and in the enjoyment of the numerous privileges which our chivalrous gentlemen are so ready to accord; many of us who feel a wish for freedom, do not venture even to whisper a single word about our rights.[34]

It is hard to tell whether Mrs. Merrick's plea, during which she played the seemingly incongruent roles of slave, gentle rebel, and mistress of an old plantation, was sincere, spurious, or ironically cajoling.

However, the notion of woman as black slave slowly slipped from feminist thought and rhetoric. Soon the white working-class girl was to replace the slave as the object of the privileged woman's sympathy. The movement also turned against the black man: the once heroic slave became the besotted freedman. Women angrily compared themselves to the voting black. There was no reason, they argued, why an illiterate black man should exercise a power the educated woman lacked. "You have lifted up the slave on this continent," said Madam Anneke, an ardent German feminist from Milwaukee, "listen now to woman's cry for freedom."[35] The women also deeply resented the potential power a black man might exercise over them. Elizabeth Cady Stanton asked sardonically:

> Are we sure that the (Negro) once entrenched in all his inalienable rights, may not be an added power to hold us at bay? . . . Why should the African prove more just and generous than his Saxon compeers?[36]

She also said, a strong elitism mingling with her racism:

> Think of Patrick and Sambo and Hans and Yung Tung, who do not know the difference between a monarchy and a republic, who can not read the Declaration of Independence or Webster's spelling-book, making laws for Lucretia Mott, Ernestine L. Rose, and Anna E. Dickinson. Think of jurors and jailors drawn from these ranks to watch and try young girls for the crime of

infanticide, to decide the moral code by which the mothers of this Republic shall be governed?[37]

For a while most feminists preserved a vague ideal of sisterhood. They kept some faith with black women. Matilda Joslyn Gage, before a congressional committee in 1876, observed: "I know colored women in Washington far the superiors, intellectually and morally, of the masses of men, who declare that they now endure wrongs and abuses unknown in slavery."[38] Yet sisterhood proved fragile. The old moral solidarity between feminists and blacks gave way to a sexual solidarity, which, in turn, gave way to a primitive racial and class solidarity. A thoroughly ugly white supremacy infested the movement. Frederick Douglass had once said that "The government of this country loves women. They are the sisters, mothers, wives and daughters of our rulers; but the Negro is loathed."[39] The white Anglo-Saxon sisters, mothers, wives, and daughters, hoping for self-rule, or at the least a joint throne, used the loathing of their brothers, fathers, husbands, and sons for political gain. Transforming the Negro's hour into the woman's, they sacrificed the black.

White racism was consciously manipulated as early as 1867. Henry B. Blackwell, a New Englander married to Lucy Stone, wrote an open letter to southern state legislatures. Some of the arguments of "What the South Can Do" were blatantly expedient. Give women the vote, Blackwell urged, and rest in peace. The combined vote of white men and women will always outnumber the combined vote of black men and women. "In the light of the history of your Confederacy, can any Southerner fear to trust the women of the South with the ballot?" he crooned. If white supremacy were so guaranteed, the South could live with the Fourteenth Amendment. Neither its basis of representation in Congress nor its congressmen need be reduced. Moreover, "the Negro question would be forever removed from the political arena." The North would ignore southern politics, but confident of stable politics, it would invest in the South. Blackwell then gilded realpolitik with morality: "If you must try the Republican experiment, try it fully and fairly."[40]

The most leprous racism appeared in the last part of the nineteenth century as the movement suffered a serious ideological shift.[41] The older feminists lost their vision of a seamless web of human rights, and accepted the argument of younger women that the rights of women were separate from those of blacks. The movement also concentrated its energy on suffrage, since its members were convinced that unless women found the grail of the vote, they would lack both equality and the muscle to bring about reform. Suffrage would help women bring right into a wrongful world: northern women might abate the evils of industrialism, southern women might shore up white supremacy. Such ends would justify a number of shabby means. Feminism also simply reflected its age: the northern refusal to see the black, the southern demand to dominate him, and the gluttonous national need to expand, which used white hatred of blacks as a sick psychological rallying cry.

The more popular the movement became, the more conservative its leaders and members were. During the 1890s chapters of the National American Woman Suffrage Association were organized in the South despite rigid regional resistance.[42] In 1895 the National Association met in Atlanta; in 1896 the national board elected its first southern officers. The older feminists, some of them abolitionists, were quiescent. Susan B. Anthony attacked Jim Crow laws, in private. She spoke before the black Phyllis Wheatley Club in New Orleans in 1903, unofficially. The club president, obviously a person of great dignity, told her guest that black women had "a crown of thorns continually pressed upon their brow, yet they are advancing and sometimes you find them further on than you would have expected." The president then assured Miss Anthony that she had helped the club to believe in the Fatherhood of God, the Brotherhood of Man, and "at least for the time being in the sympathy of women."[43]

The records of the feminists' national conventions make sorry reading. In 1899 in Grand Rapids, Michigan, the women refused to support the resolution of a black woman delegate, Mrs. Lottie Wilson Jackson, that protested Jim Crow laws on trains. In 1903 in New Orleans, the national board of directors promptly denied a local newspaper's charge that they were soft on race. The national association only cared about suffrage; state chapters could do what they wanted about race. The directors hastened to add:

> Like every other national association (we are) made up of persons of all shades of opinion on the race question and on all other questions except those relating to its particular object. The northern and western members hold the views on the race question that are customary in their sections; the southern members hold the views that are customary in the South. The doctrine of State's rights is recognized. . . . The National American Woman Suffrage Association is seeking to do away with the requirement of a sex qualification for suffrage. What other qualifications shall be asked for it leaves to other states.[44]

On the last evening of the convention in New Orleans, Miss Belle Kearney, a famous Mississippi orator, spoke, advocating woman's suffrage as the national hope for government by the educated, propertied white. To great applause she warned:

> Just as surely as the North will be forced to turn to the South for the nation's salvation, just so surely will the South be compelled to look to its Anglo-

Saxon women as the medium through which to retain the supremacy of the white race over the African.[45]

The response of the national president, Mrs. Carrie Chapman Catt, queasily allied a nod to principle and a low bow to pragmatism. She first affirmed the principle of state's rights. Then, as a woman who found Negrophobia Neanderthal, she added that Anglo-Saxons were "apt to be arrogant" about their blood. She reminded her audience that the Romans thought Anglo-Saxons too "low and embruted" to be slaves and suggested that Anglo-Saxons would cease to be dominant if they proved unworthy of the honor. Finally, she concluded brightly:

> . . . the race problem is the problem of the whole country and not that of the South alone. The responsibility for it is partly ours but if the North shipped slaves to the South and sold them, remember that the North has sent some money since then into the South to help undo part of the wrong that it did to you and to them. Let us try to get nearer together and to understand each other's ideas on the race question and solve it together.[46]

In 1904 in Washington, D.C., Mary Church Terrell, the first president of the National Association of Colored Women, took the floor. The editor of the *History of Woman Suffrage*, exposing editorial pathology, describes Mrs. Terrell as "a highly educated woman, showing little trace of Negro blood."[47] Mrs. Terrell asked the feminists to support blacks:

> You will never get suffrage until the sense of justice has been so developed in man that they will give fair play to the colored race. Much has been said about the purchasability of the Negro vote. They never sold their votes till they found that it made no difference how they cast them. My sisters of the dominant race, stand up not only for the oppressed sex but also for the oppressed race.[48]

The convention, neatly juxtaposing present policy against past radicalism, swept on to adopt resolutions of regret for the death of many pioneer suffragists.

In other ways white feminists insulted black women and evaded the support of black organizations. Now and then, if black women seemed middle class, if black women escaped the white charge of sexual promiscuity, the movement patronized them. Ironically, the most ebullient white supremacists almost wrecked the national movement. Its grand strategy had been to make woman's suffrage a matter for state conventions and constitutions, but it became clear that it might be quicker to make woman's suffrage a matter for the federal Constitution. Some southern women deplored the notion of a federal amendment, because it might violate the principle of state's rights, might help Republicans hurt

Democrats. In 1913 they organized the Southern States Woman Suffrage Conference with Kate M. Gordon, an energetic civic leader from New Orleans, who helped bring a sewer system to her city, as its prime mover. Only a revitalized national association, only a determined Mrs. Catt, fully committed to a federal amendment, subdued the Southern Conference.

The suffrage movement was no worse than other women's groups. Mrs. Josephine Ruffin, an early black suffragist in New England, the editor of a black newspaper, was verbally and physically attacked in 1900 in Milwaukee at a convention of the General Federation of Women's Clubs. The Women's Christian Temperance Union and the Young Women's Christian Association put black women in segregated units. The elite northern women's colleges, which had endured the most massive sexual prejudice, rarely rose above racial prejudice. By 1910 Smith and Radcliffe had each graduated four black women, Bryn Mawr, Mills, and Barnard none.[49] Nor, if such forces can be measured, was the women's racism as virulent as that of many of their opponents. Indeed, some women even clearly tried to shake off the disease.

What is sad is that woman's rights leaders, who had such a vivid sense of right, and woman's suffrage leaders, who worked so hard for a civil right, should have succumbed willfully to the corrupting gods in the Anglo-Saxon pantheon. What is instructive is that a coalition of the oppressed fell apart when the vital self-interest of one group collided with that of another. In 1865 blacks could hardly have been expected to wait for the vote for their men until the nation was willing to grant it to women. No group can reasonably be asked to stay either slaves or political beggars. What is appalling is how quickly morality and compassion went underground when anyone began to taste of power.

A black liberation movement has been active in America since the first black arrived in Virginia; only white belief in it has been erratic. The liberal civil rights movement which began in 1960, during the Greensboro, North Carolina sit-ins and ended around 1966, during the healthy purge of white power and participation, helped to generate contemporary women's liberation. The growth of women's liberation has imitated that of modern black protest. Civil rights activity, which demands equality within a system, breeds revolutionary activity, which demands a radically new system. Civil rights and liberation groups live together, more or less uneasily, their common enemy forcing a loose loyalty. The public, insensitive to bold differences of ideology and tactics, thinks of them as one.

There are really no formal bridges between integrated black civil rights groups and white women's liberation groups as there were in the nineteenth century, as there are in contemporary white radical gatherings. Reliable people also think that surprisingly few of the new feminists were seriously involved in civil rights. More came out of the New Left or in response to discriminatory post-World War II work conditions. The women who were committed to black causes, if they could shake loose from the roles of Lady Bountiful, Sister Conscience, or Daring Daughter, each in its way an archetypal woman's role, gained political and personal consciousness.

For many of us, civil rights activity was only a part of the interminable process of wooing knowledge, courage, and self-esteem. Other influences on our feminism may have been the psychological and moral need to have a cause, especially an impeccable but unconventional one; emotional or intellectual insults from the masculine world; and, to an interesting degree, a mother, grandmother, or aunt who, whether she wanted to or not, rebelled against woman's business as usual. For others, civil rights activity may have been crucial. It was, I am sure, different for northerners and southerners.

All learned something about the ideal of equality and how to organize to get it. Sensing the limitless possibilities of the protest movement also made us sense the impossible limits of old sex roles. Lillian Smith talks about the genteel church ladies who organized the Association of Southern Women for the Prevention of Lynching. No feminists, the ladies still helped to corrode the iron myth that white women were chaste butterflies. They had realized "that all a woman can expect from lingering on exalted heights is a hard chill afterwards."[50]

Like their ancestors in the antislavery movement, some women in the civil rights movement felt abused. They were given work supportive in nature and negligible in influence; they were relegated to the "research library and to the mimeograph machine."[51] If they were sexually exploited, their own sexual exploits were judged according to a double standard that let men sow wild oats but told women to reap the whirlwind. Not only did movement men tend to be personally chauvinistic, but many of the movement's ideals— strength, courage, spirit—were those society attributes to masculinity. Women may have them, but never more than men. The more paramilitary, the less nonviolent, black protest became, the less women and the putative womanly virtues were honored.

Still another pressure upon women in civil rights was the virility cult of white liberals officially concerned with the "Negro Problem." In 1965 the Moynihan Report made its notorious to-do about strong women and weak men. Behind its analysis lurked a grim belief in the patriarchal family. The report declared:

> When Jim Crow made its appearance towards the end of the 19th century, it may be speculated that it was the Negro male who was most humiliated thereby; the male was more likely to use public facilities, which rapidly became segregated once the process began, and just as important,

segregation, and the submissiveness it exacts, is surely more destructive to the male than to the female personality. Keeping the Negro "in his place" can be translated as keeping the Negro male in his place; the female was not a threat to anyone.

Compounding its errors of fact and spirit, the Report went on:

Unquestionably, these events worked against the emergence of a strong father figure. The very essence of the male animal, from the bantam rooster to the four-star general, is to strut.[52]

A brief, appealing memo illustrated the complex mood of some women in the peace and freedom movements at this time. Written by Casey Hayden and Mary King to other women, it asked how we might "live in our personal lives and in our work as independent and creative people."[52] The women quietly admitted that working in the movement intensified personal problems, especially if people start applying its lessons to themselves and if women assume a new role which is only, ironically, the logical consequence of the ideology they have been preaching. Hayden and King, writing before the new feminism became a coherent force, felt alone. No one talked publicly about women; no one organized them. Few men took the issue seriously, even though it involved the "straight-jacketing of both sexes," even though it involved the kind of private agony that the movement wishes to make a public responsibility. Lacking a "community for discussion," Hayden and King hoped to create a community of support.

Their ideas now seem mild. A few years ago they were whispers. Women, caught up in a sex caste system, must work around and outside of hierarchical structures of power. Their subordination is also assumed in their personal relationships. If they wish to struggle against their situation, they find few laws to attack; the enemy is more elusive. If they wish to work, they find only "women's" jobs. They have trouble asserting themselves against the world, let alone over others. Yet Hayden and King asserted that women cannot realistically withdraw from the system. A solution is to rethink the institutions of marriage and childrearing and the cultural stereotypes that bind.

The influence of black protest on women's liberation is more pervasive than the effect of one public event on the private lives of some valuable, interesting women. The civil rights movement scoured a rusty national conscience. Moral and political struggle against a genuine domestic evil became respectable again. The movement clarified concepts of oppression, submission, and resistance and offered tactics—the sit-ins, boycotts, demonstrations, proofs of moral superiority—for others to use to wrest freedom from the jaws of asses. Confrontation politics became middle class again as the movement helped to resurrect the appealing American tradition of rebellion. The real domino theory deals with the collapse of delusions of content. Once these delusions are exposed for one group, they tend to be obvious for others. The black became, as he had been before, the test of white good will. Being treated like blacks became proof of exploitation.

All of the women's liberation groups, even the more conservative, have drawn deeply on the inadvertent largesse of the black movement. Some women look to it for encouraging political lessons. It teaches that the oppressed must become conscious of their oppression, of the debasing folly of their lives, before change can come. Change, if it does come, will overthrow both a class, a social group, and a caste—a social group held in contempt. For those who place women's liberation into the larger context of general revolution, black people "have exposed the basic weakness of the system of white, Western dominance which we live under."[54] Brutal versions of the theory of the survival of the fittest have been refuted: the weaker can defeat the stronger. Their tactics will prove the virtue of flexibility, speed, and cunning. Those who were expelled from the civil rights movement are grateful for being forced to take stock of themselves, instead of taking stock of blacks. So isolated, they often go on to praise black models of the doctrine of separatism.[55]

Even more commonly, women use blacks to describe themselves. They draw strenuous analogies between themselves and blacks, between women's civil rights and black civil rights, between women's revolution and the black revolution. The metaphor litters even the most sensible, probing, and sensitive thought of the movement. One influential pamphlet, which I like, deploys it no less than eleven times:[56]

1. Women, like black slaves, belong to a master. They are property and whatever credit they gain redounds to him.

2. Women, like black slaves, have a personal relationship to the men who are their masters.

3. Women, like blacks, get their identity and status from white men.

4. Women, like blacks, play an idiot role in the theatre of the white man's fantasies. Though inferior and dumb, they are happy, especially when they can join a mixed group where they can mingle with The Man.

5. Women, like blacks, buttress the white man's ego. Needing such support, the white man fears its loss; fearing such loss, he fears women and blacks.

6. Women, like blacks, sustain the white man: "They wipe his ass and breast feed him when he is little, they school him in his youthful years, do his clerical work and raise him and his replacements later, and all through his life in the factories, on the migrant farms, in the restaurants, hospitals, offices, and homes, they sew for him, stoop for him, cook for him, clean for him, sweep, run errands, haul away his garbage, and nurse him when his frail body alters."

7. Women, like blacks, are badly educated. In school they internalize a sense of being inferior, shoddy, and intellectually crippled. In general, the cultural apparatus—the profession of history, for example—ignores them.

8. Women, like blacks, see a Tom image of themselves in the mass media.

9. Striving women, like bourgeois blacks, become imitative, ingratiating, and materialistic when they try to make it in the white man's world.

10. Women, like blacks, suffer from the absence of any serious study on the possibility of real "temperamental and cognitive differences" between the races and the sexes.

11. The ambivalence of women toward marriage is like the ambivalence of blacks toward integration.[57]

The potent analogy has affected the liberal conscience. A national news program declared that people who object to women entering an all-male bar are as reactionary as people who approve of Lester Maddox keeping blacks out of his chicken restaurant.[58] The analogy has also been the root of a favorite educational device. People are told to substitute the words "black/white" for the words "female/male" in their statements. Or, the person saying, "Women love having babies," is asked if he would burble, "Negroes love chopping cotton." The point is to use public disapproval of discrimination against blacks to swell public consciousness of discrimination against women.

However, I believe that women's liberation would be much stronger, much more honest, and ultimately more secure if it stopped comparing white women to blacks so freely. The analogy exploits the passion, ambition, and vigor of the black movement. It perpetuates the depressing habit white people have of first defining the black experience and then of making it their own. Intellectually sloppy, it implies that both blacks and white women can be seriously discussed as amorphous, classless, blobby masses. It permits women to avoid doing what the black movement did at great cost and over a long period of time: making its protest clear and irrefutable, its ideology self-sufficient and momentous, its organization taut. It also helps to limit women's protest to the American landscape. The plight of woman is planetary, not provincial; historical, not immediate.

Perhaps more dangerous, the analogy evades, in the rhetorical haze, the harsh fact of white women's racism. Our racism may be the curse of white culture, the oath of an evil witch who invades our rooms at birth. Or our racism may dankly unite culture and the way in which white infants apprehend their bodies, the real biological punishment in the myth of the Fall from the Garden of Eden. Whatever the cause, the virus has infected us all. One story may symbolize its work. Castration, when it was a legal punishment, was applied only to blacks during the period of Western slavery. In Barbados in 1693, a woman, for money, castrated forty-two black men. White men made the law. Their fear dictated the penalty. Yet a woman carried it out. White skin has bought a perverse remedy for the blows that sex has dealth.[59]

The racism of white women dictates more than a desire to dominate *something*; it also bears on her participation in what Eldredge Cleaver calls "the funky facts of life." For the black man she may be the sumptuous symbol of virtue, culture, and power, or she may be a sexual tempter and murderer, or she may be an object upon which revenge may fall. She may think of the black man as the exotic superstud, the magic phallus. A union with him may prove her sophistication and daring. She may perceive the black woman as a threat, a class and caste hatred rooted in sexual jealousy and fear.[60] I frankly dislike some of the assumptions about white women I find in black writers. I am neither the guiding genius of the patriarchy nor the creator of my conventional sex role nor a fit subject for rape. Being "cleanly, viciously popped," which LeRoi Jones says that I want, but which my culture provides for me only in "fantasies" of evil, is in fact evil. Yet white women do have deeply ambiguous sexual attitudes toward black people which often have very little to do with love.

My generalizations, which obviously ignore the idiosyncratic, subtle mysteries of the psychology of individual persons, may partly explain the tensions between members of the black movement and of the woman's movement. There are also political reasons for incompatability. The logic of the ideology of separatism is one. Blacks must liberate themselves from whites, including white women; women must liberate themselves from men, including black men. Everyone's liberation must be self-won. My brief narrative of the nineteenth century surely warns us against proxy fights for freedom. The result is that black liberation and women's liberation must go their separate ways. I would be ridiculously pre-sumptuous if I spoke for black women. My guess is that many will choose to work for the black movement. They will agree with the forceful Sonia Sanchez Knight poem "Queens of the Universe":

> . . . we must return to blk/men his children full of our women/love/tenderness/sweet/
> blkness ful of pride/so they can shape the male children into young warriors who will stand along side them.[61]

They will accept the theory that "any movement that augments the sex-role antagonisms extant in the black community will only sow the seed of disunity and hinder the liberation struggle."[62] Any black woman's movement will also have a texture different from that of a white woman's movement.

The logic of the ideologies of class improvement also makes an alliance between blacks and white women seem ultimately unstable. Both classes suffer from irrational economic discrimination: black men the least, black women the most. If society rights this wrong, it may only multiply the competition among the outcast for the cushy jobs. More dangerously, society may fail to change its notions of work. It must begin to assume, especially in a technological age, that ability is an asexual happenstance; that doing housework and raising children are asexual responsibilities; that the nuclear family, in which a father, whose sex gives him power, guarantees the annual income, is only one of several ways of leading the good life. Changing these notions means uprooting our concepts of sex and power. Such assumptions are axioms to members of women's liberation. Whether they are or not to members of black liberation, or any other political force, is unclear to me.

Finally, those of us in women's liberation have tasks independent of those confronting black liberation. We must do much more arduous work to persuade women to recognize the realities of their life. Few blacks still need consciousness-raising. Our job is harder because white, middle-class women have so many privileges and because the national impetus toward suburbia makes each home, embracing its homemaker, not just a castle, but a miniature ghetto. Blacks have long celebrated their culture. We must discover if women have a commonly felt, supportive culture, a fertile, if academically disdained, cluster of responses and beliefs. We must also confront the moral and strategic necessity of building a revolution that rejects violence. A black man, carrying a gun, despite horrified warnings that armed blacks make white backlashes, is effective. A woman, carrying a gun, despite the fact that women can and do shoot, is politically ineffective in America. Our culture finds it bizarre, and I, for one, find it regressive.

However, people in the black movement and in the woman's movement can work together on civil rights. Nearly everyone, except the crackers of both sexes, professes belief in civil rights. However, getting them is still a matter of hard work, imaginative administration, gritty willfulness, and often despair. Once, fighting miscegenation laws together would have been appropriate. Now raising bail money for Panther women is necessary. The movements can also form coalitions to struggle for specific ends. Such goals must appeal to the self-interest of both blacks and women. Among them might be decent day-care centers, humane attitudes toward prostitution, the organization of domestic workers, and the recognition of the dignity of all persons on welfare. Insisting upon these goals must lead to a real guaranteed annual income.[63]

What, at last, we have in common is a gift to America from its haphazard and corrupt revolution—the belief in human right that makes civil right imperative. We also share, if we are lucky, a vision of a blessed and generous and peaceable kingdom. If not for us, for our children. In *Prison Notes*, Barbara Deming, the poet and activist, talks about a feeling she had when she was in the city jail of Albany, Georgia, in 1964. She had been marching for peace between Quebec, Canada, and Guantanamo, Cuba. She writes:

> A kind of affection flows between us that I have known before only on other ventures like this—born in part of enduring together discomfort and danger . . . and born in part of one thing more, too: our common attempt to act toward our antagonists with sympathy. This daily effort, however clumsy, to put from us not only our fear of them but our hostility draws us closer still, as we reveal ourselves to one another, disarmed and hopeful. I have never felt toward a group of people a love so sweet and so strange. The emotion of it is as sharp as though I were in love with each of them. It has astonished me to feel so sharp an affection that was not (a possessive love). And what astonishes me is to love so intensely so many people at the same time.[64]

Perhaps Deming is too tender for those immediately caught up in a violent struggle to survive. Yet the love she offers must surely be the heart and skeleton of any peaceable kingdom. The notion of such love, as well as a passion for liberty, are what women's liberation must keep alive during the turmoil and chaos which we call revolution and during which we long for companions which present realities must deny.

3

WHAT MATTER MIND: A THEORY ABOUT THE PRACTICE OF WOMEN'S STUDIES (1973)

I write as a feminist and as an assistant professor of English who teaches a Women's Studies course at a traditional women's college.[1] I believe that impulses within the Women's Studies movement may force it to destroy itself. The impulses reflect many of the more highly-publicized tensions within feminism as a whole. My purpose is to picture them and to prescribe a tentative strategy for survival. My method is impressionistic rather than scientific.

My essay has three parts: I, the internal disruptions within the Women's Studies movement; II, the external opposition to the movement; and III, a political strategy that might survive the troubles described in (I) in order to handle and confront the troubles described in (II).

I

A vocabulary of crisis may seem apocalyptic. After all, Women's Studies is apparently flourishing. In 1969 only a handful of courses existed. In 1971 there were roughly 600 courses in roughly 200 institutions.[2] The number is apparently increasing. A group now planning a Women's Studies program at the University of Pennsylvania finds Women's Studies so widespread that it surveys current, national programs before devising one of its own. The courses have infiltrated public and private schools, prestigious and struggling schools, places as disparate as Yale, Kent State University Experimental College, and Diablo Valley College in Pleasant Hill, California. Sarah Lawrence, the University of Iowa, and Goddard/Cambridge are among the institutions that offer graduate work.[3]

The people who start, support, and teach Women's Studies are energetic, honorable, and tough. They have resolved to put the serious study of women into the academic curriculum. Useful services—journals, presses, women's commissions and caucusses within professional organizations, conferences— are beginning. Nor do women shrink from the politics of Women's Studies and from the political demands of starting them. Moreover, few assume that knowledge is really powerful enough to make a Women's Studies program the remedy for inequality. On the contrary, they fear that people will ignore the pervasive inequality of women if a narrow scholarly program about them is there.

Given such growth, given such women, my concerns need clarification. They arise because of the nature of the sour, internecine quarrels that drain Women's Studies and because of the nature of its external opposition. Quarrels haunt all political movements. The more radical the movement the more vicious the internal struggles seem to become. One suspects that hostility first compels radicalism and then allies compel each other's hostility. The fights within Women's Studies have a unique flavor; the dislike women evidence for other women, which makes collective action emotionally perilous. To that dislike, women often add an atavistic, but well-documented, distrust of women in authority, which transforms potential leaders into possible ogres whom we hound. Women have apparently accepted the theory that womanliness and power may never converge in one person. The distrust has a special mode within academic circles: the public denunciation of women who have conventional credentials (e.g. publications or the Ph.D.). As feminism has become more fashionable, some women get attention, job offers, and mildly grave requests from foundations for advice. Such favors, if favors they be, become as suspect as a bibliography or a doctorate. Every woman knows the language in which these charges are coded and publicized: "star," "elitist," "someone who rips off the movement," or "academic." The charges are pressed against women who have some influence, no matter how small, or some reputation, no matter how minor, or some credentials.[4]

To be fair, women have asked for it, as we said in childhood fights. Nearly every Women's Studies meeting has had its share of reprint-pushers, title-mongers, and bookpeddlers. Part of this is the natural exuberance of women who, after years of being ignored by colleagues simply because they were women, find themselves within an acceptable, even an exciting, public force. They have come alive. Part of this, more sinister, is the vulgar egoism of any person who suddenly picks up power in a society that values power and revels in it. All credentialed women are also suspect because of the mewing and cowardice of many women scholars in the past. Modeling their careers on those of male scholars; believing that women must adapt themselves to the demands of the university; accepting the ways and means of a modern university, such academics have given the woman scholar a reputation so suspect that women who lack a Ph.D. assume that having one must be tantamount to disliking feminism, or any activism.

Women new to success, which the women's movement may have helped them to achieve, often experience still other difficulties with women. Making it in the academic world is far easier if one has secretarial help and psychic support. The more successful the career, the more accessible such aids. Women have traditionally given both. A woman may find herself, for the first time, in a position to employ, to use, even to exploit other women, for apparently decent ends. Her position is awkward. Her discomfort may congeal into personal awkwardness.

Yet the women who accuse other women of elitism, of being neo-Lionel Trillings or neo-Robbin Flemings, often mask personal fear behind their aggressive political rhetoric. The way in which the word "intimidate" is deployed among people in Women's Studies is suggestive. A woman who says that another woman is intimidating her is admitting to fear. However, she glamorizes her panic as she transforms her self-image from a frightened person into the harried victim of a tyrant.

In my experience, the women most quick to rebuke other women for elitism are graduate students; women uncertain about taking on an academic career; women who have interrupted their career for more conventionally "feminine" pursuits; or women committed to large educational reforms. The woman whose commitment to a seemingly routine academic career is firm may implicitly reproach them, offering a symbol of a success about which they may feel insecure and ambivalent. Lashing out at the Ph.D., they then lash down guilt and self-contempt.

People also falsely assume that learning and activism are incompatible; that the woman who goes to the library in the morning will never emerge to demonstrate in the afternoon; or that going into the library at all will infect going out into the streets. The assumption, oddly totalitarian, implies that there is only one pure way to either justice or perfection. It both denies feminism the fertility of *avant-garde* thought and takes up the energy of women who must repeatedly defend their good faith. It creates an inner contradiction. The women who say that any scholarship is inevitably politically sterile are themselves a part of the academy. Degrading the academy, they degrade their own place. Ironically, they often patronize non-academic women. Announcing that a Ph.D. can only befuddle an ordinary housewife, they put down the housewife as much as the Ph.D.

The situation that I outline is psychological. Suspicion, fear, and distrust; the need to boast and the need to climb that provoke much of the suspicion, fear, and distrust are feelings, emotions, responses. The conflict they arouse may submit to consciousness-raising, therapy, good faith, and good will. However, other quarrels are political. The conflict of ideologies is so severe that it may be beyond reconciliation.

People in Women's Studies tend to belong to one of five categories: (1) The pioneers, who took women as a subject of academic concern before the New Feminism became a public force; (2) The ideologues, who were feminists first and who then tried to adapt their feminism to their work, their politics to their profession; (3) The radicals, who place their feminism within a theoretical context of demands for revolutionary educational, political, and social overhaul; (4) The latecomers, who recently discovered that women were an interesting academic subject, and who may become ideologues as they experience sexual discrimination when they try to set up a Women's Studies course; and (5) The bandwagoneers, both men and women, whose interest in Women's Studies is more in keeping up with fashion and in bucking up enrollment than in Women's Studies. I am an ideologue who wavers towards radicalism. A commitment to institutional change, as well as temperament, keeps me from a hardening of radicalism.

The most bitter quarrel, because its antagonists are in ways the closest, is between the ideologue and the radical. The pioneer tends to stay aloof. The late-comer is busy with discoveries. The bandwagoneer either drops out or fails to understand the elementary terms of the quarrels. The radicals are the most apt to accuse others of elitism, of political cowardice, and of betrayal of equality in general and equality for women in particular. The ideologues are the most nervously sensitive to those charges.

A practical question, which programs have actually confronted, dramatizes the political quarrels. Should a Women's Studies program take foundation money? An ideologue, though she might hesitate, would probably answer yes. She would argue that a Women's Studies program can use the money; that it can evade foundation control; that women might as well take what support is around. A radical would probably answer no. She would argue that foundations, like the universities, share in the moral, economic, and political sins of America; that they have been racist as well as sexist; that they have done little but salve the conscience of people in power in a society that brutally misuses power. Rockefeller, Ford, Carnegie, Sloan—all were rapacious destroyers of the earth, rapacious creatures of international empires. To take their money would be to accept a tainted bribe, to assume the rewards of a privileged class, and to submit to the control of a corrupt group.

The quarrel, and the animating visions behind it, are clearly beyond compromise. Either a Women's Studies program takes foundation money, or it does not. I can hardly reject foundation money for six months and then accept it for the next six, a Persephone living first with the Ceres of righteous poverty and then with the Hades of dark affluence.

A more theoretical question, which men and women often raise, symbolizes the complexity of ideological conflict. Should the members of a Women's Studies program celebrate if a woman became, say, the president of General Motors or a member of the Joint Chiefs of Staff. Here ideologues differ. Some say yes. They reason either that a woman would do the job better than a man, a version of the theory of the moral superiority of women; or that women must penetrate every American institution; or that women must have as many choices as possible. A woman who chose to become a five-star general might have made a regrettable choice, but the intrinsic ability to choose is what matters, particularly if the choice is one previously closed to women. Other ideologues, I among them, say no. They reason that some choices, such as that of a high military career, are so antithetical to the principles of the women's movement that to make them is to drop out.

Nor is the radical answer simple. Every radical says that the American military and that American capitalism are obscene. No person should work for them. However, radical women differ on the use of violence to bring about revolutionary change. Some approve of violence, which the military also use, as a tool. Some do not. The former idealize North Vietnamese and Viet Cong women, who seem to embody revolutoinary morality, feminism, and legitimized violence. Too often the American feminist/ revolutionary confuses honoring the Vietnamese, which I do, and believing that to imitate them would make America a revolutionary society, which I find fantastic.

The identification with the Vietnamese, or Algerian, or other Third World women, of the white, American, middle-class feminist/revolutionary, is part of the larger, popular analysis of all women as members of a single, oppressed class. But the white American, thinking of herself as a Vietnamese or stressing her sisterly links with a woman Arab guerilla, is actually inflating her own sense of oppression. It is sad, if only because a realistic assessment of her own life would give its own evidence of repression. It is also intellectually sloppy.

Psychological and ideological conflicts are part of the classroom as well. Some Women's Studies teachers try to blend the drama of the Women's Studies class and the drama of the women's movement as do some students. The students whom I have known are either the curious, who think a Women's Studies course might be fun; the committed feminists, who take Women's Studies because of their moral, intellectual, and personal devotion to the New Feminism; or feminist radicals, who find Women's Studies one of the few fluid programs in a rigid university. The curious often become feminists. The feminists usually stay that way. The radicals may become disgusted. Their suspicions—that a classroom is a refuge from a tough, political struggle; that any classroom clamps down self-expression—are confirmed. The curious and the feminists unite in boredom with what they politely call "radical rhetoric."

One example: in the spring of 1971 I was teaching "Images of Women in Literature" for the first time. About twenty-five women were enrolled. A boyfriend or two usually came as well. I had assigned Virginia Woolf, *To the Lighthouse*. We argued about Mrs. Ramsay, a quarrel at once moral and literary. The radicals, who hated Mrs. Ramsay, called her a sheltered *bourgeois* wife who submitted to Mr Ramsay's intolerable demands. Some feminists, while they agreed that Mrs. Ramsay played a traditional role, saw agreable virtues in it: the wish to unify the fragments of experience; the effort to bring together alienated men and women. The curious said that Mrs. Ramsay was a character in a beautiful novel. To read the novel as a tract was to misread it and to annoy them.

As the debate went on and on, the class looked to me to end it, to impose a professional right to ring down the curtain. I refused. Though I was trying to be consistent with my tentative theory that a Women's Studies teacher dissolves classroom authority, I doomed us to repetition and confusion. The next year no one fought very much at all. Neither the curious nor the radicals were as dogmatic. I am unsure whether this was an anomaly or part of a trend.

Psychologically at odds, hiding our fears behind political rhetoric, politically at odd as it is, people in Women's Studies go on to indulge in the flimsiest of self-congratulatory talk about intellectual adventurousness. We hurt ourselves because we deceive ourselves and because we risk contempt as we promise a Utopia of the mind and build another suburban tract. The current promises are: (1) interdisciplinary work, which will give the most spacious possible view of women and society, adequate knowledge, and rich conceptual models; and (2) team teaching and research, which will provide the human resources for interdisciplinary work, while it will eschew the figure of the entrepreneurial scholar who treats a seminar as if it were an oil field and he a Rockefeller with a doctorate.

The tributes to interdisciplinary work are more odes to an ideal than analyses of practice. Our actual interdisciplinary feats, so far so tame, have consisted of remarks about the same subject (e.g. sexual initiation or the figure of the lady) made at one time by persons from several disciplines; or the resurrection of old practices within certain disciplines (e.g. a revived interest in the sociology of literature); or a simple blurring of strict disciplinary lines (e.g. using literary autobiography as a primary source in a history class).

When persons from disparate disciplines do get together, they find that they know little or nothing about each other's jargon, models, and methods. I sat in a meeting of women scholars and watched an economist become more and more bemused as the literary critics divided the past into the Middle Ages, Renaissance, 17th-century, Augustan Age, Victorian Period, and Modern Literature. Then the critics listened and puzzled as the economist divided the past into pre- and post-Industrial Revolution. The struggles that Women's Studies practitioners have in cross-fertilizing disciplines is less a comment about them than about the extreme specialization of American scholarship, often dangerous to accept, and about the need for specialization of any scholarship, dangerous to reject.

The most ingenious team research seems to be done within one discipline, a practice scientists have long followed. Except for that, except for the odd biology course, Women's Studies has had little to do with science. This is ironic, if only because of the role of science in liberating women. A necessary condition of the New Feminism has been birth control, which did give women control over their own bodies and sexuality. So doing, it helped to release the energy for a broad political movement.

I sampled two-hundred of the Women's Studies courses in Female Studies III. Over one-fourth were in literature, the theatre, or the media. Nearly one-fourth were in sociology. Another fourth were in history, political science, or law. Psychology, anthropology, and "interdisciplinary" each had one-twentieth. The rest of the courses were in sexuality (including homosexuality and gay liberation); philosophy, religion, fine arts, education, and Oriental Studies.

The ratios were probably predictable. Women have had easier access to the humanities and softer social sciences. "Nationally, the proportion of women on college and university faculties is usually cited as between 18 percent and 22 percent. The comparable figure for the modern language fields is 37 percent. . . . Most political science departments have no women faculty."[5] More women teachers and students are available to sponsor courses. Notions about women are abundant in the humanities and softer social sciences. If anything, an excess of material exists for study, repudiation, and revision. The subjects have a close relationship to everyday life. People pass easily from theory to practice, material to self, idea to action. Finally, many people in Women's Studies believe in educational reform. They distrust the process of rational thought as a process of consciousness. Finding modern science the smug fortress of rationality, they avoid it.

I advocate, not that all women become scientists, but Women's Studies treat science more respectfully. To substitute a feminist humanities program for a masculinized one is good, but incomplete. Unless women enter fully into science and technology, they will remain outside a source of power in modern society. They will also perpetuate the ugly myth that women are too weak for the rigors of scientific thought and unfit for the management of its apparatus.

II

I am sorry about the suicidal impulses within Women's Studies—not simply because I would mourn any such impulse; not simply because they reinforce the tired old theory that women are good only for food, sex, and babies; not simply because they hurt the most humane movement I know; but because they personally hurt me. The New Feminism has given many of us our life's work. It has helped to make our lives work. The self-destruction of the movement would spell our destruction, too.

Moreover, Women's Studies has too many enemies outside of the movement who can and will harm it. The dangers out there demand vigilant attention. The resistance to Women Studies has grown, not shrunk, as Women's Studies has grown. Its mode ranges from passive skepticism to active hostility, a skepticism and hostility inseparable from negative feelings about the New Feminism and women.

Opponents of Women's Studies are effective without having exercised too vulgar or too massive a display of strength. The non-tenured and marginal status of many of its supporters, the weakness of the divisions of a university that may sponsor a course, and the volatile nature of student politics make Women's Studies unusually vulnerable. Administrators, too, may put in a course only to pacify the protesting feminists. When calm seems restored, the course goes.

Some shows of resistance look comic. Hearing about them, one feels a twinge, not unmixed with snobbery, of ironic amusement. I think of the sociologist from Texas who told me that when she mentioned some of the ideas of the New Feminism in a class, some of its members set up a prayer session to save her soul. However, the sources of resistance are usually either too powerful to be ignored or too sympathetic on other grounds to be rejected. They include: institutional conservatives of both sexes, who find curricular change as alarming as dogmatic Christians did the challenge to the infallibility of Scripture; women who fear the tumult of altering the definition of sexuality their society has given, and they have taken; and blacks, who find Women's Studies the newest toy of the protected, white, middle-class woman greedy for more status. The ignorance of white women about the black struggle and the competition between blacks and white women for jobs that affirmative action programs have opened up only pulls the snare of tension tighter. And on several campuses, sisterhood has become hard to sustain as the quiet, malleable women get the jobs, promotions, and rewards the militant women have won for the movement, and then fail to support the militants.

The most virulent opponents of Women's Studies are probably none of the above, but younger, male faculty members. They fear women as colleagues. Their anxiety is partly rooted in the neurotic conviction that losing to a woman is far more disgraceful than losing to a man. Such men believe that Women's Studies will bring more women into their departments. They fear, too, that they will be forced to recognize the insights of the new woman scholars and to talk about women as seriously as they might about the Corn Laws or Metaphysical Wit. The contraction of the current academic job market only inflames resentment. They see women, often because of government pressure, getting the scarce jobs that would otherwise have been theirs. The job has both economic and symbolic importance. It announces that the young male Ph.D. can support a wife and family. If he is using the Ph.D. as an agent of upward social mobility, it also proclaims that he has made it out of the lower or lower-middle class.

In brief, the young men think of Women's Studies as the wedge of a force that will threaten their personal security, their intellectual principles, their ambitions, their ability to fulfill obligations, and life itself. Cornered, anxious, angry, they fight as if they were fighting for survival—which they very well might be. Either too unsure or too shrewd to be innovative, they use conventional weapons of academic warfare: hostile wit and little jokes at faculty departmental, and committee meetings; quiet, man-to-man maneuvers, such as a visit to Professor X to warn him about Mrs. Y; appeals to "academic standards"; and reliance on the protection of a powerful, prestigious patron. The weapons still work.

People in favor of Women's Studies must assess how much harm their opponents have done. A quick, accurate count of the number of Women's Studies courses that have been dropped and the number of Women's Studies faculty who have been displaced is overdue. My hunch is that the count will shock women as much as the action of the New York State legislature when it overthrew abortion law reform in the spring of 1972. Certainly a number of stories are now circulating.

I heard one recently from a faculty woman at a large, Midwestern university. In two semesters there the Women's Studies courses dropped from six to zero. The woman had several explanations. (1) Her non-tenured slot made her a strategic weakness; (2) the male members of the committee that administered the unit that sponsored the courses were implicitly hostile to women; for example, their attitude towards day-care was either angry or contemptuous; (3) other women on the faculty, who might have helped, were "fearful of giving time to work which (did) not advance them professionally . . . they seem(ed) loath to call attention to their femaleness by associating with women's studies. They want, they often say, only to be judged professionally 'as if they were men.'"; (4) pervasive distrust of *any* new program; (5) students "were too easily discouraged by all the above factors. One student gave up when her request to a woman faculty member to advise a course was answered by an abrupt NO!"[6]

The alliance of people who oppose Women's Studies is more often implicit than explicit, more a quiet, mutual recognition than a public pledge of common interest. What they share, and another weight that Women's Studies must bear, is the cultural bias against intelligent women. Most feminists—including men like John Stuart Mill—have long complained about it. They have beaten their fists against the exclusion of women from the body of received knowledge and from its bureaucracy. In 1792 Mary Wollstonecraft was asking bitterly why "women should be kept in ignorance under the specious name of innocence."[7] In 1872 George Eliot was wryly defining provincial society as one in which "Women were expected to have weak opinions, but the great safeguard of society and of provincial life was that opinions were not acted on."[8] In the twentieth-century, Virginia Woolf was dissecting the education of the Englishwoman, protests now revered as prophecies.

The bias is deep enough in the marrow of society's bones to inspire forgetfulness. It is so morally disreputable, so socially stupid, so intellectually false, and so personally unjust for women that most people are ashamed to admit it influences them. The bias is one aspect of the ideology that assigns men to one sphere and women to another, which asserts that men are spirit, women flesh; men think, women feel; men act, women respond; men command, women obey. Not only are women incapable of rational thought, but they are downright irrational. They no more belong in a university than does an animal or a storm. The phrase "head of the household," which we usually apply to men, even though women head 10 percent of American households, fuses the "masculine" qualities of brains and power in a revealing pun.

The ideology is internally self-justifying. Rational man is logical, sensible, reflective, capable of abstract thought. He manipulates the world of the mind. So doing, some doctrines aver, he is like God himself. Active man is energetic, virile, efficient. He manipulates nature and society. So doing, the same doctrines aver, he is again like God. Since men are rational, active, and godlike, they must be sanctioned to command. As Aristotle writes:

> . . . although there may be exceptions to the order of nature, the male is by nature fitter for command than the female.[9]

In sum, men are mind, women matter. Women should neither mind this matter, nor think it matters. Either a Divine Intelligence or hormones meant the sexes to be this way. The theory even has a depressing corollary: men create, women breed; men are artists, women mothers.[10]

In *Genesis*, for example, God, a sacred masculine authority, brings order out of chaos, time and space out of undifferentiated murk, Eden out of muck. Then he makes Adam out of dust. Adam, a profane masculine authority, engages in reasonable activities. He organizes, generalizes, uses language, names. The profoundly rational power of coherent speech is masculinized. "Dumb broad," though slang, is another of the revealing puns ordinary language yields up. The woman the pun evokes is stupid, mute, animal, thick. Even the speech of wise women is gnomic, gnarled, utterances from the mysterious earth that gush forth like blood from the womb, indecipherable except through the exegesis male priests perform—the speech of the Delphic Oracle, the Sibyl, or a Molly Bloom.

Eve substitutes, not only will for obedience, but appetite for reason. To add to her danger, she tempts Adam away from reason. So in *Paradise Lost*, Eve tells Adam:

> God is thy Law, thou mine; to know no more
> Is woman's happiest knowledge and her praise.
> (Book IV, 11:637–38)

Yet Adam is wary. He understands that he is her superior in "the mind and inward Faculties," but her loveliness is so absolute that when he approaches her, everything she says seems "wisest, vurtuouest, discreetest, best." He tells Raphael:

> All higher knowledge in her presence falls
> Degraded, wisdom in discourse with her
> Looses discount'nanc't, and like folly shewes;
> Authoritie and Reason on her waite . . .
> (Book VIII, 11:551–54)

Ironically, women, who apparently emasculate the brain as well as genitalia, symbolize intellectual activity, poetic inspiration, and the imagination in their mythic guise of Muse.

The most influential modern spokesman for the ideology of man/mind, women/matter is probably Jean Jacques Rousseau. In his erratic masterpiece, *Emile* (1762), Roussea plays God. Here creates Eden, Emile a modern Adam, Sophie a modern Eve. He optimistically refuses to redesign the tragedy of the serpent. However, the priest of equality believes women incapable of abstract thought. They can be consulted in "bodily matters, in all that concerns the senses."[11] The female wit is a scourge to her husband, children, friends, servants, and the general public. Girls need learn only the secrets of virtue, beauty, and chastity. The faculties they may cultivate are wit, guile, and cunning: the defenses of the weak against the strong. Rousseau throws women some bones, upon which they munch still. They are the mothers of the race, and unless they mother well, the race will not do well. Paradoxically, the inferior best nurture the young. Next, women's sexual allure will give them power over men. They are at their most alluring when they seem most weak. In effect, if Sophie will only lie at Emile's feet, she will have him throwing himself at her feet—a neat gymnastic trick.

Rousseau anticipates one of history's ironies. Women, damned for centuries because they were irrational and carnal, are now damned if they are insufficiently irrational and carnal. The jeremiad, of which Norman Mailer is now the best known voice, claims that rational man has unleashed the monsters of science and technology. Women are still unscientific, atechnological, natural, carnal. The last defense of a humane society is for them to stay that way.

Some other voices make women, as muse, the symbol of destructive science. Edgar Allen Poe begins "Sonnet—to Science," with the line "Science! True daughter of Old Time thou art!" before he goes on to describe science as a vulture. Mailer and Poe have more in common than it seems. Both reveal the post-Romantic fear of science, which women share, and the post-Romantic refusal to believe that calculated reason and spontaneous imagination may work together, which women share. Both reveal a traditional fear of women so haunting that women symbolize whatever force a man finds threatening.[12]

III

The people who resist Women's Studies are so numerous, the affection for intelligent women so frail, the self-destructive impulses within Women's Studies so tempting, the unanswered questions so complex, that it seems obvious that Women's Studies is in a position of weakness. A preliminary to shoring up that position is to add up what the believers in Women's Studies have in common. Surely everyone would assent to these hypotheses:

1. American colleges and universities and their support services—repositories of sophisticated knowledge, factories of new ideas—have either warped what we know about women or behaved as if women were hardly worth knowing about at all. The process is parallel to the process through which women have been trivialized in the academy itself. That process is parallel to the processes of society-at-large. A primary task is to rectify error and to fill lucanae. Many subtle insights will come from the outcast (e.g. servants, lesbians, domestic workers, old women).

2. The drama of the classroom has been largely barren. The structure, the master professor's domination of an apprentice pupil, whether the professor is a man or a woman, is interestingly like the structure of the

patriarchy. (One of the multiple ironies of the women's colleges is their devotion to such a classroom.)

To fracture and reset an ossified pedagogy, we need:

a. To learn more about a student's conscious and unconscious needs. A woman student wil probably have to be encouraged to believe that she has the talent to learn: that society will reward her if she does; and that if society does not, it may be society's fault.[13] A man will probably have to learn that the capacity for intellectual rigor and play is less a cruel competition to be won than a humane skill to be sought. If a woman is asked to live more freely, a man is asked to discover how often his free life has been rooted in the subordination of a woman. Unhappily, few male professors set their male students exemplary attitudes of self-reform.

b. To bring women of several ages, circumstances, and economic groups into the classroom. The monochromatic American school isolates persons of one age, often to turn them into one class, if they are not already members. One result is that women learn only from their peers. In need of multiple visions, they receive mirror images. A way to enlarge the classroom is to take it off-campus and into the community. Women should, however, distrust glib references to "the community." Not only may they reflect a white, middle-class condescension towards non-white or lower-class women, but they ignore a serious problem of community colleges. The community college is a tool which a student can use to achieve the legitimate security of the middle-class. The person who teaches Women's Studies has a hard job of both pointing out the defects of middle-class sexual roles and encouraging ambition.

3. Women's Studies, or at the very least its proponents, find acceptable a minimal political program: it is bizarre to alter the knowledge of women without altering the psychological, educational, social, and political context within which knowledge is garnered, passed down, and received. The minimal political tasks are: work against sexual bias in the primary and secondary schools so that college may be more than remedial aid; a guarantee that the university itself is fair to women students and employees in hiring, promoting, admissions, counseling, access to facilities, financial aid, health services, and pensions; and access for women to the facts they need to fight discrimination outside of the university. As Ann Scott, who was a member of the English Department of the University of Buffalo, who is the vice-president of legislation of the National Organization for Women, writes:

> I believe that a university must equip women to survive in our world of the overpowering institutions which have historically excluded them (including the university itself). It can do this through adopting a variety of intervention techniques designed for enabling women to intervene for themselves, through using its own resources to intervene for them, and through using its own structure as an arena for training in

intervention. ("Educating American Women for the Leisure Class," *Educational Leadership* [October, 1971], 30).

Common assent to these propositions should be enough to start flexible coalitions among disparate groups of women from one campus or from several campuses. Men—who give political support, who suspect masculinity as usual, who encourage younger men to rebel against its strictures—can be engaging allies. If women need a coherent political strategy, I suggest they adopt the tactic of postponement. That is, they should avoid confrontation over any political or educational question that is not immediately, perceptibly related to women's issues. This excludes neither debate nor practical decisions on a local level. Indeed, it will encourage a multiplicity of local decisions. A Women's Studies program in California may reject foundation money; a Women's Studies program in Idaho may accept it. It does exclude both the use of Women's Studies as a national vehicle for any single ideology and rigidity that leads to accusations of betrayal if one group acts differently from another.

Women's Studies will embody, not a politics of chaos, nor a politics of purity, but a politics of energy. The movement will consist of a cluster of self-generating forces, a multiplicity of constellations. Each will devise its own goal and methods. One group may negotiate with conservatives. Another may consolidate the experiments of other groups. Still another may serve as a cutting edge of action and of theory. However, being a cutting edge demands a new notion of a cutting edge. It leads, but does not slash those following. Shock troops must be careful about the shock treatments they administer to other women. My admonition is less a prissy call for compromise than a reminder abot the self-proclaimed nature of feminism as a political movement: a pride in paying careful attention to the concerns of all the women whom they seek to serve and to the visceral details of their lives. The virtues of a politics of energy are the stimulus to women to be autonomous and self-defining; the creation of a number of models of local activity to test for future use; and the winning of time until Women's Studies is both more internally coherent and more muscular.

Yet, to be realistic, individuals and small groups are often isolated among the tangles of the grassroots. Women's Studies badly needs a national organization to support people in trouble locally; a national organization to provide publicity and legal aid to people in jeopardy. Such a national body might have three other functions: (1) to distribute information, tapes, bibliographies, lists of courses, films, and so on; (2) to conduct research projects, such as the actual effect of Women's Studies course on an institution at large, or the use of Women's Studies courses off-campus; and (3) to sponsor conferences on important questions. The most important questions touch on public policy (e.g. the real effect of nuclear family in contemporary society has on women, or the great demographic shifts in the ratio of men to women). They reveal the connections between the talents of the academic community and the needs of the larger community. A national office, which saw its functions as either being defensive or comparatively neutral, would avoid taking sides in ideological quarrels. The strategy is consistent with the tactics of postponement and a politics of energy.

People from Women's Studies programs, Women's Centers (whether they have a formal academic affiliation or not), journals, presses, and professional caucuses, should meet to organize a national program. The central office might move from region to region each year to avoid rigid centralization. Administration, proposals for funding, and spending of what funding there might actually be must include all positions within the Women's Studies movement. If the Department of Health, Education, and Welfare, for example, were to sponsor a series of open seminars about Women's Studies, each to last a week, one in each state, the organizers would insure that a person from a more traditional program would speak, a person from an experimental center would speak, etc.[14]

The governing structure I suggest will degenerate into bad feeling and sniping unless women recognize that the movement is at that point where no one knows what will bring the equitable future everyone wants. An attack on another women, or on a specific program, may be not simply a symptom of hostility, not simply a paragraph in a chapter of political argument, but a premature lopping off of a possibly fruitful program.

At the risk of revisionism or blasphemy, I also suggest that the merits of the star system and of elitism, which is a star system extended to a highly refined group, be recalled. The onerous dangers of the star system have been exposed: the confusion of star and movement, of elite and group; the selection of the "star" through the media or through current governors, not through the movement; the feeding of the egos of the few while the many suffer malnutrition. Yet "stars" are often smart, hard-working, courageous, and skillful. They do things. Kate Millett sat down and wrote *Sexual Politics*. I did not, nor did anyone else. Trying to abolish the star system must avoid the risk of leveling pioneers, prophets, and the odd spirits who find joy in lonely work. Trying to demolish hierarchies must avoid the risk of inhibiting skill.

Many of the attacks on the glittering and on the high also graph, as I wrote before, a fever chart of insecurity. They may also be signals of loneliness. The cry of "elitist" may represent a hope that through recimination and demand an easing of the spirit may be conjured up. Instead of crying "elitist," women might discover the creative function of insecurity. We are at a radical discontinuity with history. The past has been rejected. The future is opaque. The present is a place where insecurity and loneliness, parasites that feed on radical discontinuities, are transformed into humility, a recognition that the self cannot be an exemplum, only an experiment. Humility is a quality of the tolerance that is a consequence of reason. But then, I have faith in reason and in the benefits of rational activity. My faith reaffirms, in the teeth of an irrational educational system, that mind matters.

I am more hopeful as I finish than when I began. I have recalled how evanescent the quarrels within the women's movement have been. The fight about lesbians, for example, has faded. I remember the buoyancy that comes from sensing that to work for Women's Studies is to belong to a historical tide, a mood that injects the excitement necessary to defeat the fatigue of tedious detail and psychic conflict. Then I think that women have shown that talent for reconciliation within the movement, when they have controlled events. Women's Studies, for the most part, must survive within an institution that women do not control, in which others incite quarrels for their gain, and in which competing interests may divide women.

I console myself, during this debate taped within the mind, by picturing the great moral vision and the spacious future that the New Feminism promises. I picture a community, a collectivity, in which the physiology of birth is remarked upon, but not remarkable. The community imposes one imperative upon its members: that the shaping of the self must not demand the sacrifice of another. Both martyrdom and murder must be obsolete. In this community, a moral ecology works; the law has a little to do with justice; tenderness is the basis of all etiquette; and physical force and coercion are taboo. A community in which *The Pentagon Papers* refers to a geometry textbook, and in which women do geometry, too.

4

THE ANDROGYNE
AND THE HOMOSEXUAL
(1974)

The purpose of this excursion into cultural criticism is to clarify the figures of the androgyne and of the homosexual as models of human behavior.[1] They may be, in serious ways, incompatible. They may be, perhaps, reconciled.

A trouble with the word "androgyne" is the number of often mutually exclusive things to which it refers. To categorize them:

1. The androgyne may be a person who sleeps with members of both sexes. In some modern circles "Honor Androgyny" has the force of an Eleventh Commandment. Heterosexuals must have a homosexual foray; homosexuals a heterosexual skirmish. Androgyny, so construed, is a synonym for bi-sexuality.

2. The androgyne may be an effete male, a soft man, even a eunuch. A creature who so falls back from vigorous virility alledgedly personifies the ways in which femininity can taint and corrupt masculinity. For example, Ovid, in Book IV of the *Metamorphoses*, tells of the beautiful boy Hermaphroditus. Out wandering, he comes upon a pool. Its nymph forcibly seduces him. When she asks the gods for aid, they graft her body with his. When he calls on his mother Aphrodite and his father Hermes for revenge, they transform the waters of the nymph's pool into a liquid that will enfeeble all who touch them.

3. The androgyne may be a physical hermaphrodite. It has both female and male sex organs. This literally bi-sexed figure often has mythic and mystical meaning.[2] It may symbolize fertility, an organism powerful enough to create new life on its own. It may symbolize balance, reconciliation, and the unity of such binary opposites as female and male, earth and sun, dark and light, cold and hot. Or, it may symbolize wisdom, a creature able to grasp the totality of the experience of both sexes. In "The Waste Land," for example, Tiresias, that old man with wrinkled breasts, watches a carbuncular clerk making dull love to a bored typist. He says:

(And I Tiresias have foresuffered all
Enacted on this same divan or bed;
I who have sat by Thebes below the wall
And walked among the lowest of the dead.)

4. The androgyne may be a mental hermaphrodite. It exerts and enjoys both the "masculine" and the "feminine" spheres of the brain. A passage in Virginia Woolf's series of lecture-essays, *A Room of One's Own*, has become the classic citation for such speculative neurology. She writes:

> . . . the sight of . . . two people getting into the taxi and the satisfaction it gave me made me also ask whether there are two sexes in the mind corresponding to the two sexes in the body, and whether they also require to be united in order to get complete satisfaction and happiness. And I went on amateurishly to sketch a plan of the soul so that in each of us two powers preside, one male, one female. . . . The normal and comfortable state of being is that when the two live in harmony together, spiritually cooperating. . . . Coleridge perhaps meant this when he said that a great mind is androgynous.[3]

5. Finally, and this will be my working definition for the rest of my paper, the androgyne may be a psychological hermaphrodite. Whether female or male, biological women or biological man, the androgyne will behave as if it were both feminine and masculine. That is, in thought, feeling, and action, the androgyne will flesh out those characteristics we have subsumed under the term "feminine" and those characteristics we have subsumed under the term "masculine." Dick will live as if he were Dick and Jane. Jane will live as if she were Jane and Dick. Both will be aggressive and receptive, strong and tender, rational and intuitive.

The constellation of modern theory that has most legitimized the androgyne as psychological hermaphrodite is that of Jung. He postulates that the objective psyche of each male contains an *anima*, or feminine principle; that the objective psyche of each female contains an *animus*, or masculine principle. More recent students of androgyny, such as Carolyn G. Heilbrun or Mary Daly, are less apt to locate the capacity for androgynous action in inherited, given constructs of the self. Unlike Jung, unlike Woolf in her way, they hesitate to assign the mental or psychological hermaphrodite a quasi-biological origin. They do, however, urge us to learn to live as if we were androgynes. The possibility that Dick might act as if he were Dick and Jane, that Jane might act as if she were Jane and Dick, assumes the dignity of a moral imperative. So Mary Daly speaks eloquently of "androgynous integrity and transformation," of a therapeutic striving towards "psychic wholeness and androgyny."[4]

Some might call Vita Sackville-West, the writer who was Virginia Woolf's friend, a psychological hermaphrodite. She wrote about herself that she was both masculine and feminine; tht she could dress like a young soldier to swagger in the city with her woman lover and dress like a young housewife to garden in the country with her husband and two little boys. She predicted accurately that the psychology of people like herself would "be a matter of interest . . . it will be recognized that many more of my type do exist . . . cases of dual personality do exist."[5] Having sex with both women and men, she was also an androgyne in the sense of my Category (1). Sackville-West seems to be a sequential rather than a simultaneous androgyne. That is, particularly in her psychosexual life, she appears to be "feminine" one day and "masculine" the next, not "feminine" and "masculine" at the same moment. Unhappily, her androgyny is inseparable from her obnoxious snobbery. She thinks of her life as the invention of an enlightened elite, of the "more educated and liberal classes."

The word "homosexual" is simpler than the word "androgyne." A homosexual finds a member of the same sex erotically desirable, erotically gratifying. A lesbian is a homosexual woman. In theory, a homosexual could be an androgyne in the sense of both my Categories (1) and (5). The complications of homosexuality are less lexical than social. Homosexual practices; the attitudes they reflect and provoke; and the laws passed to control them vary from culture to culture; within cultures; from person to person; within persons.[6] Some societies enjoy homosexuals. Others permit them to exist. Still others allow them brief flings, such as the exotic lesbian interludes in pornographic books and movies. Still other societies devise rituals in which homosexual needs are acted out in translated form. Still others fear, suppress, and rigorously repress any trace of homosexuality.

In the nineteenth and twentieth centuries, the rise of a women's movement has inspired special fantasies about homosexuality. People assert that any man who is sympathetic to feminism must be a girlish male homosexual; that any woman who is sympathetic to feminism must be a mannish female homosexual. In brief, a man must be a queen, a woman a dyke. Behind such indictments is a bizarre logic. Homosexuals are both perverts and inverts. Rebels against the sexual *status quo* are perverts. Therefore, they must also be homosexual inverts. In part as a defense against such questionable logic, in part as an offense against the social and personal pathology it reveals, the New Feminism has bred the political lesbian. She cheerfully and openly supports lesbians. She identifies herself with them. So doing, she rips the word "lesbian" out of context. Homosexuality becomes less a sexual preference, which may be emotionally charged, than a political preference, which may also be emotionally charged. If "lesbian" loses its purity of meaning, so dispersed, it also loses its holophrastic intensity as a curse word.

To reassure themselves of their humanity, to remind themselves that they have a tradition, both the androgyne and the homosexual look back to Plato's *Symposium* for an endorsing myth. There the playwright

Aristophanes tells of three divided creatures, who seek their other half and the happiness it will bring: one is wholly male, the male homosexual; one is wholly female; the lesbian; and one is male/female, the androgyne. To reassure the present that they will enlarge humanity, both the androgyne and the homosexual can offer a set of appealing values and promises.

First, they believe that people can create their own character structures. At the least, they can break the gross mold of patriarchal, heterosexual convention. So believing, the androgyne and the homosexual assume that life is a loose network of possibilities and that the future is reasonably open. What Simone de Beauvoir said of the lesbian might be said of all homosexuals and of the androgyne:

> The truth is that homosexuality is no more a perversion deliberately indulged in than it is a course of fate. It is an attitude *chosen in a certain situation*—that is, at once motivated and freely adopted. It is one way, among others, in which woman solves the problems posed by her condition in general, by her erotic situation in particular. Like all human behavior, homosexuality leads to make-believe, disequilibrium, frustration, lies, or, on the contrary, it becomes the source of rewarding experiences, in accordance with its manner of expression in actual living—whether in bad faith, laziness, and falsity or in lucidity, generosity, and freedom.[7]

They must also necessarily rebel against the binding constraints of the present. People may find that rebellion gloomy. Baudelaire's voluptuous condemned women, for example, seem wrapped in a dark, velvet cloak of doom. But whether the rebels seem wretched or redemptive, they attract the interest of restless or agnostic minds.

Next, the androgyne and the homosexual value freedom, if not intrinsically, then as a prerequisite for self-creation, for being at once a more affable Pygmalion and a more willful Galatea. In practical terms, they translate their support for an ethic of freedom into support for a platform of civil liberties. They also, at best, endorse an ideology of human rights. They tend to reason that sexual preference is a matter of mature choice. To have that choice is a human right. A climate of freedom and civil liberties will best nurture its exercise.[8] The apparent fact that some homosexuality is obligatory, that some people sleep with members of the same sex because they cannot sleep with members of the other sex, fails to diminish the worth of a morality and politics of sexual freedom. The androgyne, however, must ultimately face a logical dilemma. It may endorse freedom of erotic preference, but it cannot support freedom of sexual role. By definition, the androgyne demands the blending and merging of masculine and feminine roles.

Finally, the androgyne and the homosexual can expediently argue that they embody the potential for a creative life. A body of empirical evidence suggests that clever people act out both putatively masculine and putatively feminine traits. The psychologist Eleanor E. Maccoby writes:

> The studies cited so far indicate that analytic thinking, creativity, and high general intelligence are associated with cross-sex-typing, in that men and boys who score high are more feminine, and the women and girls more masculine, than their low-scoring, same-sex counterparts.[9]

A body of empirical achievement suggests how much homosexuals can do, much of it done in a culture hostile to homosexuality and to the independence for women that most lesbians need in order to survive. Obviously, not every homosexual is an André Gide or a Gertrude Stein, but enough gifted persons have been homosexual to show that it has been, for many, not incompatible with creative accomplishment.

Oddly, the homosexual is a far more threatening figure than the androgyne. Society after society has passed laws against homosexuals, but not against androgynes. Homosexuals are more menacing, in part simply because they exist. They are a fact of life that heterosexuals must confront. The androgyne is nothing more, or less, than an idea. More accurately, the androgyne is the result of the adding together of two ideas: the idea of the feminine, the idea of the masculine. Optimistic theoreticians of androgyny hope that the illusory total will be more that the sum of the illusory parts, even as they overlook the contradictions between some of the parts.[10] Many people erroneously believe that the concepts of femininity and masculinity denote something natural, a biological given. Those interested in the psychological hermaphrodite tend to make the same mistake. They talk as if their idea were a part of the natural world. On the contrary. If the homosexual is an outlaw of many cultures, the androgyne is their unicorn.

Another reason why the homosexual is more threatening than the androgyne is because the homosexual, by self-definition, rejects the heterosexuality that is the dominant sexual patterning of most societies. So doing, the homosexual also rejects the ordinary family and the children it sustains. The androgyne, on the other hand, may reject the patriarchy, but not heterosexuality, home, and babies. It gives itself permission to think that biological men, even if they have both feminine and masculine traits, and biological women, even if they have both feminine and masculine traits, will continue to sleep together, have children, and marry.

Moreover, the androgyne still fundamentally thinks in terms of "feminine" and "masculine." It fails to conceptualize the world and to organize phenomena in a new way that leaves "feminine" and "masculine" behind. The theoreticians of androgyny resemble poets who have been writing about two lovely beasts: winged horses and centaurs. People come to them and say, "We're tired of winged horses and centaurs. What about a new beast?" And the poets reply, "Great, I'm tired of the old beasts myself. What about this fabulous creature with the head of a man, the body of a horse, and the wings of an angel?"

The ironic tragedy of homosexuality, as Westerners tend to know it, is that it has itself kept the stereotypes of "feminine" and "masculine" spinning. Though reaching toward erotic freedom, the homosexual often lapses back into the safety of received psychosexual identities and becomes "butch" or "femme." To add intricacy, the games of "butch" and "femme" may also serve as explorations into the games of domination and submission, activity and passivity, and parent and child. The male homosexual has even transmogrified patriarchal preference for the phallus into an exclusive worship, a syndrome that Jean Genet and Alfred Chester have dramatized. It is mystifying why the homosexual should rebel against the erotic demands of heterosexuality, but not against its behavioral modes. Perhaps the struggle against homophobia is so exhausting that the homosexual can do no more now than to break loose from the codes that govern sexual passion. Perhaps freedom is so terrifying that the homosexual clings to the old roles for some security. Or perhaps some myths and theories are correct: the structure of human life is profoundly heterosexual. No-one can defy that structure fully.

The ironic tragedy of androgyny, apart from its inherent limitations, is that it has itself kept a patriarchal bias.[11] Men may incorporate feminine virtues, but women must remain content with being wholly feminine. John Crowe Ransom, for example, believes that male poets, to be poets, must be womanly. He also admits that female poets, like Marianne Moore, can be manly. Yet his rhetoric implies that men are more apt to be good poets and to take on the mental habits of women than women are to be good poets and to take on the mental habits of men. He says:

> . . . man, at best, is an intellectualized woman. Or, man distinguishes himself from woman by intellect, but it should be well-feminized. He knows that he should not abandon sensibility and tenderness, though perhaps he has generally done so. But now that he is so far removed from the world of simple senses, he does not like to impeach his own integrity and leave his business in order to recover it . . . his problem does not arise for a woman. Less pliant, safer, as a biological organism, she remains fixed in her famous attitudes, and is indifferent to intellectually, I mean, of course, comparatively indifferent.[12]

Popular culture is more apt to produce an Alice Cooper, a man who flaunts certain feminine characteristics, than a Marlene Dietrich, a woman who puts on top-hat and tails from time to time. Happily, some women writers are now working to correct that male bias in the tradition of androgyny. In her poem, "Report from Inner Space: Seagoddess, muse," Alicia Ostriker begins by listening to two male poets—Allen Ginsberg and Robert Creeley—say how much they want to return to their mother's bodies and to grow "more feminine." Then Ostriker claims equal psychic time. She declares that she wants the traits and prerogatives of a man.

> Let me out, man, I do need
> to evolve lungs & legs & give it a try—
> I want some cold wheels
> and a technological freeway
> I want a gun like everybody else.

Other theoreticians of androgyny might wince at Ostriker's militant desires. They assume, as an article of faith, that the pacific in the "feminine" will cancel out the delight in guns and violence in the "masculine". One purpose of that serious, ingenious piece of speculative fiction, *The Left Hand of Darkness*, by Ursula K. LeGuin, is to explore such an assumption. LeGuin neither fully endorses, nor abandons, it. A larger purpose of the novel is to imagine what an androgynous world might be like. LeGuin, unlike many speculative writers, has the wit to envision a new sexual order. Yet the book exemplifies that tendency I mentioned before, that interest in androgyny that excludes or evades homosexuality.

In *The Left Hand of Darkness*, LeGuin postulates a cosmos that contains a number of planets that the human race has colonized and settled. Among them is Gethen, or Winter. Its landscape has features like those of Iceland, Greenland, and Antarctica. Its nations are like medieval Iceland or a totalitarian state minus technological overload. Perhaps because of early sexual/genetic engineering, the Gethenians are ambisexual. Everyone has a female *and* a male biological system. Everyone embodies "feminine" *and* "masculine" traits. During most of a month, the period of "somer," their sexuality is latent. Then, during a period of "kemmer," a Gethenian's sexuality is overt and potent. If two Gethenians in kemmer meet, they first indulge in foreplay. Gradually, one becomes male, the other female. If the temporarily female Gethenian becomes pregnant, she gives the child "her" family name after the pregnancy comes to term. After intercourse, or after the pregnancy, is over, each Gethenian returns to the ambisexual state.

LeGuin points out the good of such an androgynous world. Gethen has no rapists. People in kemmer respond only to other people in kemmer. Sexual fulfillment demands mutual desire. All Gethenians have equal work opportunities. Work cannot be divided up along sexual lines. Gethen has neither the Oedipus nor the Electra complex. Little Gethenians lack "psychosexual relationship to mother and father." Moralists are unable to sex-link any human excellence, or human folly. The citizens of Winter are also sterling heterosexuals. A woman, an early visitor to the planet, records that if there are kemmer-partners of the same sex, "they are so rare as to be ignored."[13]

In brief summary, the homosexual, who promises to go beyond androgyny, often fails to come near it. The androgyne, though poetic fiction, promises to go beyond patriarchy, but often fails to abolish that, or to explore alternatives to heterosexuality. Even if their promise were to be fully realized, both homosexual and androgyne would share a quality that makes them less than Utopian figures to persons who care about large-scale, structural social, political, and economic change. They are primarily models for private behavior, for private change, for private action. They enter our culture either as such models or as subjects for aesthetic play. The real connection among androgyny, homosexuality, and the reconstruction of institutions except for the family now remains largely in the world of rhetoric. The androgyne may talk of "human liberation" gilding and suffusing the future, or the androgyne may speak of the diminuation in suffering that a severing of the nexus of virility and violence might bring. However, the question, "What, if anything, does androgyny really have to do with politics?," has not yet been explicitly answered. Because laws bind them, because prejudices scar them, because rights are deprived them, homosexuals have a clear political mission. Yet the question, "After gay liberation, what?," is also in need of a full answer.

At their best, the androgyne and the homosexual, as such, have a special sensitivity to the details of a decent private life. For most people, a decent private life has something to do with sexuality. The androgyne and the homosexual may be able to explore the land between sexuality and love. They might seek an ethic of love expansive enough to translate from private to public behavior, from persons to institutions. The question of love in the post-modern world often oozes into sentiment, curdles into cliche, or poeticizes the possessive. Though he astounds me in other chapters, other verses, St. Paul offers a vision of charitable love that is fertile ground in which to sow the seeds of speculation.

> I may speak in tongues of men or of angels, but if I am without love, I am a sounding gong or a clanging cymbal. I may have the gift of prophecy, and know every hidden truth; I may have faith enough to move mountains; but if I have no love, I am nothing. I may dole out all I possess, or even give my body to be burnt, but if I have not love, I am none the better.
>
>   Love is patient; love is kind and envies no one. Love is never boastful, nor conceited, nor rude; never selfish, not quick to take offense. Love keeps no score or wrong; does not gloat over other men's sins, but delights in the truth. There is nothing love cannot face; there is no limit to its faith, its hopes, and its endurance.[14]

5   ON WORK
(1977)

I am a member of an elite. My grandparents were not. I am single. My grandparents were not. what, then, unites us, besides skin, genes, and blood? Devotion to a theory and practice of work. Their work has helped to generate mine.

My father's father, as a boy in the 1880s, herded cattle in Dakota. Later, he dug graves, waited on tables, and cleaned furnaces to earn his way through medical school. My mother's mother got up every morning at four o'clock to do the baking for the little restaurant she and my grandfather ran next to the train station in Nashua, Iowa. Work was, for them, the cause of survival; the effect of necessity. Whether they were happy or not was irrelevant. Success was a guarantee— of sorts—against disaster.

However, my grandparents were not raw materialists. They wanted to give their children more than they had gotten from their parents; to be active links in the chain of being upwardly mobile. By 1905, for example, my mother's parents had saved enough money to move West. There, they figured, they might do well enough to send their children to college. My maternal grandfather had graduated from high school; my grandmother had not. Doing well also meant working with skill and character. Rewards might be gained at the price of mercy toward oneself, but never at the price of justice and legality.

Even after they had found some security, even after they could tell stories to grandchildren who wore Stride-Rite shoes and braces, anxiety guarded them. If one worked well, one would sever the harsh past from the less dangerous present; the present from an even less dangerous and more generous future. But if things went wrong or if one did not work well—or worse, if one refused to work at all—the present would collapse back into the past, and the future would disappear. "Shirt sleeves to shirt sleeves in four generations" was a choral refrain of the adults in my childhood. Several families in town exemplified the maxim. Once, they had made it. Then, because of sloth or lack of purpose or lazy, spoiled children,

My thanks to Kim Townsend for his comments on these paragraphs.

they had lost it: the accumulated money, local prestige, ability to pay cash, the chance to take vacations.

This ideology of work and the need to fulfill it dominate me still. Even before I saw my first Blake engraving, my picture of myself as a worker was that of an angel: wings and body on fire; shooting toward heaven, at once desperate and choreographed; longing to leave the hereness of the base world behind and go into orbit in welcoming space. Yet, my experience of work, the psychology of living out the calendar it organizes, is not that of my grandparents or parents.

For of course, they are there, a pressure from the past. If I fail—a fear that haunts me as chronic illness does the flesh—I will have failed them. Unable to redeem their sacrifices, I will have denied the gift of their denials, of their sweat and discipline. I will have abandoned them, and in the harsh, clear dialectic of conditional love, they will have the right to abandon me.

Despite such apprehensions, I expect to like what I do. Pleasure is one of the privileges of professionalism. I do like most of what I do, very much. At the end of a good lecture, or of the draft of an essay or story, I may feel a rush not altogether remote from ecstasy. I say, "It worked." One reason I can have fun in my teaching job is that it offers some protection against financial catastrophe through social security, medical insurance, a pension plan. Because of this, I am partially dependent upon an institution. However, I am not dependent upon a person. To lose the autonomy and freedom that supporting myself underwrites would be a spiritual catastrophe.

Supporting myself also underwrites my refusal to marry and have children, my cheerful social isolation. I am the second of seven surviving children, the first of five girls. Making my brother's bed, washing my siblings' diapers, helped to convince me that the sanctity of domestic love could never sufficiently compensate for the rigors of domestic service. One can have stability in love without ordinary homeyness.

Some people suspect my declarations of independence. "Evasion of maturity," they mutter. "Unnatural behavior." Because I believe in the unconscious, I will hypothetically admit that I may want a child; that such a desire may jostle with my superego in hidden psychic regions, to emerge sublimated as affection for nephews, nieces, and the children of my friends. However, the taste of self-deception is familiar. The seeming absence of that combination of marshmallow and metal when I talked about my single life and why I like it, about the personal wisdom of my rejection of roles of wife and mother, assures me that I am being genuine.

I am part of a modern historical pattern. A number of women have found a traditional female role and serious work outside of the home incompatible. So did one of my mother's sisters, a chemist, who never married. So did my father's sister, a rollicking woman who married only after she had lots of jobs, including a position with the Red Cross during

World War II and in a European refugee camp afterward. The ability to recognize a set to which one belongs is helpful for self-understanding, but the decisions through which I joined that set were made before I knew there was one.

The family member who most consistently sustained me was my mother. Though she burdened me with some of her fantasies and expectations about my future, she also freed me from a debilitating pressure to accept the dictates of femininity as usual. She urged me to have a more intellectually gratifying life than she felt that she had had. I need not imitate her life, she said, as long as I did something that was both respectable and excellent. If she encouraged me, my father did not discourage me. Indeed, he paid the bills for the ambiguously supportive and straightforwardly expensive women's college I attended.

Those of us who reject both the idea of failure and the conventional criteria of feminine success must construct our own tests of triumph. I am now trying to articulate a new set of standards which will be of fresh vitality and worth. To do so, I am pulling apart a sticky conflation of fame and success that I have made; trying to attend more strictly to things for their own sake, rather than to things for the sake of fame and success; and withdrawing from an overexacting submission to two other tests of worth I once used.

The first asked me to score as perfectly as possible at public trials such as an IQ test. They publicly measured me both against an absolute standard and against other people. The second demanded that I win as much praise and as many expressions of esteem as possible. Because such qualitative statements of esteem can be elusive, even enigmatic, victory in the second test was much more demanding than in the first.

Such examinations were exhausting. They also bred ambivalence about other people. Significant human applause metered my sense of the worth of my work. However, if that work was to win that applause, I had to better most humans. Another self-image, less hot and glamorous than that of the orbiting angel, was to stand alone on a plain—rivals vanquished, vanished, banished. At once in thrall to and at odds with others, I wanted to achieve a version of ascribed status.

Whatever the tests of success, no matter who or what the agencies of judgment may be, I am most genial and relaxed when working well. During my middle twenties, back in America after two happy years of study in Europe on a Fulbright, I was empty of both animating purpose and a job that might execute and symbolize it. The need for them was too strong to permit me to go to hell with a big splash. My dissipations were reasonably trivial, demeaning rather than tragic. My jobs were menial. During one, a secretarial position in a reform campaign, I forgot my name was "Catharine" and began to believe that I had been rebaptized as "girl." If I learned things I needed to know, my curriculum specialized more in the tacky than in the extreme. During this "lost period," I had megalomaniac fantasies about the future. At the very least, I would be a senator before I was forty. My most arrogant dreams of work were as sweetly lurid as some nineteenth-century American landscape painting. They burst forth when my guilty sense of having betrayed my promise—the assurance ot past and present generations that I had a talent the future would recognize—was at its most rapacious.

The lost period incorporated the first two or three years of Columbia Graduate School. I entered there to prepare for work that might carry with it both significance and freedom. My emergence from this period marked the end of some necessary growing up, some exploration of possibilities of not being "good." It also coincided with the growth of the New Feminism. In 1966, when I was thirty, I went to my first feminist meeting, a chapter of NOW, in a church basement near Columbia. By then I was also teaching freshman English at Barnard College. The women's movement has fertilized my consciousness and morality; without it I would still have worked ambitiously. I have an appetite for autonomy, self-expression, recognition, and for change. However the women's movement has given me dignified hopes, ideas, and a community. If my grandparents and parents worked for their blood family, I work, in part, for my political relatives.

Feminism also places me in a paradoxical position. Beyond its call for sexual equality is a legitimate skepticism of such "male values" as the love of power, endorsement of competitive zeal, and an equation of worth with worldly deeds. Still, I want my share of power; I have my share of competitiveness; I go after my share of worldly deeds. I work as a middle-class man might. I have repudiated woman's subordination and her constricted role in the home, but not the well-meaning professional's role in the world. A serious worry is that I, though an active feminist, may be phallocentric; that I may be more in love with power, victory, and the craving ego than I need to be in order to work autonomously, creatively, energetically.

This anxiety, that a discrepancy exists between my politics and my personality, is but one of several sources of psychic insomnia. Much of my life is spent in public performance: teaching, speaking, publishing. The gap between the performance and the self-doubt of the performer sometimes seems unmanageable. I like reassurance, but I hesitate to confess dependency on it. No amount of inoculation against self-pity has fully immunized me against its sickly charm. I get lonely.

One accepts such minor crises of belief and of the emotions as one does weeds. In my middle years, I think I have been fortunate. I wonder if I ought not to rearrange my occupations—perhaps to write more and to teach less. A legacy of mobility is restlessness. I often remember my mother's mother, the wonderful security of her unconditional tenderness. A world without her resilience and capacity for love would be terrible, unacceptable, but, in brief, I am glad that I am not, and will not, be her. However, I regret that as I received and achieved much of what she wanted for her family—my education, for example—I also received and achieved what my politics have ultimately taught me to suspect: that membership, albeit marginal, in an elite.

6

TILLIE OLSEN:
WITNESS AS SERVANT
(1977)

We know now, if we care to know at all, that history has spliced feminism, literature, and other politics together. The combinations and recombinations have released at least three species of the rebellious text: those that subsume anger at women's condition under an exposure of other forms of inequity and suffering;[1] those that express that anger directly;[2] and finally, those that fuse feminism and other forms of radical analysis.[3]

Tillie Olsen, like Marge Piercy, works towards such a synthesis. Her story "O Yes," for example, is about both the socialization of children, a feminist concern, and racism, a moral concern of writers since Aphra Behn in the seventeenth-century. Such a synthesis demands that the narratives of political literature expand to include—if not to make central—domestic life; the experience of women as a group; and the ways in which sex/gender systems function.[4] Unfortunately, trying to satisfy this demand may enmesh a writer like Olsen in contradictions, which she may either ignore or attempt to resolve. In addition, Olsen, again like Marge Piercy, is doing more than measuring wrongs. She also desires a future world—new, recreated, right. So doing, she brings together protest and dream. However, particularly in her fiction, the price of injustice that she calculates is high enough to threaten to overwhelm the assertion that dreams may be realized.

Particularly in *Yonnondio*—that fragmented tale begun in 1932, partly published and fully praised in 1934, then put aside and left unfinished until 1973—Olsen attacks capitalist industry and agriculture, their exploitation of human, animal and natural resources. Olsen, though she set *Yonnondio* in the 1920's, saw it chiefly as a novel of the 1930's, with the active consciousness of that period. Somewhat like Edith Wharton, in *House of Mirth*, who measured the corruption of New York society by observing

Some of my ideas about Tillie Olsen were published in "Three Women Work It Out," *Nation*, 219, 18, (November 30, 1974), 1565–6. A version of this paper was read at the Rutgers Interdisciplinary Conference on Politics and Literature, March, 1977.

what it destroyed, Olsen wants to teach us about the vileness of a system by dramatizing the indifference with which it victimizes human beings. In order to provoke us into a rage acute enough to want to work against the system, her victims—female and male—must be essentially decent. Her powerless miners, day laborers, and tenant farmers want to be good. One sign of that desire is the nature of their dreams. None of them want to triumph wholly within the system; that would be a tainted success.

Some protest literature may tend to tempt the writer away from the empiricism of the novel and towards the fabulousness of a kind of romance. There heroes are superior to their environment, a setting in which the laws of justice have either been suspended or wait to be summoned into being. Olsen is not immune to such a morally-charged psychology. She may sound as if she endorses the loose requirements of the realistic novel. For example, she praises Rebecca Harding Davis for maintaining "that fiction which incorporates social and economic problems directly, *and in terms of their effects on human beings.*"[5] Yet her aroused humanism insists upon the conscience, the sensibility, the worth, and the capabilities of the marginal and of the dispossessed. Because circumstances may deform adults, their children most fully embody their innate strength and promise. So a baby girl is happy as she learns to play with the lid of a fruit jar in the stinking kitchen of a slum house in a city that the meat packing industry dominates. Describing the infant's triumph, Olsen celebrates the "human ecstasy of achievement, satisfaction deep and fundamental as sex: *I achieve, I use my power; I! I!*"[6] The passage is not a warning against the unbridled ego, but a marker of a belief in the presumptive heroism of the innocent.

Olsen also knows that poor women probably have a more difficult, a harsher, life than poor men. First, women are potentially, if not actually, members of a double proletariat. They must work at home, without wages, and then, if necessary, work outside of the home for whatever wages they can get. Anna Holbrook, the besieged wife and mother of *Yonnondio*, must go from door to door, to beg for piecemeal jobs as a laundress. Next, women are sexually more vulnerable than men. Not only does a Jim Holbrook's desire to have sex with his wife overpower her need to be physically left alone, but an Anna must then carry the children sex generates. Next, women cannot succumb to an escape men have: the chance to run away from home, temporarily or permanently. Jim Holbrook gets drunk in a bar; he disappears, without explanation, for ten days. Anna, at once stranded and rooted at home with the children, can only flee into illness and depression. A feminist might use a Jim Holbrook to make palpable a theory, like that of John Stuart Mill, of a cross-class male drive towards rule; of a cross-class male fear, at once brutal and skittish, of sexual equality. However, Olsen's belief in the goodness of her subjects renders full allegiance to such a theory logically impossible. The fact that poor women are more victimized than the poor men, who help to victimize the poor women, cannot obscure, for her, the fact that poor men are victims too.

In her sense of domesticity and family life Olsen must also balance possibly conflicting perceptions. She is hardly a Maribel Morgan, giddy and atwitter with the delights of a prettily old-fashioned womanhood. Unsentimentally, Olsen's fictions present family women who, as they succor others, are themselves starved for comfort; women who have sickened of moving to the rhythms of others; women who are left alone after those whom they have so passionately attended go elsewhere; women who are forced to choose between conjugal intimacies and the autonomous claims of their own intelligence. Eva, the heroine of "Tell Me a Riddle," old and dying of cancer, remembers being a young wife. Then, while nursing one baby and holding another, she would still try to stay awake to read. Her husband, coming home "late from a meeting . . . stimulated and ardent, . . . " would promise to take the baby to its bed if only she would put aside Chekhov and come to their bed. As unsparingly, Olsen's essays eloquently state that, for most women, the life of art and the life of domesticity have been irreconcilable. The claims of creativity have had to give way to the claims of femininity, too often construed as synonomous with domesticity. In her well-known morphology of silence, "Silences: When Writers Don't Write,"[7] Olsen outlines the ways in which the demands of home, husband, and children push women into silence, or into a prattling, specious speech. She notes how many creative women have been childless.

However, Olsen has also happily commented on the fact that during the course of the twentieth-century, more women seem to have been able to combine the roles of artist and mother. For Olsen also offers up domestic life as a rich and necessary existence. She seems to reserve a special respect for the mother who—despite poverty, "humiliations and terrors," and endless struggles against physical and spiritual grime—keeps the home going. Such a mother is a major symbol of the battered, ennobled will, and when she fails, Olsen assigns to her fall the dignity that tragedy once reserved for kings. So she mourns Anna Holbrook after her bloody miscarriage and nervous breakdown:

> It was not any and it was all of these things that brought her now to swaying in the middle of the floor, twisting and twisting the rompers in soundless anguish. It was that she felt so worn, so helpless; that it loomed gigantic beyond her, impossible ever to achieve, beyond any effort or doing of hers; that task of making a better life for her children to which her being was bound. (*Yonnondio*, p. 127)

Her homeless characters—the sailor in "Hey Sailor, What Ship?" or the husband about to become a widower in "Tell Me a Riddle"—perhaps best feel, through a process of negation, what home might signify and mean.

First, the home is the arena in which the daily survival tasks of life are done; in which food, shelter, clothing, and sleep are provided for, in which the angel in the house bears Ajax. Next, the home can offer love, quotidian caring, hard to sustain, hard to do without. Between husband and wife there can be a closeness, a unity, that both includes and transcends erotic sexuality. The old man in "Tell Me a Riddle" is miserable when his wife wants to sleep alone:

> After all the years, old harmonies and dependencies deep in their bodies; she curled to him, or he coiled to her, each warmed, warming, turning as the other turned, the nights a long embrace.[8]

Next, parents can transmit a moral sense to their children, a mingling of compassion, experience, and commitment to social justice. The ideology a family hands down may be at odds with and better than the dominant society. A mother, caressing a daughter, thinks:

> . . . caring asks doing. It is a long baptism into the seas of humankind, my daughter. Better immersion than to live untouched. (*Tell Me a Riddle*, p. 61)

Finally, the family can be an instrument of hope. Parents may continue to struggle because they believe that if they do so, their children's lives will be better than their own; because they believe that their energetic sacrifices will stimulate history into a progressive movement that will prove more benign for the children than their own historical phase proved to be for them.

Because Olsen construes the family as such a conduit of improvement, her sense of domesticity is inseparable from that dear, tired subject: the American dream—that vision of a peaceable kingdom; that combination of Thomas Jefferson, Paul Bunyan, Thomas Edison, and Horatio Alger, which, on the surface, has very little to do with Sigmund Freud. The personal contents of the American dream for her characters are modest. They want their children to be healthy, at ease, with wholesome and reliable food and shelter. The Holbrooks, particularly Anna, believe that schools and libraries wil be the means to such ends. Anna tells her daughter Mazie:

> An edijication is what you kids are going to get. It means your hands stay white and you read books and work in an office. (*Yonnondio*, p. 4)

The Holbrooks begin to realize the dream, with its European roots, on a farm in South Dakota. There they share a brief, peaceful interlude between life in a mining town and an industrial city. Anna permits herself to think that she might have:

> School for the kids, Jim working near her, on the earth, lovely things to keep, brass lamps, bright tablecloths, vines over the doors, roses twining. (*Yonnondio*, p. 39)

Amidst such tranquillity; such unity of marriage, family, nature and work, sex divisions of labor are less the mark of a patriarchal hierarchy than the social equivalent of the aesthetic fact that harmonies are blends of different pitches.

The political contents of Olsen's dreams are also straightforward. They seem naive in comparison to a sophisticated ideal of the state, but they also seem idealistic in comparison to the possibility of realizing them. They include generous and egalitarian human relations; an individual freedom, for members of both sexes, that does not swell up into domination of others; "light and cheering throngs and happiness" (*Yonnondio*, p. 8). Olsen embodies such public visions in metaphors, in pictures of small groups that fuse self-expression and group ritual: a family singing; the members of a farm community dancing.

Olsen reveres the capacity for aspiration as well as its particular forms. She admires a young girl in a tent in a garbage dump who exercises the faculty of desire, though she regrets that Hollywood has given the child shoddy counters with which to dream. However, Olsen's analysis forces her, as it has others, to recognize the double meaning of the word "dream." It may signify a vision, be it of a new heaven or a new earth or both; or the word may signify a nightmare, the negation of the happy vision. In *Yonnondio*, Maize hopes that the reality of her life will prove to be such a nightmare, from which awakening will release her. Given her sense of American politics, Olsen cannot show the achievement of the good dream, only its transformation into terror or its dissolution. When the dream is dissipated, as it is for the American-born children of Russian revolutionaries in "Tell Me a Riddle," its political contents, its sense of "the flame of freedom, the light of knowledge," are lost. Only its personal contents are gratified. Without the political, the personal is merely materialistic.

For most, the dream is taken, not thrown away. People are sold out. They do not sell out. For example, Rebecca Harding Davis succumbs to a self-destructive feminine role because of false consciousness and circumstances, not because of avarice or malice. Because she deals with "what should have been and what cannot be helped," a general sense of irrevocable, blameless loss pervades Olsen's work. Her literature is profoundly elegiac. She suspects Walt Whitman because he lacks a strong

enough sense of the holocaust of industrialism, but she takes the title
Yonnondio from his poem/dirge of the same name. The word means
"lament for the aborigines," for vanished chieftains, medicine men, and
warriors who have gone by like "clouds of ghosts." They have neither
record nor permanence.

As Olsen lists the causes of the loss of talent, love, promise, energy,
adventurousness, power and creativity; as she enumerates the "inequities,
restrictions, penalties, denials, leechings";[9] her voice moves from elegy to
accusation; from lament to anger; from grief to a controlled jeremiad. What
has died in some of those for whom she mourns is the capacity for action.
They will do nothing more. What has died in others of those for whom she
mourns is the capacity for creating genuine art. They will sculpt or say
nothing more. In the case of Rebecca Harding Davis, she will say only
nothings. What has vanished in all is the capacity to imagine the future
honorably, ambitiously.

For all the victims, there may be periods between silence, or its
equivalents, and the full articulation of their dreams— periods of
stammering, of fragmented speech. For the physically living, the internal
pressure to use the language of desire exists, but both psychic stress and
external forces clamp speech back as it struggles to emerge. For the
physically dying, such stresses relax and such external forces lose their
suffocating strength. For the dying, then, fragmentation is not a stylistic
marker of autonomy succumbing, but of autonomy appearing before life is
extinguished. So Eva, in "Tell Me a Riddle," dying of the cancer that a
doctor has diagnosed too late, lapses back into her past as various forms of
censorship abdicate their power. The long-suppressed contents of
consciousness erupts in flares and dashes. In yet another example of
Olsen's belief in the helpless excellence of the powerless, they are pleas for
the possibility of social virtue:

> No man one   except through others
> Strong with the not yet   in the now
> Dogma dead   war dead   one country
> (*Tell Me a Riddle*, p. 109)

Given the relationships between the home and the dream, a violation to
one is a violation to the other. Both wounds are regrettable. Olsen's
attraction to the home—no matter how sorrowfully or frequently or
regretfully she qualifies it—helps to distinguish her ardent feminism from
that which would abolish the family, be it nuclear or extended, altogether.
Since the domestic sphere has such promise, its difficulties must be
attributed to other institutions. The organism of domesticity must be
remedially diseased, not intrinsically destructive. If husbands beat wives,

and wives then beat their children, their domestic violence must be construed as their release from external tensions. When mining becomes unendurable, Jim Holbrook:

> . . . had nothing but heavy blows for the children, and he struck Anna too often to remember. Every payday he clumped home, washed, went to town, and returned hours later, dead drunk . . . Anna too became bitter and brutal. If one of the children was in her way, if they did not obey her instantly, she would hit at them in a blind rage, as if it were some devil she was exorcising. Afterward, in the midst of her work, regret would cramp her heart at the memory of the tear-stained little faces. "'Twasn't them I was beating up on. Something just seems to get into me when I have somethin to hit." (p. 9)

The alienation that family members feel from each other, the alienation within intimacies they ought to share, is numbing enough to obscure its social and economic origins. At the same time, the responsibilities of intimacy are strong enough to bind good men to bad jobs. Jim Holbrook would like to stop working on a sewer construction crew, but cannot. The same complex sense of "manhood" that inspires resistance to exploitation also subdues it. Caught between signals, Jim can only transform the demands of manhood that call for resistance to demands for endurance. He also consoles himself with the rare pleasures of paternity. He tells himself:

> "All right for Tracy to talk, but he doesn't have a wife and brats. But no man has any business having 'em that wants to stay a man. Not unless he knows he's goin' to hafta take crap . . . Not that they aren't worth it though," thinking of Jimmie, "what else you got?" (*Yonnondio*, p. 87).

If fathers find their children one of the few rewards of the otherwise punishing toil of their lives, mothers may find their toil a punishment for their children. A mother's entrance into the labor force, out of economic necessity, demands that she exchange a rich, if problematic, psychic support system for a sparser physical one. A regretful woman muses about her oldest daughter:

> She was a child seldom smiled at. Her father left me before she was a year old. I had to work her first six years when there was work, or I sent her home and to his relatives . . . She was a child of anxious, not proud, love. We were poor and could not afford her the soil of easy growth.[10]

Olsen is angrily aware that the exploitation of workers— female and male—in the sphere of production is not the only service they "give" to the powerful. Their miseries in the sphere of reproduction also sustain those

who, controlling social and economic structures, block the dream: then
Olsen must confront the conflict that animates Western feminism itself:
what about the bourgeois woman? What about her class status and
privileges? Women may be members of the same sex, but they are also
members of different classes. Consequently, they both mirror and maim
each other. Olsen's attitude towards bourgeois women is necessarily
contradictory. In her fiction, they are victimizers. In "*I Stand Here Ironing*,"
a working-class child must go to a clinic in the country. Helping to
underwrite this loveless, demeaning place are charitable balls that "sleek
young women" plan when they are not decorating Easter eggs and filling
Christmas stockings for the objects of their sterile philanthropy. In
Yonnondio, Anna takes her children for a walk through a "nice"
neighbourhood on a quest for greens for supper. First, two girls snicker at
them. Then, "a woman putting on white gloves" smiles at them. As a
resentful Mazie moves to protect her mother, she represents the child who
must nurture the adult woman against the assaults of class.

Yet, in Olsen's non-fiction, all women are victims of male hegemony. Olsen
writes, with taut lyricism, of the constraints upon the bourgeois woman that
objectify, trivialize, infantalize, and diminish her. Her essay on Rebecca
Harding Davis brilliantly anatomizes such a process. In Olsen's feminism,
what binds women together is loss. If only some women are members of the
double proletariat, from which other women profit, all women can share a
sense of violation of the potential self, of deprivation. As they are psychologically wounded, so may their capacity for physical passion be suppressed
if their bodies do not fit "the prevailing standards of female beauty or
behavior."[11] In effect, what Olsen grants working-class men in her fiction, a
latitude of forgiveness, she grants to bourgeois women in her non-fiction.

How far a sense of shared misery can go as the glue for political action
is uncertain. Olsen, in her writing, is less a source of pragmatic advice on
ways to enact feminism or other dreams than of the affective perception of
a community of sorrow. One female loss that she mourns most acutely is
that of the potential writer and artist. She laments both the women who
were kept from the aesthetic lives they might have had and the literature
they might have produced, particularly rich, accurate descriptions of
domestic life itself. In one of her turns against the home, Olsen plausibly
suggests that the neglect of housework as a literary subject has had political
effects. The writer has not really helped to "create an arousing awareness
(as literature has done in other realms)." This lack of consciousness of
women's chores "has contributed to the agonizingly slow elimination of
technologically and socially obsolete, human-wasting drudgery."[12] She
implies that if housework had not been too lowly a subject for political
writing as usual, women would have been able to write more and exhaust
themselves for the household less.

Olsen, of course, does not limit her ideas about the writer to women. Everyone, she believes, responds to their world aesthetically. Every child can create assemblages out of junk piles and be among the "nameless Frank Lloyd Wrights." Such a conviction about sensitivity parallels the democratic theory that everyone can dream of a fairer life than he or she now has. However, for Olsen, the artist has a stronger sense of beauty; a more compelling need to form artifacts out of life's jumbled facts. Mazie Holbrook's wish to fit language to reality as poetically as possible is more passionate than that of her brothers. On the other hand, her brother Jimmie's ability to sing is purer than her own.

The romantic figure of the artist as someone of special sensibility could prove problematic for an egalitarian. Olsen is aware of one danger: that the artist might become enmeshed in bourgeois needs and flattery and become the plaything of the pampered. Describing the death of a miner, Andy Kvaternick, she writes sarcastically:

> Earth take your dreams that a few may languidly lie on couches and trill 'How exquisite' to paid dreamers. (*Yonnondio*, p. 8)

A second danger is less consciously examined that sensibility might demand its own privileges, not of affluence, but of cultivated isolation. Olsen may skimp this subject simply because the sense of loss in her work is so pervasive that the difficulties of gain, of a life spent in a plentitude of creativity, is not available to her as subject matter. Yet, as if she felt the danger, she responds to it by postulating several roles for an artist. They do not require the artist to be a propagandist, but to explore beauty and to aid the community and its needs simultaneously. Such a reconciliation between aesthetics and group service is similar to the reconciliation that Olsen hopes contemporary women writers will achieve between literature and family service, between the private world of art and the little public world of domesticity.

First, the artist must serve as witness. Olsen would mock the evil, and argue with them, but otherwise, her sense of the writer as witness derives from that of Walt Whitman in "Song of Myself." However, the writer must witness a particular set of memories, lives, and dreams: those of the "despised people." They may be in special need because they themselves have been rendered inarticulate. Despite her failures as a feminist precursor, Olsen finds in Rebecca Harding Davis a model of the writer who watches the reality of such lives so closely that she transforms sight "into comprehension, Vision."[13] In *Life In The Iron Mills*, the novella Olsen helped to restore to public attention, Davis gives us a potential witness who has been destroyed; 19-year-old Hugh Wolfe. He carves figures from korl, the refuse from steel mill ore. In order to continue his sculpture, he steals

some money. Legally culpable, morally blameless, he is sentenced to a
19-year-term. In his jail cell, he commits suicide with the rough instrument
that has been his artist's tool.

To write about the despised and the silenced is to record that they were
present in history. Then, though a particular text becomes a part of the
past, it can still be read in the constantly new present. In effect, it
reproduces one generation— its hopes and its defeats—for the next. Eva
thinks, in "Tell Me a Riddle," that "stone will perish, but the word remain"
(p. 90). The text will then serve, not only as history, but as answer to those
who might ask, "But what is to be done?" They are to perpetuate the hope
and to redeem the defeats.

However, if literature is to have these profoundly educational functions,
it must be read as well as written. A Rebecca Harding Davis must be
accorded more than one or two sentences, if that, in a history of the radical
novel.[14] Not only individual talents must be made visible, but the traditions
in which they were created. Olsen's experience has taught her that schools
may break down even for those whom they pretend to enlighten. For
example, she had to discover Rebecca Harding Davis' work in an Omaha
junkshop amidst a pile of old magazines. As a result, the artist must
continually invent extraordinary classrooms and curricula. He or she must,
in life, become an intellectual alternative.[15]

In Olsen's case, the writer does not serve as witness and servant simply
to avoid the theoretical dangers of detachment, of a severance of the realm
of literature from that of politics, culture, and society. Olsen has also
participated in the exclusions and constrictions and losses she dramatizes.
She writes of "myself so nearly remaining mute and having let writing die
over and over again in me" (*Yonnondio*, p. 153). She is, then, a survivor,
whose responsibility is to honor those who, though equally worthy, did not
survive.

The act of witnessing, when it returns to the shadows of the past and
becomes elegiac, sees possibilities of wretchedness that, somehow, the
witness evaded; the final losses that the ego did not, after all, have to
endure. The act of witnessing, when it records the dreams that animated
the past and were a source of its dignity, sees possible alternatives to
wretchedness. In both cases, the witness is, in effect, saying, "I wish my
work to so alter circumstances that if I were to be born again, I would not
have to fear death, and the death of my dream, as I once did."

7

SHAKESPEARE AND THE SOIL OF RAPE (1980)

Shakespeare's sympathy toward women helps to create an attitude toward rape that is more generous and less foolish than that of many of our contemporaries. He never sniggers and assumes that women, consciously or unconsciously, seek the rapist out and then enjoy the deed: brutal, enforced sex; the ghastly tmesis of the flesh. He never gives "proud lords" the right to "Make weak-made women tenants to their shame."[1] Nor does the act dominate his imagination, as it might that of a lesser writer as concerned with violence, war, and sexuality as Shakespeare is. In the complete works, the word "rape" occurs only seventeen times; "rapes" three; and various forms of "ravish" thirty-eight.[2] "Ravish" is perhaps like a poetic gloss that both hints at and denies rape's brutal force.

When rape occurs, it is terrible in itself. Like murder, it displays an aggressor in action. Shakespeare and his rapists use stridently masculine metaphors of war and of the hunt to capture that flagrant energy. Tarquin

> . . . shakes aloft his Roman blade,
> Which, like a falcon tow'ring in the skies,
> Coucheth the fowl below with his wings' shade, . . .
> (*Lucrece*, lines 505–7)

Like murder, rape also pictures a helpless victim, powerless vulnerability. Because rape's violence is sexual, an audience watching it can live out voyeuristic fantasies. Moreover, Shakespearean rape signifies vast conflicts: between unnatural disorder and natural order; raw, polluting lust and its purification through chastity or celibacy; the dishonorable and the honorable exercise of power; "hot-burning will" and "frozen conscience" (*Lucrece*, line 247); and the sinful and righteous begetting of children. A

An earlier version of this essay was presented at the International Shakespeare Association Congress, April 20, 1976, Washington, D.C. The author is grateful to Allison Heisch and Carol T. Neely for their helpful comments.

chaste wife, a "clean" marriage bed, guarantee that property rights will pass
to a man's blood heirs. For a man to rape a woman, then, is to take sides;
to make a series of choices. Rape tempts and tests him, physically and
morally.

The structure of Shakespearean rape scenes itself embodies a conflict.
The language in which rapes are imagined and then enacted is vivid,
immediate, extended, garish, sometimes hallucinatory: "Night-wand'ring
weasels shriek" (*Lucrece*, line 307); Lucrece's breasts are "like ivory globes
circled with blue" (line 407). The breast, at once erotic and maternal, swells
to symbolize the body that will be overcome. However, the setting of the
rape scenes in the plays is remote in time or place or both, usually near
Italy, if not actually within it. The result is a dramatic sexuality that has the
simultaneous detail and distance of a dream/nightmare. The dream/
nightmare also contains frequent references to past rapes, to the Trojan
War, to the legend of Philomel. Shakespeare compares Lucrece to
"lamenting Philomele" (line 1079), a bitterly poignant allusion she herself
will make. In *Titus Andronicus*, both Aaron and Marcus will join Philomel
and Lavinia in a female community of suffering (II.iii.43; II.iv.26). Aaron
judges Lavinia as pure as Lucrece. (II.ii.108.) Such reminders give the
dream/nightmare the repetitive weight of myth and history, of experiences
that have occurred before and will occur again.

When a man pursues, besieges, and batters a woman's body, he assaults
a total world. The female flesh is a passive microcosm. Lucrece is a world,
a "sweet city" (line 469). In *Coriolanus*, Cominius says to Menenius:

> You have holp to ravish your own daughters
> and
> To melt the city leads upon your pates,
> To see your wives dishonour'd to your noses—
> Your temples burned in their cement, and
> Your franchises, whereon you stood, confin'd
> Into an auger's bore.
>
> (IV.vi.81–8, 85–87)

In *Titus Andronicus*, "Lavinia and Tamora may be seen as symbolic
personifications of female Rome."[3] The question then becomes, "To whom
does the world belong?" The order of Cominius's clauses, as well as his
pronouns, provides an answer. The world belongs to men: fathers,
husbands, lovers, brothers. Because in Shakespeare only well-born women
are raped, their violation becomes one of property, status, and symbolic
worth as well. The greater those values, the greater the sense of power
their conquest confers upon the rapist.

Because men rape what other men possess, rape becomes in part a
disastrous element of male rivalry. The woman's body is a prize in a zero-

sum game that men play. Collatine's boasting about Lucrece, an act of excess that is a rhetorical analogue to Tarquin's sexual will, helps to provoke the ruler's desire to conquer the pride of his subordinate. In *Titus Andronicus*, the vicious competition of Demetrius and Chiron parallels the sibling hostilities between Saturninus and Bassianus. However, Demetrius and Chiron stop fighting over Lavinia when it comes time to rape, mutilate, and humiliate her. The joys of controlling a woman together subsume the difficulties of deciding which one will control her independently. Their horrible, giggling plan—to use Bassianus's "dead trunk" as "pillow to our lust" (II.iii.130)— deflects and satisfies their need to defeat other men, to deprive them of their rights and gratifications. When their mother gives birth to Aaron's child, their half-brother, Demetrius and Chiron also unite in their disgust, an emotion that yokes Oedipal jealousy, racist revulsion at miscegenation, and fear of the Roman political consequences of their mother's adultery.

Such rivalry can occur within a man as well as between men. Tarquin, in his long internal debates, struggles between the good self, who argues against rape, and the bad self, who demands sexual triumph. Tarquin is unable to use the common justification for rape: political or familial revenge. He is equally unable to forget that Collatine is a principal man in his army, a kinsman, and a friend; these are male bonds that invert and undermine male rivalries. Tarquin mourns:

> Had Collatinus kill'd my son or sire,
> Or lain in ambush to betray my life,
> Or were he not my dear friend, this desire
> Might have excuse to work upon his wife,
> As in revenge or quittal of such strife;
> But as he is my kinsman, my dear friend,
> The shame and fault finds no excuse nor end.
> (lines 232–38)

In psychoanalytical terms, Tarquin's ego is torn between the demands of a libido and a superego whose appeals Lucrece vainly tries to reinforce. After the rape, the superego takes its belated revenge. Guilt immediately deprives Tarquin of any sense of sexual pleasure. In *Measure for Measure*, Angelo will later act out Tarquin's struggle. He will put Isabella in the position of a potential rape victim, for the "choice" he offers her—submit to me sexually or commit your brother to death—is a version of the "choice" Tarquin presents to Lucrece—submit to me sexually or commit yourself to death.[4]

For women, rape means both submission, death, and more. Shakespeare never falters, never hedges, as he shows how defenseless women are before sexual violence and the large destructiveness it entails. Forced sexual submission enforces female death. For the loss of chastity, "a dearer thing than life" (*Lucrece*, line 687) stains women irrevocably. Lavinia knows that being murdered is better than being subjected to a "worse than killing lust" (*Titus*, II.iii.175) that will deprive her of her reason for living. Women are unwillingly responsible for a "cureless crime" (*Lucrece*, line 772). Lucrece, her act at once sacrificial, redemptive, and flamboyant enough to make her husband's friends wish to revenge her, must kill herself. Because "the girl should not survive her shame" (V.iii.41), Titus stabs Lavinia. Their deaths purge the lives and honor of the men whom they have ornamented: Lucrece's husband and father, whose mournings mingle over her corpse; Lavinia's father alone, her husband being dead.[5]

Few of Shakespeare's dramas about traumatic injustice are as clear, or as severe, as those about the raped woman who must be punished because she endured an aggression she never sought and against which she fought. Shakespeare deploys the voice of moderate men to comment on such unfair expiations. In *The Rape of Lucrece*, Brutus thinks Lucrece's suicide a final act of excess in a Rome Tarquin and his family have ruled. Discarding the mask of silliness he has expediently worn to now reveal an authentic self, he tells Collatine not to "steep thy heart/In such relenting dew of lamentations . . . " (lines 1828–29). He urges Collatine to abandon private grief for political action and rid Rome of Tarquin. In a sense, Brutus uses Lucrece's anguish as a weapon in a struggle betwen men for power. In *Titus Andronicus*, Marcus asks for compassion for his niece and shows her how to publicize her plight. The reasonableness of a Brutus or Marcus contrasts to the despicable excesses of will of the rapist and the dangerous excesses of rhetoric of husbands who brag about their wives' chaste fidelity. Oddly, moderate women (like Paulina) who play prominent, articulate roles defending the victimized woman in Shakespeare's explorations of sexual jealousy, are missing from the examinations of rape.[6] Their absence starkly points to women's inability to control and to influence in benign ways the public structures that judge rape and the psychosexual needs that generate it.

Indeed, women assist in the rapes that attack other women. In *Lucrece*, night is allegorically female, a sable "mother of dread and fear" (line 117). In *Titus Andronicus*, Tamora wants to destroy Lavinia. Like Clytemnestra, she seeks revenge for the sacrifice of her children. She is also annoyed and threatened because Bassianus and Lavinia have discovered her sporting with Aaron in the woods. However, Tamora's encouragement of her sons to rape not simply Lavinia but any Roman woman has a lascivious quality that flows beyond these motives. Letting her boys "satisfy their lust" (II.iii.180) expresses her enjoyment of her sons' potency, which veers toward and approaches a sublimated incest.

Tempting such taboos, Tamora deliberately turns away from Lavinia.

She ignores the plaintive cry, "O Tamora! thou bearest a woman's face—"
(II.iii.136) and denies, as Lady Macbeth will do, her own femaleness. This is
but one act in a series that will end when she eats her dead children; when
she incorporates them back into her body it is an inversion of the release of
a living child that marks natural maternity. The forest setting of Lavinia's
rape increases the play's sense of distorted, squalid sexuality. The soil is
soiled in a perversion of nature comparable to the perversion of
domesticity Tarquin creates in Collatine's and Lucrece's marriage bed. The
pit that becomes Bassianus's grave, "unhallowed and blood-stained"
(II.iii.210), symbolizes the violated female genitalia and womb as well.

Self-reflexive Shakespeare, ever rewriting his materials, also offers a
darkly comic study of imagined rape. In *Cymbeline*, Posthumus flaunts
Imogen's virtue before Iachimo and dares him to assail it. Iachimo does not
physically rape Imogen, but his theft of her good reputation, like his
penetration of her bedchamber, is a psychic equivalent. He admits this
when he compares himself to Tarquin. Learning that Posthumus thinks her
a strumpet and her sex a regiment of strumpets, Imogen begins to imitate
Lucrece by stabbing herself in the heart. In addition, clod Cloten sees
Posthumus as his rival. Cloten's fantasies parody a conflict between men in
which victory means the right to assume the identity of the vanquished, to
wear his clothes, to have his wife. Cloten also desires to revenge himself
upon the woman who, defending herself against his advances, has
offended him. With the encouragement of his mother, he imagines his
sexuality as a vehicle of punishment. So he mutters:

> . . . With that suit [Posthumus's] upon
> my back will I ravish her; first kill him, and in her
> eyes. There shall she see my valour, which will then
> be a torment to her contempt. He on the ground,
> my speech of insultment ended on his dead body,
> and when my lust hath dined (which, as I say, to
> vex her I will execute in the clothes that she so
> prais'd), to the court I'll knock her back, foot her
> home again. She hath despis'd me rejoicingly, and
> I'll be merry in my revenge.
>
> (III.v.140–50)

However, crude Cloten cannot transform fantasy into act. Such inadequacies become a grossly comic figure. In *Cymbeline*, comedy blunts
the force of Shakespeare's analysis of male enmity and the reunion of
Posthumus and Imogen mitigates the force of his brief against the wagers,
literal and figurative, that men place on women's virtue.

The fact of having been raped obliterates all of a woman's previous
claims to virtue. One *sexual* experience hereafter will define her. Such a

strict interpretation of rape may be an index to a shift in the position of women during Shakespeare's time. One historian has suggested: "What the Reformation era witnessed was the changing delineation of women's roles. As this period drew to a close, women's roles became defined increasingly by sex—to the detriment of all women—rather than by class."[7] Other historians have postulated that the more controlled female sexuality is in particular societies, the less power women have. Shakespeare warns his audience about breakdowns in the boundaries on male sexuality, showing rapists as vicious and out of control. However, he also reminds his audience about the boundaries that marriage places on female sexuality. His protest is not against such confinements, but against assaults upon them. If Shakespearean rape does indeed signify such a double retraction—of female identity to sexual identity, of female sexual expressiveness to marital fidelity—it might illustrate the intricate development, between 1580 and 1640, of what Lawrence Stone has named the Restricted Patriarchal Nuclear Family. Stone writes: ". . . both state and Church, for their own reasons, actively reinforced the pre-existent patriarchy within the family, and there are signs that the power of the husband and father over the wife and the children was positively strengthened, making him a legalized petty tyrant within the home."[8] Coppélia Kahn then correctly reads *The Rape of Lucrece* as the poetic version of an ideology that justifies this male power through imputing "a sort of natural inevitability to the relationship between men and women as the relationship between the strong and the weak. . . . "[9] In brief, the rape victim may be painfully emblematic of the plight of women during a period of constriction. Her sexual terror stands for the difficulty of her sex. Men, who have more power than women, abuse it. Women, who have less power than men, must absorb that abuse. In Shakespeare, women also have language and the dignity of stoicism as well as the choral commentary of decent men to provide a sympathetic response to their condition.

Psychologically, Shakespeare's rape sequences shrewdly unravel some of the reasons why men rape and the justifications they offer for such exploitation of their strength. Morally, the sequences compel sympathy for women, though they offer, as an inducement to the audience, some recoiling titillation. Shakespeare acutely shows—through Lucrece's speeches, through Lavinia's amputations—the agony a woman experiences after rape. Yet breeding that agony is the belief that the unwilling betrayal of a man's patriarchal position and pride matters more than the destruction of a woman's body and sense of being. Shakespeare deplores warped patterns of patriarchal authority but not the patterns themselves. I cannot prove that the Judith Shakespeare Virginia Woolf imagined in *A Room of One's Own* would have more skeptically asserted that patriarchy itself, not simply malicious and overweening representatives of it, helps to nurture rape. No fabulist, I cannot manufacture texts for history, a "Lucrece" by Judith Shakespeare. We must attend to what we have: Shakespearean victims to mourn, victimizers to despise, and a hierarchical order to frame them both.

8

AD/D FEMINAM: WOMEN, LITERATURE AND SOCIETY (1980)

Bacon's idols of the Tribe, the Cave, the Market-place, and the Theater stubbornly dominate our thinking about women, literature, and society. This error offends intellectual propriety and the demands of the issue itself. For contemporary forces are generating both a compelling need to reconstitute our sense of the female subject and a number of women writers, with a maturing tradition, who have begun that task. Among those forces are the development of a class of literate, educated women; the entry of women into modern public life and its labor force; and the formation of feminist ideologies that construe culture as potentially useful and liberating, not as necessarily futile and alienating. Consciously or unconsciously, many critics confuse what they are saying about women and literature, if they are saying anything at all, and what there is to be said.

To help reduce that disorder, I want to offer three questions, a set of co-ordinates, that people can use to place women and literature in a social context. Applying my method of interrogation, as I will briefly do, will not reveal a single definition of women's literature, a woman's book. Rather, women's literature will consist of those texts that my questions may most lucidly reveal. I will distinguish between *female* and *male*, terms that refer to biological classes, and *feminine* and *masculine*, complementary terms that refer to social constructs that have governed and interpreted those biological classes. We write about, not simply from, our bodies.[1] However, my queries may be put to texts that more arduously conflate nature and culture, sex and gender, the flesh and history.

Regulating my interrogation is the conviction that women writers have had to overcome a devaluation of them as producers of public culture. Balancing this, as matter does antimatter, has been the pervasive insistence

A version of this essay was given at Princeton University in November 1978 at a seminar sponsored by the Council of the Humanities.

that women's primary work ought to be that of eros and of reproduction. Obviously, the degree of devaluation has varied from society to society, historical moment to historical moment. Some salons, for example, fathered women, culture, and politics in ways that render "devaluation" too superficial a description.[2] As obviously, certain women, such as George Eliot, have been exempted from those assessments that judge "woman" and "serious writer" an odd coupling. Yet, most women writers have confronted a trivialization of their textual ambitions, whether they attribute this to divine displeasure, constricting social structures, or their own lacks, their own castrating wounds.

If a woman, then, has been literate, she has had to work to be educated. If she is educated, she has had to work to be published and criticized justly; if she has been published, she is more welcome in "empty fields" than in prestigious ones. She has been more able to "move into an area of endeavor when it is not valued. As it becomes more esteemed, the field is increasingly populated by men."[3] If she wishes to extend respected genres, she experiences the skeptical pressure of a patriarchal tradition.[4] She is left with the more despised forms: letters, diaries, children's stories, modern Gothics, or "feminine" texts. In the American tradition, the "feminine" signifies vapidity, gentility, conformity, sentimentality, mawkish morality; in early-twentieth-century France, a lyrical celebration of nature, the body, and tender flights from male brutality and from life's more tragic, existential tests.[5] Because public acts of the imagination are stifled, like fallopian pregnancies, many women writers anxiously inhabit a realm between the to-be-said and the not-said. They are like a Mary Wollstonecraft heroine: "She could not write any more; she wished herself far distant from all human society; a thick gloom spread itself over her mind: but did not make her forget the very beings she wished to fly from."[6]

The responses of women reflect strategies with which people integrate deprivation into their lives, rebel against it, or balance submission and subversion. Some writers, like the Brontë sisters, though not always as modestly as they did, deny a female identity. Pseudonyms have been a helpful device in achieving this. So have been the romantic and modern myths of the artist as a privileged figure who soars beyond the vulgarities of imposed labels and identities. The woman who calls upon these myths trades the recognition of her female birth for the chance to express herself publicly. So doing, she risks indifference to social issues about women. Other women acknowledge the significance of sex and gender, but speak for, to, and from the self. They explore the subjective consequences of female birth, but refuse to project themselves as citizens of a sexually bounded community that society has also helped to structure. They tempt lapses into a lyrical solipsism. Perhaps deceptively, *Aurora Leigh*, that epic about the woman artist, begins:

Of writing many books there is no end;
And I who have written much in prose and verse
For others' uses, will write now for mine,—
Will write my story for my better self, . . .[7]

To speak, as I have done, about the female writer as a figure separate
from the male writer is the inevitable heritage of cultures that have made
much of sexual differentiation. Indeed, the first of my questions accepts the
necessity of confronting that legacy. It asks what notions of sexual
differentiation, which must entail mutually dependent senses of the female
and male, a text embodies. If a woman writer replicates an ideology that
suspects women as public voices, contradictions will bloody her. She will
be saying that she ought to be silent. The status of her text will resemble
that of a bastard. Its mere existence challenges hegemonic notions of
appropriate birth, but its acceptance of the label of bastard, if done without
the ironic self-consciousness of Lear's Edmund, will simultaneously
endorse those notions. If, however, a male writer replicates the same
ideology, he will have the luxury of being congruent with tradition.

Implicit in every notion of sexual differentiation is a sense of time, an
attitude about the permanence of difference. Historical processes may
create and then amend differences, except for obvious anatomical ones. If
so, difference belongs within the domain of the temporal and of specific
societies.[8] Men and women may have dissimilar experiences and histories,
which the content of literatures will reflect, even perpetuate. But such
diachronic asymmetries and inequalities may dissolve, even disappear. A
writer—from a Charlotte Brontë to a Carolyn Keene, from a John Stuart
Mill to a Frank O'Hara—may help that process along.

However, others believe that supernatural forces, or psychic and
somatic structures, or the overwhelming evolutionary needs of the species,
are responsible for sexual differences. They belong, then, within and
beyond the domain of the temporal and of specific societies. Female and
male subjects will have states of being that persist across time and space.
The content and the forms of literature, perhaps even of language itself,
will reflect this. Among the markers that distinguish interpretations of
women and literature, and the presentation of women in literature, from
the interpretations of class and literature, and the presentation of class in
literature, is the frequency of the assumption that differences of sex and
gender are immutable, asocial, atemporal—a human embodiment of
natural law. Ironically, both sexual conservatives and certain radical cultural
feminists share an attraction to such assumptions. The former tends to prize
the male; the latter certainly celebrates the female, but both seek
synchronic securities in dimorphism.

A powerful conceit magically lifts the artist from society and stabilizes the assignment of creativity to an ahistorical realm. Using metaphors from nature, it conflates pen and penis, writing and maleness. Modern technology (the typewriter, electronic voice-processing machines) is pushing the pen, and the pencil, toward obsolescence. As they wither away, the easy jump in English from pen to penis will seem less and less a sanctifying metaphor, more and more a curiosity. Nevertheless, it persists, to compel some women to find substitutes, signs of female creativity that draw on female biology, on blood, ova, genitalia. Such efforts repeat the pattern of using organic language of the body to transform a social role into a transcendent calling.

The belief in difference influences the perception of the audience of a text, the concern of the second of my critical questions. Because a sociology of reading is imperfect; because "uses and gratification" research is incomplete; and because reading, particularly about a subject like sexuality that is both a code and encoded, is indeterminate, no one can fully analyze the patterns of consumption a text might stimulate. This holds true for individuals and groups. Nor, because of the inadequacies of self-consciousness, can any writer say precisely for whom a text came into being. Despite these theoretical and practical strictures, we can tell, roughly, if a text is written for women, and for what kind of women. It suggests if it is meant to be instructive, a command to ego and superego, an exortation of obedience to the reality principle; if it is meant to be gratifying, an appeal to eros and thanatos, a suggestion of cultivation of the pleasure principle; or if, like *Clarissa*, a text claims to be both. To ask about the woman reader ascribes to her the dignity of being a subject and involves the book in an active social relationship, in which the primary bond is that of consciousness.

My third question inquires more specifically about the sense of community a writer establishes with other women, the projection of a shared society or of shared experiences. The male writer, to do so, must deal with a difference rooted in the body.[9] He may translate and inflate a lack of biological identity with the female into the verbal space between subject and object that characterizes scientific discourse; didactic tales; narratives of Oedipal disenchantment; romances of domineering or unrequited love; phenomenological analyses of the Other; or pornography. Writing to or of women, he implicitly or explicitly accepts socially maintained distinctions between feminine and masculine behavior. Other male writers—a Genet—can appropriate the feminine as a stance for the male through which to express receptive subordination before God or a godlike phallus. Self-consciously sacrificial, they speak from the feminine. Because chosen, this placing of the self is paradoxically confident and assertive. It lacks the nervousness of male artists in modern capitalist societies that denigrate them as womanish or infantile.[10] Still other male writers, like a Henry James, write about women, particularly lovely victims. Self-consciously empathetic, they speak of and for the feminine.

Each of these strategies is limited, if only because of the obvious anatomical differences I mentioned, perhaps too cursorily, before. A male writer may speak of, for, to, and from the feminine. He cannot speak, except fictively, of, for, to, *and* from the female. This inability hardly has the dignity of a tragic fact, but it does have the grittiness of simple fact. The woman writer—because she can speak of, for, to, and from the female; of, for, to, and from the feminine—has a wider choice of genres in writing about women in general. She also becomes more existentially plausible if she chooses to establish any sort of community among them. If she does so, she can, as Aurora Leigh sometimes does, accept the gravities of leadership. She serves as vanguard, witness, and chorus. She constitutes her social responsibility as the naming of a reality that has been pushed to the edge of invisibility; as the reclaiming of names that have been obliterated. As Virginia Woolf wrote bitterly in 1929, "I would venture to guess that Anon, who wrote so many poems without signing them, was often a woman."[11]

But this posture can become arrogant. A writer can become cannibalistic, devouring her collective subject. Without much theoretical fanfare, women writers have devised the strategy of the synecdochical voice to avoid such difficulties. In "Prologue," for example, Anne Bradstreet exemplifies this tactful performance. She pictures herself as a woman writer; to forestall charges of preposterous presumption, she cleverly manipulates an ironic self-deprecation. She refers to "my mean pen," to "my obscure lines." She says she is "obnoxious to teach carping tongue/Who says my hand a needle better fits." Then, shifting from the first-person singular to the third-person plural, from a private to a collective identity, she generalizes about the sex of which she is a part. "Men can do best," she moralizes, acidly aflutter, "and women know it well."[12] The synecdochical voice is hardly the property of women writing about women. "I, too, dislike it . . . " is a statement of personal and group taste. However, an Anne Bradstreet is special because she negotiates both the hazard of speaking for herself, a violation of social authority, and that of speaking for other women, a reinforcement of the enforced practice of having others speak for them. Her text itself displays the process of those negotiations.

If the woman writer is conscious of Western cultural tradition, she must ask if she wishes to include the Muse—that figure of memory, speech, inspiration, and reward—in a community of women. Women writers— Sappho, Anne Bradstreet—have been called the Tenth Muse. The apposition controls as it flatters. For the Muses, though charming personifications of creativity, are not themselves strenuously creative. If a woman is to be actively aesthetic and intellectual, she may renounce the

myth of the Muse and other acculturating myths. If such a stripping away of
tradition is impossible, she can practice an imaginative form of sexual
inversion and declare the Muse male. She then may inadvertently
reincarnate the inhibitions of patriarchal tradition in the Muse himself. If she
retains a female Muse, she may shift the sexual metaphor for writing from
heterosexuality to homosexuality and drape her text in wisps of social
deviancy.

Let us think, then, as if the classes in a taxonomy of a women's literature
are attitudes toward sexual differentiation: projections and recognitions of a
female audience: and some sense of community or society between author
and audience. Women's literature will organize a multiplicity of conventions, forms, and genres. It will include the mass media. Popular novels,
women's magazines, and the women's pages of newspapers have
provoked critical contempt and the professional jealousy that Hawthorne
expressed and James parodied.[13] However, they have given women a
profession and a living. Because they depend on sales for survival, they
have to be alert to female audiences. Becuase of this, they provide
sensitive, shifting registers of an audience's tastes and beliefs, needs and
aspirations, fears and desires. If texts from the mass media are less
visionary, imaginative, and strange than those from "literature," they may
be more cunning guides to social realities.

I will first apply my questions, then, to a . . . copy of the Ladies Home
Journal. A purpose of the professional men and women who manage, edit,
and write for the Journal is to help their readers manage their own world in
ways profitable to the Journal. Producers and consumers apparently both
act on the assumption that men and women inhabit the same society, but
in ways so dissimilar that each sex needs its own pragmatic counsel. The
Journal has some ideas about the cause of sexual differentiation. A feminist
editor, associating herself with her readers through their common training
in appropriate gender roles, blames socialization. "While boys and men
were taught to ask themselves, 'Who am I and what do I want to be when I
grow up,' girls and women—no matter what our unique talents—were
taught that it was enough to grow up to be women, wives, and mothers."[14]
However, to explore the origins of sexual differentiation fully demands
logical rigor, anthropological zeal, biological awareness, and historical
knowledge. Such scholarship might alienate readers. To end the unfairness
of institutionalized differentiation demands political commitment—if only to
a modestly feminist ideology. Such a program might divide readers whom
domestic interests unite. Shrewdly, the Journal avoids too much attention
to the beginnings and to the end of differentiation. It concentrates on the
energetic administration of its effects.

The title, Ladies Home Journal, both evokes and reassuring moral and
social status for its readers and reminds them of their proper sphere. The

same melding of idealization and bluntness appears in advertisements. They emblazon pictures of competently sleek, physically comfortable, wholesomely healthy women—generally between twenty and forty years of age, almost always white. The ads also iconographically gloss the domestic contents of a reader's world: animals: husbands and father: appliance repairmen: an enormous number of things: items of clothing, toys, food, furniture. They apparently make the home at once attractive and inevitable. So do features. A male writer muses about "What Marriage Means to Men." Sitting next to his wife on a sofa, a setting that evokes intimacy and evades naked passion, he is "stunned by how much [he loves] her." A female model on the cover wears an exotic headdress that is at once alluring helmet and erotic wimple. A line of print counsels, "Crochet this stunning outfit from our do-ahead Christmas boutique."

However, the contemporary *Journal* reader/buyer inhabits a world in which the meaning of sexuality and the demands of gender are irrevocably changing. The *Journal* cannot underwrite any of several competing ideologies of women's nature too rigidly. As a result, a male doctor anoints divorce as an appropriate solution to a bad marriage. A woman professional and her male collaborator discuss incest, a devastating critique of family life. A special section, "The Complete Working Women's Guide," helps women enter the public labor force. Famous working women, such as movie stars or the *Journal*'s editor herself, stress the anxieties of success, the joys of family tradition, but they also remind their audience that they have conquered public domains. For women in the paid labor force, the *Journal* erratically subscribes to a sliding scale of sexual differentiation: more of it at home or between lovers than at work, where equality of opportunity has become a social goal.

The *Journal* publishes its contradictions without comment, without apparent shame.[15] So doing, it becomes a collage of possibilities. If readers are to mediate the contradictions and choose among the possibilities, they must primarily do it themselves. Individual effort, the autodynamic will, not politics, must resolve conflict, strain, and the clash of heterogeneous roles. Such sources of authority as magazines provide enlightened guidance for self-reliant deeds. Yet, the *Journal* reader must exercise only a moderate self-reliance. She must eschew both solitude and excessive solicitations of subjectivity. She must continue to serve others and an ego ideal. The *Journal* is also chary about publishing flagrantly emotional material, though its poetry and fiction can be sentimental. It is wary of too much Gothic or romantic fantasy, though it dreams of moral and social mobility. Brisk, jauntily productive readers are to consume the *Journal* and to honor the home without excluding the world beyond the home; to improve family and society without disrupting them; to applaud the female and the feminine without obvious masochism. From time to time, the *Journal* will soothe and console them as they do so, but a more primary pact is to be reliable.

That assurance of trustworthiness links the *Journal* to more seriously regarded mimetic texts that promise to describe women's lives as honestly as possible. If the *Journal* helps women to do things, these texts help readers to see situations. At one extreme, that of Colette, they may be lyrical. At the other extreme, that of Mary McCarthy, they may be ironic. Between them is Doris Lessing's *The Golden Notebook*. Firm, compassionate, judgmental, it is a noncommercial commodity that asks to be read for the enhancement of consciousness and conscience. Lessing also tests herself against an ideal text: "a book powered with an intellectual or moral passion strong enough to create order, to create a new way of looking at life."[16]

The Golden Notebook names aspects of sexual discrimination that make women second-class citizens. The modern woman feels "emotions of aggression, hostility, resentment." In theory, a woman writer ought to express them: if she can, she will speak for her contemporaries as well as for herself. Lessing believes in a literary adaptation of theories of an organic relationship between microcosm and macrocosm. However, the inferiority of women means that their thoughts and perceptions will be disregarded. Aware of this, the woman writer, an Anna Wulf, fears using language publicly. Though the author of one novel, she now "stammers," an act that lacks the mystery of silence and the power of confident speech.

Yet, in *The Golden Notebook*, sexual discrimination fails to explain all of sexual differentiation. Women bear children; men do not. Women have intuitive, emotional, vaginal orgasms; men do not. Sexuality binds women with entangling cords of familial and personal dependency men escape. Reformers may dismantle inequities, but they cannot abolish all difference. An Anna may eventually write a second novel, but both Anna and Saul will retain some elements of self that the other can perceive in intersubjective transactions but never fully experience subjectively.

Curiously, in 1971, nine years after its publication, Lessing repudiated *The Golden Notebook* as a woman's text. Declaring that people had misread it, she said its central concern was not sex and gender, but fragmentation and reintegration. She admitted that she was chary about issuing such a public denial, because she did not wish to reject women. With her usual dogged candor, she said:

> . . . nobody so much as noticed this central theme, because the book was instantly belittled, by friendly reviewers as well as by hostile ones, as being about the sex war, or was claimed by women as a useful weapon in the sex war.
>
> I have been in a false position ever since, for the last thing I have wanted to do was to refuse to support women.
>
> (p. viii)

Yet Lessing did not stop there and leave a double text: the public *Golden Notebook* and her private interpretation. She consistently endorses a morality of generosity. For example, in *The Golden Notebook*, Saul and Anna give each other the first sentence of the book each will write. Lessing extends to her readers the enabling charity Saul and Anna have shown toward each other. She alters her charge of misreading to the more benign one of multiple rereadings. If women wish to use the novel as a document in the sex war, they may. If an "old Red" wishes to use it as a political memoir, he may. Lessing gives up a community organized on the principle of sex or a shared interpretation of sex and gender to accept one based on the values of perceptiveness, thought, and discussion.

The Virginia Woolf of *A Room of One's Own* speaks for women, of women, to women far more unequivocally. She refuses to separate herself from them as Anna and Molly part from each other at the end of the *Free Women* portions of *The Golden Notebook*. The actual audience for the first version of her text were women at Cambridge University. Her implied audience consists of persons interested in women and fiction. Woolf and both audiences are meant to share an affection that history has repressed: a "common life" history has ignored; and a hierarchal structure of sexual differentiation that history has enforced. Following John Stuart Mill, preceding Simone de Beauvoir, Woolf explores men's apparent psychic need to dominate women. Longing for self-esteem, they construct women as the Other, "by nature" inferior. "Women," she notes sardonically, "have served all these centuries as looking-glasses possessing the magic and delicious power of reflecting the figure of man at twice its natural size."[17]Dramatizing her sexual protest, Woolf offers the parable of Judith, Shakespeare's sister, an extraordinary fiction of grievance, a compressed historical novel about the tension between social structures and the aspiring woman artist. She pictures as well the forms the language of the frustrated woman writer might take: witchcraft, the laments of the mad, folk songs, lullabies.

However, Woolf's community of women shares a tradition of resistance and triumph as well as one of suffering. The members have appropriated whatever cultural and economic opportunities their days have given to them. Having claimed their right to public language, they now need privacy, economic independence, and a self-determined isolation in order to exercise it. An exemplary synecdochical voice, Woolf urges women further into language, into the imagining of the possibility that this exploration will end in the articulation of women's forms, perhaps even of a women's syntax, "a women's sentence."

Even as *A Room of One's Own* exhorts women to adventure—as recorders, architects, and prophets—into a woman's world, it contains a second, strangely inconsistent message as well. For Woolf also advocates androgyny as an ahistorical description of the artist's state of mind. Her comments about androgyny are tentative, perhaps playful. It is unclear whether she believes that artists are neurologically wired as both "male" and "female" or if she believes artists perceive and balance contradictions, a feat of consciousness that androgyny metaphorically represents. Nor are the motives for her flight from a society of women into a theory of androgyny wholly deciphered. Elaine Showalter, Adrienne Rich, and others have argued persuasively that if Woolf were to have investigated a woman's world too deeply, be it that of the devalued past or of the to-be-transvalued future, she would have been forced to encounter feelings of anger that would prove too threatening. In addition, I believe, such investigations might have pulled her too close to other difficult regions: to public discussions of female homosexuality, which, in Woolf's fiction, rarely goes beyond a kiss; to memories of grief and of the loss of women, her mother, her half-sister; and to sustained thought about an intimate unit that might replace marriage and the family. Significantly, in *To the Lighthouse*, published only two years before *A Room of One's Own*, a married couple with children, Mr. and Mrs. Ramsay, form an androgynous whole.

Whatever her reasons, Woolf, who writes so eloquently about male social control of women and the woman artist, who claims the female subject as the great subject for that woman artist, also asks that she integrate the male for the sake of that art. Lily Briscoe cannot finish her painting until she incorporates Mr. Ramsay into her vision. As Woolf instructs other women artists in *A Room of One's Own*, the "I," the controlling voice, sinuously advances, and then withdraws. It alternates between assertion and qualification.

More than thirty years after *A Room of One's Own*, Adrienne Rich's poems, in *Diving into the Wreck*, explicitly continue its feminist analysis of sexual differentiation as a hierarchy that men dominate.[18] Women must succor them psychically, protect them from the "abyss," keep their houses, bear their children, and provide the substance of their dreams. For men to be free, women must be constrained. For men to "see," women must be blinded. Like Woolf, Rich offers women her text as a weapon in the struggle for consciousness, in their review of patriarchal culture that serves as a life-saving prelude to abandoning it. Words "are purposes./The words are maps." Like Woolf, Rich also plays with the androgyne as a redeemed, redemptive figure. In "The Stranger," a speaker serves as a synecdochical voice for both sexes. The woman writer who accurately weighs sexual iniquities becomes capable of transfiguring differentiation. The androgyne becomes "the living mind you fail to describe/in your dead language."

However, *Diving into the Wreck* reverses Woolf's flight from a woman's world into the myth of androgyny. A text from a period of transition in which definitions of sex and gender are increasingly unstable, it moves closer and closer toward a woman's world. The androgyne is less an endgame than a midpoint between an attempt to live with men and the need to be with women. These principles of differentiation are not sex and power: but experience, politics, and personality. One major poem suggests, "I would have loved to live in a world/of women and men gaily/in collusion with green leaves," but men have rendered nature barren, civilization a technological monstrosity, paternity possessive, and the male principle suspect. The first poem in *Diving into the Wreck* is "Trying to Talk with a Man," but the next is "When We Dead Awaken," spoken to a "fellow-creature," a "sister." Rich borrows from Ibsen, neither to mimic nor to serve, but to show how some cultural remnants may serve women. The growing community of women has several modes of discourse available: dialogue, song, prophecy, open protest. Unlike Woolf, Rich, through precept and percept, encourages her readers to express their rage against male outrages. "Fire" signifies the anger that will purge anger's cause. Rich's text is to prove as contagious as flame for a reader who will consume language to escape from the present.

Like Rich, Hélène Cixous allies herself with a public women's movement, for Cixous *écriture féminine*, the extraordinary attempt to discover what community of discourse women, freely writing "as women," might build.[19] "The Laugh of the Medusa" expands the revisionary demands of *Diving into the Wreck* into deconstructive explosions. Her text pulsates with the rhetoric of rebellion, insurgency, militancy, rupture, demolition. She then stretches beyond anger at the male to celebrate the female. Feminizing the ideology of the avant-garde, she proclaims the joyous primacy of a future in which women, singly and collectively, will discover, through writing, their previously repressed bodies; psyches; memories. *Diving into the Wreck* tells of women as mothers. The female world embraces children through bearing them, through raising them and through a shared status as patriarchal possessions. "The Laugh of the Medusa" also promises that language will reveal the female's own creative response to the presence of the primordial, the maternal.

Obviously, "The Laugh of the Medusa" exuberantly proclaims the ahistorical strength of sexual differentiation and of feminine and masculine writing. "In the beginning are our differences." The historical repression of the female has simply blurred our vision of differentiation and blocked feminine writing. After women have flown from men; after they have reveled in their love for each other; after they have seized language: an authentic, dynamic bisexuality will be available to us. Moreover, Cixous asserts, the release of the female will be of such bounty, such fluent plentitude, that it will spontaneously revolutionize all structures and movements. "The Laugh of the Medusa" lacks the detail of the Utopian

narratives of Ursula LeGuin or Marge Piercy, but it states that the praxis of
the boldly linguistic woman will mutate politics: "Because the 'economy' of
her drives is prodigious, she cannot fail, in seizing the occasion to speak, to
transform directly and indirectly *all* systems of exchange based on
masculine thrift. Her libido will produce far more radical effects of political
and social change than some might like to think" (p. 882).

Casually Cixous assumes that men might read her lyrical, linguistically
complex polemic. A footnote warns with some indifference that men, too,
will have everything to write about themselves if phallogocentric laws are
deregulated. As women transform what men have said about them, men
must transform what they have said about themselves. However, her
primary audience is female. Passionately, charismatically Cixous is writing
from herself to other women to bring them to self-revelatory writing. She
urges them to inscribe themselves. She is a singular participant, witness,
and synecdochical voice in the process of recognizing the vibrant grammar
of self and differentiation. Like those of Wittig, Cixous's own text is a
kinetic sculpture. Its rhythms replicate the flight from repression toward the
expression of an atemporal female that will live itself out in history. As
Cixous constitutes herself through her language, that language summons
other women to follow her, without being followers. Cixous and her
reader/writers will form a community that neither psychoanalysis, nor
literature, nor sociology, nor philosophy has yet discerned.

Cultural history demonstrates that the genderized ways in which men
and women have construed themselves as writers has been a social
product. History in general shows that the human body has natural
elements, but that "woman" has been a socially produced concept, role,
metaphor, fantasy, and set of statistics as well. I have suggested a critical
method that assumes the validity of such instruction. Yet, texts that
represent "women's literature" often deny the primacy of social forces.
Some rebel magnificently against their society, anathematizing it as
destructive to women. Others submit that society alone cannot explain the
sexual differentiation that has required a separate category of women's
literature. Too often, such a conviction sustains powerful, discriminatory
ideologies, but it may also valorize the female as women attempt in clear
and coded ways to overthrow their place.

To mediate among hypotheses about the origins and perpetuation of
differentiation, of the feminine and the masculine, may not lie in the
province of literary criticism. That task may be claimed by the biological
and neurological sciences, history, anthropology, or even, as some believe,
by cosmology. However, literary criticism, when ambitious, has proposed
that the study of texts and languages will reveal the structure of human
nature and the meaning of our social patterns. If that is true a fresh,
scrupulous attention to "women's literature" will tell us if our dimorphic

bodies have pertinently, permanently generated our culture, or if, as I believe, our vast social capacities have done so, too often unscrupulously assigning a permanent significance to human physical forms.

9   ZERO DEGREE DEVIANCY: THE LESBIAN NOVEL IN ENGLISH (1981)

In her poem "Diving into the Wreck" (1972), Adrienne Rich imagined a descent into the sea of history that might see the damage that was done and the treasures that prevail. The poem has been a mandate for feminist critics as they measure the damage patriarchal cultures have inflicted and the treasures that a female tradition has nevertheless accumulated. We have yet to survey fully, however, the lesbian writers who worked under the double burden of a patriarchal culture and a strain in the female tradition that accepted and valued heterosexuality.[1] It is these writers whom I want to ground more securely in the domain of feminist criticism.[2]

My definition of the lesbian—as writer, as character, and as reader—will be conservative and severely literal. She is a woman who finds other women erotically attractive and gratifying. Of course a lesbian is more than her body, more than her flesh, but lesbianism partakes of the body, partakes of the flesh. That carnality distinguishes it from gestures of political sympathy with homosexuals and from affectionate friendships in which women enjoy each other, support each other, and commingle a sense of identity and well-being. Lesbianism represents a commitment of skin, blood, breast, and bone. If female and male gay writings have their differences, it is not only because one takes Sappho and the other Walt Whitman as its great precursor. They simply do not spring from the same physical presence in the world.

To my lexicographical rigidity I will add an argument that is often grim. Because the violent yoking of homosexuality and deviancy has been so pervasive in the modern period, little or no writing about it can ignore that conjunction. A text may support it, leeringly or ruefully. It may reject it, fiercely or ebulliently. Moral or emotional indifference is improbable. Few, if any, homosexual texts can exemplify writing at the zero degree, that

Early versions of this paper were read at Brown University, Hampshire College, the Columbia University Seminar on Women in Society, and the Modern Language Association. I am grateful to Adrienne Rich, Elizabeth Wood, and Elizabeth Abel for their comments.

degree at which writing, according to Roland Barthes, is " . . . basically in the indicative mood, or . . . amodal . . . [a] new neutral writing . . . [that] takes its place in the midst of . . . ejaculation and judgements; without becoming involved in any of them; [that] . . . consists precisely in their absence."[3] Lesbian novels in English have responded judgmentally to the perversion that has made homosexuality perverse by developing two repetitive patterns; the dying fall, a narrative of damnation, of the lesbian's suffering as a lonely outcast attracted to a psychological lower caste; and the enabling ecape, a narrative of the reversal of such descending trajectories, of the lesbian's rebellion against social stigma and self-contempt. Because the first has been dominant during the twentieth century, the second has had to flee from the imaginative grip of that tradition as well.

If the narratives of damnation reflect larger social attitudes about homosexuality, they can also extend an error of discourse about it: false universalizing, tyrannical univocalizing. Often ahistorical, as if pain erased the processes of time, they can fail to reveal the inseparability of the twentieth-century lesbian novel and the twentieth century: " . . . in the nineteenth century . . . homosexuality assumed its modern form," which the next century was to exhibit.[4] One sympton of modernization, of the refusal to exempt the lesbian from the lurching logic of change, was a new sexual vocabulary. Before the end of the nineteenth century, homosexuality might have been subsumed under such a term as "masturbation."[5] Then lesbians became "lesbians." The first citation for lesbianism as a female passion in *The Shorter Oxford English Dictionary* is 1908, for "sapphism" 1890.

The public used its new language with pity, hostility, and disdain.[6] The growing tolerance of an optionally non-procreative heterosexuality failed to dilute the abhorrence of a necessarily nonprocreative homosexuality, especially if practicing it threatened to mean social as well as sexual self-sufficiency. In her study of birth control, Linda Gordon states: "We must notice that the sexual revolution was not a general loosening of sexual taboos but only of those on nonmarital heterosexual activity. Indeed, so specifically heterosexual was this change that it tended to intensify taboos on homosexual activity and did much to break patterns of emotional dependency and intensity among women."[7] Both female and male writers absorbed such strong cultural signals. If "guilt and anxiety rarely appear in homosexual literature until the late nineteenth century, . . . [they] become the major theme of *Angst* . . . after 1914."[8] Evidently, freedom in one place may serve as an inoculation against its permissible appearance elsewhere. The more autonomy women claim in one sphere, the more they may enter into an obscure balancing act that may lead to tighter restrictions upon them in another.

Such an environment nurtured external and internal censorship. During a century in which the woman writer as such became less of a freak, the lesbian writer had to inhibit her use of material she knew intimately but which her culture might hold to be, at best, freakish. She learned that being quiet, in literature and life, would enable her to "pass." Silence could be a passport into the territory of the dominant world. In a quick-witted recent novel, June Arnold's *Sister Gin*, an aging mother responds to her middle-aged daughter's attempt to talk to her about her lesbianism: "But she shouldn't say that word. It isn't a nice word. 'People don't care what you do as long as you don't tell them about it. I know that.'"[9] Such silence signifies a subterranean belief in the magical power of language. If the lesbian were to name herself, her utterance might carry a taint from speaker to listener, from mouth to ear. Silence is also a shrewd refusal to provoke punitive powers—be they of the family, work-place, law, or church. Obviously this survival tactic makes literature impossible. Culture, then, becomes the legatee of linguistic zeros, of blank pages encrypted in tombs critics will never excavate.

If the lesbian writer wished to name her experience but still feared plain speech, she could encrypt her text in another sense and use codes.[10] In the fallout of history, the words "code" and "zero" lie together. The Arabs translated the Hindu for "zero" as *sifr* ("empty space"), in English "cipher." As the Arabic grew in meanings, *sifr* came to represent a number system forbidden in several places but still secretly deployed, and cipher became "code." In some lesbian fiction, the encoding is allegorical, a straightforward shift from one set of terms to another, from a clitoris to a cow. Other acts are more resistant to any reading that might wholly reveal, or wholly deny, lesbian eroticism.

Take for example "the kiss," a staple of lesbian fiction. Because it has shared with women's writing in general a reticence about explicitly representing sexual activity, the kiss has had vast metonymic responsibilities. Simultaneously, its exact significance has been deliberately opaque. Look at three famous kiss scenes:

> It was a very real oblivion. Adele was roused from it by a kiss that seemed to scale the very walls of chastity. She flung away on the instant filled with battle and revulsion. [Gertrude Stein, *Q.E.D.*]

> Julia blazed. Julia kindled. Out of the night she burnt like a dead white star. Julia opened her arms. Julia kissed her on the lips. Julia possessed it. [Virginia Woolf, "Slater's Pins Have No Points"]

> Then came the most exquisite moment of her whole life passing a stone urn with flowers in it. Sally stopped; picked a flower; kissed her on the lips. The whole world might have turned upside down! . . . she felt that she had been

given a present, wrapped up, and told just to keep it, not to look at it—a
diamond, something infinitely precious, wrapped up . . . she uncovered, or
the radiance burnt through the revelation, the religious feeling! [Woolf,
Mrs. Dalloway]

Does the kiss encode transgression or permissibility? Singularity or
repeatability? Impossibility or possibility? The same character, "O," can
stand for both the zero of impossibility and for the possibilities of female
sexuality.[11] Does the kiss predict the beginning of the end, or the end of
the beginning, of a lesbian erotic enterprise? Or is it the event that literally
embraces contradictions?

Still, the overt will out. As if making an implicit, perhaps unconscious
pact with her culture, the lesbian writer who rejects both silence and
excessive coding can claim the right to write for the public in exchange for
adopting the narrative of damnation. The paradigm of this narrative is
Radclyffe Hall's *The Well of Loneliness*—published, banned in England,
and quickly issued elsewhere in 1928, by which time scorn for lesbianism
had hardened into orthodoxy.[12] Novelist as well as novel have entered
minor mythology. Hall represents the lesbian as scandal and the lesbian as
woman-who-is-man, who proves "her" masculinity through taking a
feminine woman-who-is-woman as "her" lover. In a baroque and savage
satire published after *The Well of Loneliness*, Wyndham Lewis excoriates a
den of dykes in which a woman artist in "a stiff Radcliffe-Hall collar, of
antique masculine cut" torments a heterosexual fellow and dabbles with a
voluptuous mate.[13] He is too jealous and enraged to recognize either the
sadness of costume and role reversal (the stigmatized seeking to erase the
mark through aping the stigmatizers) or the courage of the masquerade (the
emblazoning of defiance and jaunty play).[14] Be it mimicry or bravery, the
woman who would be man reaches for status and for freedom. The man
who would be woman, because of the devaluation of the female and
feminine, participates, in part, in a ritual of degradation.

Comparing *The Well of Loneliness* to Hall's life reveals a discrepancy
between the pleasures she seems to have found with her lover, Una
Taylor, Lady Troubridge, and the sorrows of her hero, Stephen Gordon.
Hall offers a parallel to the phenomenon of the woman novelist who
creates women characters less accomplished and successful than she. In
addition the novel is more pessimistic about the threat of homosexuality as
such to happiness than Hall's earlier novel, *The Unlit Lamp* (1924). Set in
roughly the same time period as *The Well of Loneliness*, *The Unlit Lamp*
dramatizes a triangle of mother, daughter, and governess. The daughter
and governess have a long, unconsummated, ultimately ruptured lesbian
relationship. Their grief is less the result of a vile passion and the reactions
to it than of the daughter's failure of nerve, her father's patriarchal

crassness, her mother's possessive manipulations, and the constrictions provincial England places on the New Woman.

In brief, *The Well of Loneliness* tends to ignore the more benign possibilities of lesbianism. Hall projects homosexuality as a sickness. To deepen the horror, the abnormal illness is inescapable, preordained; an ascribed, not an achieved, status. For Stephen is a "congenital invert," the term John Addington Symonds probably coined around 1883 and Havelock Ellis later refined: "Sexual inversion, as here understood, means sexual instinct turned by inborn constitutional abnormality towards persons of the same sex. It is thus a narrower term than homosexuality, which includes all sexual attractions between persons of the same sex." The congenital female invert has male physical traits—narrow hips, wide shoulders—as "part of an organic instict."[15] Stephen also has a livid scar on her cheek. Literally, it is a war wound; socially, a mark of the stigmatized individual who may blame the self for a lack of acceptability;[16] mythically, the mark of Cain *The Well of Loneliness* stresses the morbidity of a stigma that the politics of heaven, not of earth, must first relieve.

Yet Hall planned an explicit protest against that morbidity. Indeed, having Stephen Gordon be a congenital invert who has no choice about her condition strengthens Hall's argument about the unfairness of equating homosexuality with punishable deviancy. The novel claims that God created homosexuals. If they are good enough for Him, they ought to be good enough for us. Hall cries out for sacred and social toleration, for an end to the cruelties of alienation. In the novel's famous last paragraph, Stephen gasps, "God . . . we believe; we have told You we believe. . . . We have not denied You, then rise up and defend us. Acknowledge us, oh God, before the whole world. Give us the right to our existence."[17] Ironically, the very explicitness of that cry in a climate increasingly harsh for lesbians, combined with the vividness of Hall's description of homosexual subworlds, propelled *The Well of Loneliness* into scandal while the far more subversive, if subtle, *Unlit Lamp* was a success. To double the irony, Hall's strategies of protest against damnation so entangled her in damnation that they intensify the sense of its inevitability and power. The novel's attack on homophobia becomes particularly self-defeating. The text is, then, like a Janus with one face looming larger than the other. It gives the heterosexual a voyeuristic tour and the vicarious comfort of reading about an enforced stigma—in greater measure than it provokes guilt. It gives the homosexual, particularly the lesbian, riddling images of pity, self-pity, and of terror—in greater measure than it consoles.

The Well of Loneliness lacks the intricacies of Djuna Barnes' *Nightwood*, another parable of damnation, published eight years later. Its lack of intricacy, plus its notoriety and the way in which it inscribes damnation, helped to transform its status from that of subject of an obscenity trial to that of an immensely influential, token lesbian text. As one historian writes, "most of us lesbians in the 1950s grew up knowing nothing about lesbianism except Stephen Gordon."[18] Despite, or perhaps because of, its reputation, critics have ignored its structural logic, an error I want to remedy now.

Each of the novel's five sections (or acts) ends unhappily, the parts replicating and reinforcing the movement of the whole. Book 1 begins with Stephen's birth to a loving, rich couple.[19] The happiness of their legitimate, heterosexual union is the positive term that opposes the woe lurking in wait for illegitimate, homosexual ones. Although Sir Philip Gordon had wanted a son, he loves his daughter. Wise, courageous, kind, honorable, attentive, athletic, he embodies a fantasy of the perfect father Hall never had, the perfect man she could never become. Lady Anna, however, who had simply wanted a baby, instinctively repudiates her "unnatural" daughter. Though mother and child are of the same sex, they share neither gender nor love. Hall's idealization of Sir Philip and her regrets about Lady Anna are early markers of a refusal to link a protest against homophobia with one against patriarchal values.

During her late adolescence, Stephen meets a visiting Canadian, Martin Hallam. They become the best of brotherly friends—until Martin falls in love with Stephen. His emotions shock her; her shock stuns him; he leaves the neighborhood. Stephen's introduction to heterosexual passion, to her a form of homosexual incest, confirms her inability to pass even the most benign of initiation rites for girls. The loss of her "brother," however, is far less painful than the accidental death of her father, which ends book I: it deprives her of "companionship of mind, . . . a stalwart barrier between her and the world, . . . and above all of love" (p. 121).

So bereft, Stephen behaves blindly. She falls in love with Angela Crosby, fickle, shallow, and married. As Angela strings Stephen along with a few of those conventional kisses, she sets her up as a rival of two men: husband Ralph and lover Roger. The masculinized lesbian has few advantages in competition with natural males. To keep Ralph from finding out about Roger, Angela shows him a love letter from Stephen and claims to be the innocent victim of odd affections. Ralph takes the letter to Lady Anna, who gives Stephen the choice of leaving her beloved ancestral estate or watching Lady Anna leave it. Finding her "manhood," Stephen accepts exile. With a loyal governess, a favorite horse, and a private income, she abandons Eden for London. Hall concludes book 2 with the punishment of expulsion, proving that even the aristocratic homosexual must suffer.

In the city, Stephen completes the rites of maturity for inverts. She finds a home: Paris, the center of literary lesbianism in the first part of the twentieth century. She finds work: literature itself. She writes a wonderful and famous novel. As Cain's mark was from God, so both Ellis and Hall give their inverts some compensations: intelligence and talent. If the body is negatively deviant the mind is positively so. Hall demands that the invert use that intelligence and talent. Hard work will be a weapon against the hostile world; cultural production an answer to the society that repudiates a Stephen because she has been forced to repudiate reproduction. Finally, serving a larger cause, Stephen becomes a valiant member of a World War I women's ambulance corps. (Hall here explores, if peripherally, that standard setting of the lesbian text: a community of women.) But despite the personal bravery of both female and male warriors, the war is a wasteland. Stephen's personal anguish and confusion over her sexuality, then, find a larger, historical correlative in the trenches, as Hall ends book 3 with a lament for the dead.

During the war, however, Stephen has met a poorer, younger, Welsh woman. Mary Llewellyn, whom she takes to a Mediterranean villa. For a while they suppress their physical longing. In Stephen's fears that sex will destroy love, ecstasy intimacy, Hall is suggesting that the stigma of homosexuality is tolerable as long as the erotic desire that distinguishes the lesbian remains repressed. The conclusion—that a released eros will provoke the destructive potential of the stigma—places Hall in that Western cultural tradition that links sex and death. In addition, she is attributing to lesbianism a conventional belief about female sexuality in general: that women prefer love and romance to physical consummation. Ultimately Mary's needs overwhelm Stephen's chivalrous hope to protect her from them. Though their bodies, like those of any homosexual couple, are anatomically similar, their relationship embodies a number of dyadic roles. Into their closed and exclusive world they structure multiple polarized differences, primarily that between female and male. Hall exults:

> Stephen as she held the girl in her arms, would feel that indeed she was all things to Mary; father, mother, friend and lover, all things; and Mary all things to her—the child, the friend, the beloved, all things. But Mary, because she was perfect woman, would rest without thought, without exultation, without question; finding no need to question since for her there was now only one thing—Stephen. [P. 134]

Seeking metaphors for their passion, Hall, like many lesbian novelists, turns to nature, both tamed and untamed: to vineyards, fruit trees, flowers, the four elements, the moon. Such standard tropes carry the implicit burden of dissolving the taint of "unnatural" actions through the cleansing power of natural language.[20]

Most idylls, even those of refound Edens, must end. Hall concludes book 4 with the ominous "And thus in a cloud of illusion and glory, sped the last enchanted days at Orotava" (p. 317). Stephen and Mary return to Paris. There, with their loving dog, they are happy—for a while; but Mary, restless, begins to seek diversion with other lesbians and in the homosexual underworld, particularly in the bars that modern cities nurture. Bars can serve as a source of warm, egalitarian *communitas* for the marginal homosexual who must also aspire to the far more prestigious heterosexual world that is a structural reference group.[21] But the fearful, puritanical Stephen despises them; like many fictive lesbians, she finds security in a sanctified domesticity. Though a friend reasonably tells Stephen that Mary has too little to do, especially when Stephen is obsessively writing, Hall just as reasonably locates the primary source of strain between the lovers in the tension between their little world and the larger world of society and family that fears them.

Whatever the cause, Mary mopes and hardens. Then, a secular *deus ex machina*, Martin Hallam returns. Stephen's alter ego, he, too, has been wounded in the war. He, too, falls in love with Mary. The two fight it out for her. Though Stephen wins, the price is too high: where she once had Mary's soul but feared possession of the body, she may now possess the body but not the soul. For God's scheme includes congenital heterosexuals as well as congenital inverts. Mary has, somewhat belatedly, realized that she is one of them. Martyring herself in the religion of love, Stephen pretends to be having an affair with a woman friend, Valerie Seymour. She stays out for two nights. When she returns, her mock confession of infidelity drives the distraught Mary into the night and the arms of the waiting Martin, whom Stephen has posted in the street below.

Throughout book 5, Hall's religiosity has become more and more omnipresent: her attraction to Catholic theology, architecture, and liturgy; her anxious queries about God's real allegiance in the war between Stephen's little world and that which would damn it. As Stephen renounces Mary, she has a compensatory vision, at once hallucination, inspiration, and conversion experience. She will become the voice of the voiceless stigmatized; she will help them break through to a new, sympathetic recognition. So willing, Stephen finds that "her barren womb became fruitful—it ached with its fearful and sterile burden" (p. 437).

That juxtaposition of fruitfulness and aching burdens is a final bit of information about the unevenly balanced duality of Hall's text. Yet she does create the figure of Valerie Seymour, a charismatic teetotaler who keeps a famous Parisian salon. Amidst the volatile gloom of Stephen's histrionics, she is serenely sunny. She, too, finds homosexuality congenital, but she lyrically interprets fate as a friendly boon: "Nature was trying to do her bit; inverts were being born in increasing numbers, and after a while their numbers would tell, *even with the fools who still ignored Nature*" (p. 406). Though Hall does little with Valerie, she signifies the presence of a second consciousness about lesbianism that *The Well of Loneliness* and the forces surrounding it helped to submerge, screen, and render secondary during the mid twentieth century. This consciousness, aware of the labelling of lesbianism as a pollutant, nevertheless chose to defy it.

The "Kinsey Report" suggests the existence of such a mentality. Of 142 women with much homosexual experience, 70 percent reported no regrets.[22] This consciousness has manifested itself in literature in two ways. First, in lesbian romanticism: fusions of life and death, happiness and woe, natural imagery and supernatural strivings, neoclassical paganism with a ritualistic cult of Sappho, and modern beliefs in evolutionary progress with a cult of the rebel. At its worst an inadvertent parody of *fin de siècle* decadence, at its best lesbian romanticism ruthlessly rejects a stifling dominant culture and asserts the value of psychological autonomy, women, art, and a European cultivation of the sensuous, sensual, and voluptuous. Woolf's *Orlando* is its most elegant and inventive text, but its symbol is probably the career of Natalie Barney, the cosmopolitan American who was the prototype of Valerie Seymour.[23]

The second mode is lesbian realism: the adaption of the conventions of the social and psychological novel to appraise bonds between women and demonstrate that such relationships are potentially of psychic and moral value. The slyest realistic text is Stein's *Autobiography of Alice B. Toklas*, but less tricky examples include *The Unlit Lamp* and another ignored novel, Helen R. Hull's *Labyrinth* (1923). There one sister marries an ambitious, egocentric man. A second sister lives with an ambitious, generous woman. The first sister is unhappy and confined; the second happy and productive.[24] What *Labyrinth* implies, other realistic texts state explicitly: even though the lesbian may have children whom she loves, she must reject the patriarchal family, which the stigma against her helps to maintain, if she is to reject repression as well. The tension between the role of mother, which the lesbian may desire, and the traditional family structure, in which women are subordinate, is obviously far more characteristic of lesbian than gay-male writing. A man may have both paternity and power, but a woman must too often choose between maternity and comparative powerlessness.

In 1963 Mary McCarthy's *The Group* brought that submerged, screened, secondary consciousness to public prominence. Second on the fiction best-seller list for its year, selling well over 3,000,000 copies by 1977, *The Group* showed that lesbianism could be an acceptable, even admirable, subject—particularly if a writer of unquestioned heterosexuality served as the gatekeeper. Moreover, McCarthy was tactfully judicious about the erotic details of lesbian sexuality. Cleverly, if perhaps inadvertently, McCarthy fused lesbian romanticism and lesbian realism. In characteriz-ation, setting, style, and some of its assumptions, *The Group* was realistic, but its heroine was wonderfully romantic. For Lakey is self-assured, intelligent, beautiful, charitable, and anti-Fascist; she wears violet suits; she has lived in Europe; she has an affair with a baroness. In brief, she personifies the most glamorous of enabling escapes from stigma and self-contempt. The members of The Group, all Vassar graduates, also prefigure the possible response of liberal readers of this novel to the claims of this secondary consciousness to primary status. Lakey, after she returns from Europe, cannot be damned; indeed, she must be respected. Yet The Group finds encounters with her awkwardly enigmatic and strange; strangely and enigmatically awkward.

Since *The Group*, a far less tormented lesbian has surfaced— to supplement, if not wholly supplant, the Stephens and the Marys. In some texts by nonlesbians, she is little more than a romp, a sexual interlude and caper. Like masturbation and the orgy, homosexuality has become a counter in the game of erotic writing. Trade fiction has claimed the provinces of pornography and sexology. Other texts, however, primarily by lesbians and sympathetic feminists, damn the lesbian's damnation. Their appearance in strength is the result of a confluence of forces. Certainly a material cause was the founding of several journals, magazines, and presses that could publish the products of a more audacious sexual ideology and practice. Among the most substantial, for the lesbian novel, was the small trade house, Daughters, Inc. Its subtitle, "Publishers of Books by Women," reflects its founders' theory that feminism would create new genres. Existing in that climate, which might have a certain early crudity, would be a "freer lesbian novel, and Daughters would be a medium that lesbian novelists could count on."[25] Among the social causes of the reappearance of a submerged consciousness and its narrative of the enabling escape have been the women's movement, more flexible attitudes toward marriage (so often contrasted favorably to the putative anarchy of homosexual relations), the "modernization of sex," which encourages a rational, tolerant approach to the complexities of eros,[26] and the growing entrance of more women into the public labor force, which gives a financial autonomy inseparable from genuine sexual independence.

The new texts are hopeful about homosexuality and confident about the lesbian's power to name her experience and experiment with literary form.[27] These novels invert the application of the label of deviant: the lesbian calls those who would call her sinful or sick themselves sinful or sick; she claims for herself the language of respectability. In a sweet novel of the 1960s, Elana Nachman's *Riverfinger Woman*, the protagonist fantasizes about enlightening some benighted heterosexuals. She and her lover will make a movie "so that people would see that lesbians are beautiful, there is nothing, nothing at all unnatural about them, they too can have weddings and be in the movies."[28] Mingling fiction, journalism, autobiography, and polemic, Jill Johnston declares in her book *Lesbian Nation* that "that awful life of having to choose between being a criminal or going straight was over. We were going to legitimatize ourselves as criminals."[29] Obviously these dreams and manifestos are still enmeshed in older vocabularies of value. A few books approach indifference. Less attracted to acts of reversal, they hint at a Barthian writing degree zero.[30]

Among the first of the more hopeful lesbian novels was *A Place for Us*, which its author (using the name Isabel Miller) published privately in 1969 and which a commercial press reissued as *Patience and Sarah* in 1972. That was the year of the Stonewall Resistance, the defense of a New York gay bar against a police raid that symbolizes the beginning of the Gay Liberation movement. The history of *A Place for Us*—the pseudonym, the dual publication—shows both the presence and the dissolution of a fear of lesbian material. Its author's comments about *The Well of Loneliness* reveal both the influence of and a resistance to Hall's earlier gesticulations: "I think Radclyffe Hall was antihomosexual. . . . I first read *The Well of Loneliness* when I was about seventeen. . . . I was very excited. But I didn't like the characters, I didn't like the arrogance of the heroine."[31] Gentle, kindly, *A Place for Us* tells of two nineteenth-century women who run away together from patriarchal brutalities to build their farm in New York State. Almost immediately after *A Place for Us*, the most successful of the new texts appeared, Rita Mae Brown's *Rubyfruit Jungle* (1973), which during the 1970s replaced *The Well of Loneliness* as the one lesbian novel someone might have read. In *Rubyfruit Jungle* (the title alludes to the female genitals), Molly Bolt (a name that alludes to freedom and flight) escapes from a seedy provincial background to triumph over mean men, shallow women, bad schools, menial jobs, and lesbian-baiting.

If *A Place for Us* adapts the narrative of the enabling escape to the pastoral domestic idyll, *Rubyfruit Jungle* integrates it with the picaresque and the *Bildungsroman*. Together these novels dramatize two contradictory attitudes about sex and gender that pervade the contemporary lesbian novel. The first of these attitudes is a bristling contempt for sexual role playing (*A Place for Us* is an exception here). The protagonist in *Riverfinger Woman* asserts: "we were too modern already to believe that one of us was the man and the other . . . the woman. We felt like neither men nor women. We were females, we were queers. . . . We knew we had the right to love whomever we loved."[32] Under the influence of an existential ethic that praises the freely forged self and of a feminist ideology that negates patriarchal practices, such novels abandon the customs of a Radclyffe Hall. Yet they are simultaneously conscious of sex. Males, particularly traditional ones, are in disrepute. Some novels, such as Arnold's *Sister Gin*, articulate punitive fantasies—some violent, some playful—which they justify as catharsis of self-defense. The female and the female world are honorable, as structural reference and source of *communitas*. Women ask not only for equality but for self-celebration; less for the rehabilitation of men than for independence from them.

Lesbian novels thus map out the boundaries of female worlds.[33] Some of the bonds within these boundaries are erotic, a proud isosexuality that separates the lesbian novel from other, more guarded explorations, such as Charlotte Perkins Gilman's *Herland*. Characters also search, however, for alter egos, moral and psychological equivalents, which the term "sister" signifies. Poignantly, painfully, they seek the mother as well.[34] A mother waits at the heart of the labyrinth of some lesbian texts. There she unites past, present, and future. Finding her, in herself and through a surrogate, the lesbian reenacts a daughter's desire for the woman to whom she was once so linked, from whom she was then so severed. Because the mother was once a daughter, a woman approaching her can serve as the mother's mother even as she plays out the drama of a daughter. In such complex mother/ daughter exchanges and interchanges, the women explore both narcissistic and anaclitic love. Of course lesbianism is far more than a matter of mother/daughter affairs, but the new texts suggest that one of its satisfactions is a return to primal origins, to primal loves, when female/female, not male/female, relationships structured the world. A lesbian's jealousy, then, spurts like blood from the cut of terror at the possibility of losing again the intimacy that has at least been regained.

To focus on mothers and daughters—or on any personal bonds—is too narrow; psychology hardly defines the totality of our lives. In several texts the world of women is also a political center of solidarity and resistance. As such it can perform social experiments that the larger culture might regard attentively. To name such communities, the lesbian writer calls on myth: prehistorical matriarchies; the Amazons; Sappho and her school. The myths, also current in contemporary feminist ideology, were popular in stylish lesbian circles in the earlier part of the twentieth century. Part of their value is their ability to evoke atemporal resonances within narratives that are separate from such patriarchal religious structures as the Catholic church before which Hall knelt. When novelists grant myths the status of history (easier to do with Sappho than with Amazons and primeval matriarchs), their error, because it occurs in the freewheeling context of fiction, is more palatable than in the stricter context of programmatic ideology, political theory, and "herstory."

The most ambitious and the cleverest of the new novels in English is perhaps Bertha Harris' *Lover* (1976). The lesbian novel has tended to be, and remains, formally staid, a conventionality that has served both a homosexual and heterosexual audience. The lesbian, as she struggles against the hostilities of the larger world, can find comfort in the ease of reading. Between text and self she may also establish a sense of community. The heterosexual, as she or he nears unfamiliar and despised material, can find safety in the same ease of reading. The continued strength of literary form can stand for the continued strength of the larger community's norms. However, Harris, an American equivalent of Monique Wittig, experiments with narrative pattern as a possible coefficient of her vision of sexuality. A modernist, she fragments and collapses characters, settings, chronology, and states of mind. Her central presence appears as Veronica (also the name of the second wife of Veronica's bigamist grandfather); as Flynn; as Bertha; and as "I." In each guise the voice is both fiction and the author in the act of writing fiction. In brief, *Lover* is another book about becoming a book.

Harris is ingenious, sardonic, parodic—an economical comic intelligence. Another cultural consequence of the stigma against the lesbian is that it deforms comedy. Those who support the stigma, such as Wyndham Lewis, may freely assault the homosexual with hostile satire and burlesque. Those who internalize the stigma use the same weapons as a form of self-assault. Only when the stigma is simultaneously comprehended and despised can the comedy of a Harris, or of a Barnes before her, emerge.[35] It is a satire, often elaborate, even grotesque and baroque, that ultimately adorns rather than mutilates its subject. Barnes' enigmatic and rich prose has deeply influenced Harris, but more immediately, so has Nabokov's, his "tricking and fooling and punning and literary joking."

Some people in the feminist and lesbian press have criticized Harris and others for these adventures. Harris has been called inaccessible, as if modernism were itself an indecipherable code. She is, therefore, supposedly ideologically unsound, stopping that illusory creature, the average lesbian, from using literature to articulate her experience and urge rebellion against its nastier aspects. Harris has explanations for such prescriptive reviews. She believes that the feminist and lesbian press still lacks an informed criticism to mediate between texts and a large audience, and she finds too few "well-read reviewers, conscious of literary traditions." The press must learn to do what modern art has done: to create a self-explanatory body of criticism. Furthermore, "the lesbian readership" wants a "positive image" in its novels. Part of the huge popularity of *Rubyfruit Jungle* is due to its ebullient self-admiration. Such easy hedonism and heroism is, of course, didactically helpful and politically worthwhile, but it also "prevents a deeper look into the nature of things and the nature of lesbianism."

The baffled response to *Lover* is ironic, for few writers have given the lesbian a more lyrical identity. Harris explores the various roles women have played: grandmother, mother, daughter, sister, wife and second wife, businesswoman in man's clothing, prostitute, factory worker, movie star, muse and tutelary spirit, warrior, artist, fake saint, martyr. She codifies difference of role in order to assess similarities of the players and to find a common basis for a community of women. There the primary difference will be between lover and beloved—though lovers can be loved and the beloved lovers. The phallus may not be unwelcome, especially if necessary for breeding, but the nonphallic lesbian has a privileged status. In loving women she exalts both self and other. Harris also anoints this paradigm and paramour as an omnipotent cosmic spirit. Capable of anything and everything, she is polymorphic, amorphic, transmorphic, and orphic. She both pictures margins and escapes them. She is the principle of creativity, of a fertility of both mind and body. As such she incarnates the genesis of the world itself, once suppressed, which might be reappearing now. In an essay about Barnes and lesbian literature, Harris might be talking about *Lover* itself:

> There is not a literature that is not based on the pervasive sexuality of its time; and as that which is male disappears (sinks slowly in the west) and as the originally all-female world reasserts itself by making love to itself, the primary gesture toward the making at last of a decent literature out of the experience of a decent world might simply be a woman like myself following a woman like Djuna Barnes, and all she might represent down a single street on a particular afternoon.[36]

Not everyone will accept Harris' only partially ironic apocalyptic fantasy. Her picture of the damned does, however, reverse that of *The Well of Loneliness*. The lesbian novel has offered up Hall's vision, but it has also sheltered and released the rejection of that vision, offering an alternative process of affirmation of the lesbian body and transcendence of a culturally traced, scarring stigma. It has been a deviant voice that has both submitted to deviancy and yearned to nullify that judgment. Feminist critics, zeroing in on that voice, can serve as its acoustical engineers. We can listen for its variations, fluctuations, blurrings, coded signals, and lapses into mimicry or a void. As we do, we must also try to hear, in wonder and in rage, words and phrases that might explain what is now a mystery: why people wish to stigmatize, to dominate, to outlaw, and to erase a particular longing for passion and for love.

10 THE COMPANY OF CHILDREN (1982)

> The great tribal forms of family may be
> vanishing, but new kinship systems flourish all
> around us."
>
> *Dorothy Dinnerstein, in "A Conversation with*
> *Robin Morgan," Ms., August, 1978*

I want to talk about family. To do so properly, I must be more personal than I am wont to be. A narrow-mouthed woman, I prefer reticence to autobiography.

Yet, too many people who talk about family are less candid, less personal, than they ought to be. Reining in fears and desire that will ride them anyway, they lie about themselves, and hurt us. I think of the man in Tampa who, in 1981, pleaded "no contest" to charges of sexual misconduct with an eight-year-old girl and a teenage boy. He was, as well, a leader of a group called Taxpayers Against Kiddy Smut. That boy, that girl, might have been spared if he had admitted how horribly he wanted to touch children instead of pretending to be their guardian.

I grew up within a family that was both huge and orderly: one father, one mother, no stepfather, no stepmother, two brothers, four sisters, aunts, uncles, cousins, grandparents. My paternal grandfather married three wives, but he was widowed twice, never divorced. Implacabilities of death, not flights of human choice, ruptured his monogamies. We picked flowers on Mother's Day, picknicked on Father's. We were together for car trips, church services and Monopoly. We were comfortable, earnest, robust, and loving. We had an environment in which to survive. The adults had space in which to suggest that their relatively unformed neonates become well-behaved members of society. The neonates had time in which to construct their identities, to stammer out their thoughts, to hammer in their fantasies.[1]

My brothers and sisters are married. Only one has been divorced. I have 13 nephews and nieces. No doubt there will be more. I have never married, nor ever wanted to, but, when 40, I began to help another woman raise several children. I have taught one to drive, another to play poker, and given another her first Nancy Drew. My love lacks any security of blood, any sanctity of law. So does the anger the kids and I bring up in

111

each other. Without such regulations, I must balance interference, intervention, and interplay. I must earn and cajole authority. My emotions have a free-floating purity, and risk.

I am a creature of tradition. When I shop with a kid, I realize how reflexively people approve of me if they believe my ties belong to a particular old school. The company of children confers an ancient, reassuring legitimacy. Sighting my own gestures, I sigh and sense a mingling of past and present as close as that of salt and flour in bread. When I arrange food, in the movement of my hands are a taste for the aesthetic, a bounty, that are my mother's. When I carve meat, in my voice is a spacious affability that was my father's. Listening to a child split hairs about hygiene, I hear a stubborn, frustrated logic that was my own.

Yet, I improvise the new. As I imitate father/mother, I am neither father, nor mother, but adult in a little group that some admire, and others—perhaps even the kids themselves when they rebel—may disdain. Moreover, I must deal out, and with, a culture my childhood never knew. I, who grew up without television, must permit the goofy returns of "Love Boat." I, who was told about the old sex intelligently, must refer now to sperm banks, Louise Brown, and adolescent diaphragms.

I have, then, both reconstituted and repudiated family history. Through that choice, I have bitten on necessity. For family life demands some giving up. It schools us in limits. A child—smaller, more dependent than adults—learns this. So do those adults who are not fugitives from realism. The family has also set up a curriculum for sacrifice. The feminine form of the Latin word for family meant household servant—before it came to include household, the retinue of a nobleman, persons of common blood or race, or any group that shares characteristics. Being in a family means serving others, especially small, dependent children. For obligation-ridden adults, there is no free lunch, breakfast, or after-school snack.

Despite my pride in my idiosyncratic, even loony, choice, I am no anomaly. Rather I am part of that social sweep that puts the ego in its place: a demographic trend. So are many of my friends. The houses that hold us are too heterogeneous, too full of permutations, for a patriarchal god and polyester gospelers to bear. In 1970, "family households," in which birth or marriage binds folk together, were 81.2 percent of all households in the United States. In 1980, they were but 73.9 percent. "Nonfamily households" grew from 18.8 percent to 26.1 percent. During the decade, 15,707,000 new households burgeoned. A majority were nonfamily; of the family category, a majority had single heads. I belong to an emerging group, to a statistic on a growth spurt.[2]

People comment on my trend incessantly. As I struggle with ordinariness, with shirts and sneakers and TV, others talk about my group, and the meaning of it all. My tedium, toil, and fun are raw material for public, and published argument.

Some people are confessional. They write of their own experiences of contemporary family life—of orgies with married couples at conference centers in California canyons; of bitter custody cases; of unions between transsexuals. Still other people are brisk troop leaders of social change. They jauntily tell us how to march through historical and psychic upheaval. One author, for example, issues a manual for divorced men in order to help them heal their suffering from a "FIR Tree" syndrome of "Failure," "Inferiority," and "Rejection."

Still other people are sober academics. Historians claim that the modern family no longer produces goods and services. Instead it consumes them. It may also be a refuge from a ruthless, competitive, loveless world, or, for black families, a legitimate source of resistance to the illegitimate racism of that world. Economists announce that it may now take $100,000 to raise a child. Psychologists theorize that such a child, as a baby, first mirrors the inchoate self in a mother's gaze.

Still other people are ideological. A privileged savant of the New Right clamors that I am committing sexual suicide. He announces that men are naked nomads whom nature has made both wilder and weaker than us girls. Men must have a home, with a wife serene within it. If they do not, the species will not survive. A pope replays St. Paul and a dogma of the Christian marriage. Legislators draft a Family Protection Act that would grant married couples, but only married couples, a special tax exemption if they bear or adopt a child. In response to such maneuvers, a man of the New Left tries to reclaim the family for progressive politics, and even to make it central to them. Among other things, he calls for an American Families Day. Answering him, a woman of the Left wisely reminds him of both visions of community that transcend family or race and visions of morality that affirm "individual desire and imagination."[3]

Because I am a woman who rejects femininity as usual, the feminist discourse has been, for me, the most searching, steadfast, and sustaining. Though feminists are hardly the only people to question the family, they have provoked the most hostile brouhaha. Plato preferred the state to the family but few censor him. Perhaps our contemporary cultural illiteracy, in which Plato is a sex club, not a philosopher, has its virtues. Feminists provoke that ire because some dare to think that the family in general ought not to survive and because all declare the health of women to be a prime test of a particular family. Indeed, only feminists—men and women alike—systematically ask if the angel of the home is really happy there, particularly if her actual stance is less that of angel than of Atlas.

Unsentimentally, feminists have documented the unhappy burden of the women, now a majority of wives in the United States, who work inside and outside the home; the inequalities of marriage and divorce codes; the horrors of the wife-beating and child abuse that make the home more violent than a factory, highway, or Army boot camp. It has been feminists who have mourned a refusal, in the United States and elsewhere, to fuse domestic life and sexual equality. They have scrutinized the social construction of sexuality that labels a woman's body the agent of the needs of others; that calls female sexuality correct within the heterosexual home, incorrect but permissible outside that home, and damnable and incorrect if lesbian. Feminists— Brownmiller, Chodorow, Dinnerstein, Rich—have mined connecting shafts between patriarchal sex roles within the home and a public life that threatens us all. They have wondered if the fact that women, but not men, are raised to nurture within the home means that men are dangerously incapable of it outside.

Even as feminists skeptically analyze a family that others fancy, they seek to imagine new communities of intimacy. To be a feminist is to move between negation and hope, betwen estrangement from time present and belief in time future. In her novels, Marge Piercy has conjured up Utopian societies that are harmonious yet egalitarian, sane yet poetic. In feminist theory, Sara Ruddick has asked why men and women cannot practice "maternal thinking," a habit of mind that respects a balance between self and others, between self-assertion and altruism. In sociology, Rosabeth Moss Kanter has listed ways in which we could integrate work and family life. To have significant labor and leisure; to enjoy dependents and dependence while rejecting the filthy luxuries of domination and submission; to be autonomous and communal; to proclaim differences and yet to sing to children—such has been a feminist ideal, as its most dangerous and lovely.

A rule of language insists that the more we talk about a subject, the more we may be trying to hide something. Some people are consciously evasive. The New Right wraps itself in the flag of the family in order to clothe its poling toward political control. Other evasions loll in the subconscious, and we must yank them to attention. As I dwell on homey details, on leftover apple cores and the cost of tube socks, my quest for tidiness and thrift may obscure more taxing questions. How eroticized are some family passions? How much must an adult guardian, with our wariness about repression, still guard against the expression of a sharp tenderness that veers toward desire? Some polymorphous sexuality is perverse. Or, a less fashionable issue, what might one do about a child whom one might not like? Whose presence, because it may too vividly mirror one's own, may be a pang? Or, a more civic concern, how much might being involved with family welfare mask a fear of other struggles, for example, about the welfare state. The lake of the everyday may be tepid, but its rafts are there, its shores known.

The answers to such queries, like the *whyness* of my present life, still elude me. Yet, I am sure that I have tested several forms of dailiness. No one chooses a family of origin. Many of us crawl into our adult arrangements, heedlessly repeating that primal place. Later, we may not select their dissolution. However, we willful plungers in families of transition have rummaged through our past to decide what we wish to preserve. We are defense witnesses for versions of family life.

Some people accuse me of acting unconsciously. My delight in a young boy, they say, represents the rediscovery of a "phallus" I lost in childhood. Buying balloons for a birthday party is compensation for the "loneliness" I felt while a striving, womb-denying, animus-mad career woman.

Maybe the amateur psychoanalysts are correct, but it all seems much simpler and less theoretical. Because I expect to be here for along while, because I have education and mobility, I see my life as a series of possibilities. Some can be, and were, deferred. I got bored with being with contemporaries. Though aging, I lacked a crucial measure of maturity. Inarticulately, I wanted a new fusion of responsibility and surprise, of routine and shock, of ritual and unpredictability; touches that did not have to be renegotiated at least for a while; jokes that did not have to be explained; and innocence. Though I will pass on little property and no name, perhaps I wished to infiltrate another's memory.

I did not actively seek the children out. Nor they me. Yet my difficulty now is that too many people—both strangers and acquaintances—perceive my politics, my psyche, and my form of parenting as an assassination attempt on "decency." Conservative scorn surrounds me. So does liberal surprise, but I can disarm that. Some days I ignore the conservative scorn, but I would be a fool to forget the burn of my anger, and the sting of my defiance. They are usable weapons.

I have stood, in the morning, telling a child she must drink her apple juice because she needs Vitamin C. She has reported that she has often ignored her apple juice, and she has survived. Such dialogues are hardly the scripts of postlapsarian sin. Like many of us, I am engaged in an experiment that is trying to write new narratives of love and freedom, of being with children without using them or using up ourselves. I have a national policy for families—as simple, as nontheoretical as a child's need for apple juice. Let no child starve—in mind or body. Let no child be beaten. Let parenters speak their name, and have enough money and flexible public services to do their chores. Then—let me alone. I want privacy, not to hide some viciousness, not to perpetuate a false division between public and domestic life, but because I need the space in which to give texture to a language of love and care that is now gossamer.

11 FEMINISM AND FEMINIST CRITICISM
(1983)

In 1861, Emily Dickinson cut one of her shard-like poems about language. "Many a phrase has the English language," she said, and added, with ironic modesty, that she had heard but one, "Low as the laughter of the cricket/Loud as the Thunder's tongue." At once monolithic and polyphonic, the phrase had broken in bright orthography on her simple sleep. It had made her weep, not for sorrow, but for the "push of joy."[1]

I place Dickinson as the first inlay in the mosaic of my argument as a tribute to the power of women writers, itself an act of feminist criticism. My argument is less a well-framed work than a rough premonition about feminist criticism. This criticism has brilliantly helped to compel both feminism and criticism to remember the push *and* joy of language. Its theories and insights matter to any analysis of language, politics, and power. Despite such achievements, in its growing maturity feminist criticism may defang its feminism. I do not want to subordinate criticism to feminism, complexity of analysis to the severities of ideology. Neither do I wish to subordinate feminism to criticism. Rather, I seek a "dialectical mediation between them."[2] A fidelity to history—in general and to that of feminist criticism in particular—can sustain this double, doubling commitment.

Since the late 1960's, the meaning of being a feminist critic has deepened.[3] It has, however, consistently entailed assuming the validity of a tough, parsimonious theory; we cannot understand history, society or culture unless we graph the causes and effects of sex/gender systems. Such systems proliferate, foliate, and vary, but they have usually pushed down on women. Rochesters have bestrode the world more firmly, and freely, than Janes. Janes have had to choose between polishing their boots or declining to do so—at the risk of a kick. The feminist critic must break such sex/gender systems, using language as weapon and tool, and then labor to renew history, society, and culture.

Accepting such a theory as axiomatic, feminist critics have exerted their energies in three fields. They have first unravelled the thick tapestries of male hegemony, and unknotted networks of conscious assumptions and unconscious presumptions about women. Nina Baym has explored definitions of American literature to show how assertions about what was "American" about "American" literature" *a priori* defeminized it.[4] Feminist critics have decomposed the representation of women in culture; the images, stereotypes, and archetypes. They have found woman as beautiful other, as aesthetic object whose power is that of eros, glamour, and fashion. They have found woman as mother, whose will and power, if checked and directed, will succour. They have found woman as schemer, whose will and power, if unchecked, will devour.

Less successfully, feminist critics have analyzed the reasons for the persistent reproduction of such patterns, their acute ability to sustain themselves. Our failure largely lies in the lack of an explanatory matrix that allies psychology, history, and a recognition of intertextualities. Whatever the causes, representations of women repeat themselves compulsively. For example, that antique, epic picture of woman as schemer now appears in "Boris," a Yale University computer program. A crude but lively critic, Boris reads and interprets stories, including one about Richard, an attorney; Paul, once his roommate; and Sarah, Paul's wife. Paul asks Richard for help because Sarah wants a divorce, ". . . the car, the house, the children and alimony." A distressed Paul must stop the greedy Sarah. After some drinks, and consultation, Richard drives Paul home. Paul walks into his bedroom and nearly has a heart attack. For Sarah is there with another man. But he realizes what a blessing it all is. "With Richard there as a witness, Sarah's divorce case was shot."[5] A good thing, too, thinks Boris.

Feminist criticism's first field of activity, then, has been generally deconstructive. Its second has been reconstructive. Feminist critics have knitted up a woman's tradition. As Elaine Showalter says, they have created "gynocritics." To be sure, many women writers have either extended "male" conventions or accepted a theory of art that degenderizes the imagination. Nevertheless, many women writers in the past have undergone a process similar to that of feminist critics today. They have cut loose from male hegemony and sought another, more authentic voice. They have demonstrated Susan Griffin's musing injunction: "We must trust in words, and the coming of words."[6] Mary Wollstonecraft, in *A Vindication of the Rights of Woman* (1792), gazes back at, and then turns away, from Rousseau. Charlotte Brontë, in *Shirley* (1849), gazes back at, and then turns away, from the Old Testament and Milton. So doing, their lot has been to become, not pillars of salt, but creatures of language. Because women have had less access to literacy and to education than men, the traditions of gynocritics are spoken as well as written, as much intervocalities as intertextualities. Whether speech or text women's seizure of language reveals the dual activity of pulling down and putting up that Gertrude Stein demands in "Patriarchal Poetry":

Reject rejoice rejuvenate rejuvenate rejoice
reject rejoice rejuvenate reject rejuvenate
reject rejoice.[7]

Such verbal negations and recreations are but a part of a larger moment
in contemporary culture that feminist criticism observes and even, in its
bolder rhetorical gestures, joins. This moment devises events and artifacts
that celebrate women's capacities for action on their own behalf. To an
unusual degree, they fuse pleasure and polemic. Once, in prison, writing to
his wife, Gramsci said that when he read, he often had to distinguish
between "enthusiasm for a work of art in itself and moral enthusiasm, by
which I mean a willing participation in an artist's ideological world . . . "[8]
The new women's culture self-consciously produces a feminist aesthetic
that reconciles the flavorful gratuitousness of style and the imperatives of
ideology. It appears in posters; clothing, such as T-shirts;[9] demonstrations
(those in Italy have a special elegance, verve, and theatricality); fine art;
films, and texts that experiment with a voice at once personal and
collective, fragmented and coherent, that alludes to riccota and Adrienne
Rich, wool and Virginia Woolf, the domestic and the public.[10]

The unravelling of male hegemony, the knitting up of a female
heterodoxy at once independent and interdependent, is inseparable from
feminist criticism's third field of activity: the study of sexual difference itself;
of what is "male" and what is "female"; of the causes and inscriptions of
difference, whether as fiat or graffiti. Because feminist criticism is feminist,
the study of sexual difference is a study of hierarchy, of power differentials,
as well.

Some critics explore difference in everyday language, in "genderlects,"
and ask about the relationships between genderlects and gender/lex. As
psycholinguists compute the burrowings and flights of speech, they print
out male dominance.[11] The revelation of inequalities has led to suggestions
for their remedies through changes in linguistic habits.[12] Other feminist
critics codify cultural productions, to see women stoking fantasies of
power where men stroke eros,[13] or to find women demystifying a New
World landscape that men were grandly mythologizing.[14]

The study of difference has provoked mingled psychic responses. Some,
who float on the anxiety principle, fear what a discovery of profound
ahistorical differences might mean. Others, who ride the reality principle,
declare that we must understand sexual difference, no matter what this
might mean. Still others, who invite the pleasure principle, vow that we will
discover a difference that we will cheerfully proclaim. Margaret Walker
declares:

Creativity cannot exist without the feminine principle, and I am sure God is
not merely male or female but He—She—our Father-Mother-God.[15]

In part because these psychic responses are so volatile, feminist critics have treated their differences about theories of sexual difference somewhat gingerly. Such reticence has also been the result of the pervasiveness of the belief that nearly all sexual differences are the consequence of social conditions, and social conditioning, which we might alter; of a stubborn shying away from theory; and of the factitious conviction that strong argument is fractious, unruly, and unsisterly.

This polite tentativeness is enervating, for theories of sexual difference have more than intellectual interest. They influence the political imagination. If I conflate sexual difference, I will prefer a political myth that praises undifferentiated and equal persons. If, on the other hand, I inflate difference, I will seek a political myth that praises differentiated, even partially separated, equal men and women. Implying that the passage of time has its progressive paces, feminist writers are now publishing Utopian narratives that provide materials for the political imagination. They offer a number of models for a new community: all-female societies; biological androgynes who avoid invidious genderizing; genuinely egalitarian cultures.[16] Even if they are to do something as simple as codifying such texts, feminist critics must confront their particular, and conflicting, sense of the structures of difference.

Even if it were to be more public and more vigorous, the debate about sexual difference would still be difficult. For its very terms—"female" and "male"—are problematic. Like the word "instinct," they are at once too smoothly universal and too roughly thickened by misuse. To think of women and men as primarily "female" or "male" blurs our vision of the historical complexities of women's identities, when it does not blind us to them altogether. Because of the legitimate pressure of such groups as black feminists, feminist critics are now more apt to remember that every woman is more than a woman. She belongs, as well, to a class, a race, a nation, a family, a tribe, a time, a place.

Less explicitly and fully, feminist critics have recognized that every woman, as language user, has multiple relationships with chosen audiences. Each will embody its own sense of language, of her place in the world, and of the possibilities of change in that place. At times, women may speak or write only for themselves. Their motives may be weariness, fear, or insecurity. More cheerfully, they may be claiming a private space in which to experiment with style, to test perceptions, to play with fantasies. Whatever the cause, the effect is to reinforce an impression of the apparent solitude of language.

At other times, women address only a significant other, or a tiny handful of others. They discuss activities that the larger society disdains, dismisses, and taboos. Though they speak freely to each other, the closed circuit quality of their discourse perpetuates society's disdain, dismissals, and taboos. In the later 1920's and early 1930's, for example, two young women, living in different cities, each getting professional training, corresponded at some length. They wrote about work and play, families and friends, courtship and sex. Even as they describe their men, they express a passionate love for each other, at once maternal and erotic, which they cannot and will not introduce into their work and play, to their families and friends. They have a public and private life, a public and a private language. One letter tells of the author's loss of her virginity, after she and a man "get around to the real fundamentals," and of a visit she makes to a fatherly doctor who advises her about methods to render "intercourse" less painful. Then, she signs her letter "Love kisses" from "Mary who loves you very much more than she can say." After that revelation of the impotence of language, she scrawls out three rows of "Xs," the sign of a kiss and of illiteracy: one of 17 marks, one of 18, a third of 17. Finally she ends:

> —if you take each kiss separately that might give you some idea. Then quadruple the number and the idea should be a little clearer. If I haven't kissed you into unconsciousness by this time repeat above formula until I do.
>
> That's about $\dfrac{1}{1,000,000,000,000}$ of how much I love my darling Jessie.[17]

At still other times, women gossip, an activity sadly devalued as the trivial chatter of those who lack headier substance. When women gossip to each other, they do more than consistently exchange ideas, judgment, and information—the data of every day. They are covertly creating a subtle, collective presence in the world.[18] At still other times, women use language far more openly to establish a more forceful, public presence. To be sure, some do so in self-contradictory ways. The nineteenth-century sentimental novelists both averred that women suffer under patriarchy and averted the logical consequences of their pleading: a call to change patriarchy. In a twentieth-century reversal of this pattern, a Phyllis Schlafly endorses patriarchy but avoids the logical consequence of her pleading: to be quiet and stay at home. Other women, however, militantly, system-atically deploy language to stimulate their audience's desire for profound political and cultural change. Like feminist critics themselves, they inscribe a "feminist polemic."[19]

Cultural productions themselves reveal change, concrete restructurings of consciousness in language, through language. They then prove that the desire for change (particularly in consciousness and culture) is plausible. It need not be aimless, feckless, wishful, wistful, Utopian. The very act of feminist criticism, its readings and interpretations, foreground these demonstrations. As a feminist critic, let me offer but two examples of such a process. The first is a series of poems, which begins with Yeats' canonical sonnet, "Leda and the Swan." It alternates between images of beauty and of terror; between images of Leda's rape and the war the rape will engender. As it reaches closure, it asks of Leda:

> Did she put on his knowledge with his power
> Before the indifferent beak could let her drop?

In 1964, a women poet, Mona Van Duyn, answered that question. So doing, she began to tug at Yeats' place as a regulator of cultural excellence and meaning. She wrote two poems about Leda, both more carefully careless than the Yeats, more rhetorically casual and ordinary.[20] In one, "Leda," she gives Leda a history. She says that Leda's life, in men's stories, ends with the swan's loss. Van Duyn's Leda, however, has her rape-engendered children. She gets horribly depressed, recovers, and finally marries " . . . a smaller man with a beaky nose/and melt(s) away into the storm of everyday life." Then, in a second poem, "Leda Reconsidered," Van Duyn returns to the rape itself. If she has given Leda a biography before, she now offers her interiority, subjectivity, the capacity for choice. Her Leda has a minute of waiting, of apparent passivity, as the swan approaches her. She uses it to decide actively how to interpret her experience. She wills an acceptance of the utter strangeness of the god, the exaltation of the divine. She permits the swan to penetrate both imagination and flesh. Then, as his shadow falls on her skin, she reaches out—to touch the plumes.

In 1972, another woman poet, Adrienne Rich, published another text, bluntly titled "Rape."[21] Like Van Duyn, she rejects the temptations of transforming women's pain into myth, into tragic grandeur. Unlike Van Duyn, she austerely refuses to give women any choice about rape, that terrible formula for a man's exercise of power over a woman. The rapist might be a prowler, or a father, or a neighbor, or a cop—who will listen later to the victim's testimony. No matter what his social role, the sperm that greases a woman's thighs will be that of an abusive maniac, not that of a god. Rich's language compels our revulsion.

My second example reveals a far more comic pattern: that of the individual who learns to exercise power, not to dominate others, but to erode illusions and the imperiled stance of the victim. *From Housewife to Heretic* is the autobiography of Sonia Johnston, a Mormon woman who became an outspoken feminist.[22] She tells her story clearly, passionately, but with an edge of happy surprise, as if the developing plot of her life still thrilled her. In bearing witness to that life, she tells of a masculine, weighty command of language. Men use words to spell out their laws, to pray to the God who gives them their laws, and to define their will. Language labels heretics and punishes women. Language also defrauds women.

Johnson's husband of twenty years, whom she loves and respects, persuades her to sign a "fake divorce" before a notary. It will, he assures her, in some dialectical swerving, renew their marriage. Two days after she gives him her signature, and her trust, he announces:

> I'm tired of working on our marriage. I don't care about it anymore. I want that divorce to be real. (p. 19)

No matter how besieged and betrayed, Johnson grasps language for herself. Indeed, the autobiography is final evidence of her linguistic achievement. She begins to write in church, in a secret act of defiance against the "voices of patriarchy" to which she has listened for over forty years. During the sermons, she scrawls poems. Writing replaces hearing. She meets with other women to engage in a shrewd, informal, communal analysis of their lives. Speaking reinforces writing. She reads feminist polemic: Kate Millett, Germaine Greer. She speaks more and more publicly about political matters. Her support of the Equal Rights Amendment will trigger her expulsion from the Mormon Church.

As language helps Johnson stabilize a new identity, she gives it more and more powers. It becomes cathartic of a still-haunting past. As she is ending a chapter about her marriage for her autobiography, her daughter enters the scene of writing. Supportive, idiomatic, her daughter says:

> You're lucky, Mom, do you know that? . . . Not many women get to do what you did. You really got to write him off! (p. 233)

Language is also the medium through which the good news of women's vitality, integrity, and strength will travel. Taking on a prophetic function, bridging the gap between her single vision and that of women's communities, Johnson writes of women's being:

> I cannot begin to express with what pleasure I now watch my sister feminists' lives, delighting in the myriads of evidences of intelligence and wisdom, of good humor, liveliness and playfulness, of loving care for women everywhere, for the children, for the men, for the old and the poor people of the world. I cannot get enough of the words written by women. Every word sounds different in my mind from the way it sounded when men used it. It is a new word, with new meaning (or the original one restored), richer, more provocative, healing, mine. My language, finally. (pp. 289–90)

My remarks about change mark my transparent, but adhesive, allegiance to placing women and language in a kinetic history that we can nevertheless map. I realize that "history" is itself a construct, a series of acts of writing. The Oxford English Dictionary's first definition of history is a "relation of incidents . . . a narrative, tale, story. . . . " Nevertheless, history is more than a construct, more than a series of acts of writing, just as a broken bone from an automobile accident is more than a police report, a hospital admissions form, or a doctor's bill. I admire the empiricism of the other Foucault, Jean Bernard Léon Foucault (1819–1868), who devised a pendulum to measure the earth's rotation, who believed material realities were there to measure.

In part, feminist critics graph private histories, narratives of character, biographies and autobiographies. Such work is less the after-image of an obsolete theory of history as the record of great personalities than it is a tribute to intention, to individual action and will. In part, feminist critics write public histories of language as a system that interweaves with other systems. An anthropologist matches creation myths with the sexual "scripts" of various cultures to show how such myths can predict a culture's commitment to gender parity.[23] A classicist excavates the literacy of women in ancient Greece.[24] A historian analyzes the reading patterns of Colonial and Revolutionary women to see how they absorbed and shaped an ideology of "republican motherhood."[25] Finally, in part, feminist critics, from their place on the margins of culture, can translate their perspective of the past into rewritten records of that past.[26] For example, in a brilliant story, "Meditations on History," at once fiction and criticism, Sherley Anne Williams savagely parodies the language of Southern white men who investigated slaves and slave revolts. She inserts, largely through indirection, the deeper, alternative history a black slave woman would have uttered.[27]

A number of ideological reasons have compelled attention to the past: the need to document feminist convictions about the degree of women's sufferings, the wish to untangle the social and cultural causes of that pain, the belief that one must act within history if one is to act politically and alter public and domestic structures of power. The feminist critic logically goes on to spurn a historiography that pictures history as repetitive, as a series of cycles or spirals or ditto marks. Any critical movement that has self-consciously distanced itself from the traditional alienation of its members (in this case, women) will think in this way. For them, fatalism is masochism. The feminist critic extolls the Adrienne Rich who writes:

> I have cast my lot with those
> who, age after age, perversely,
> with no extraordinary power
> reconstitute the world.[28]

Despite such interests and self-interests, feminist critics have often erred in their sense of the past. Those whose literary training has been in texts and textualities have frequently been ignorant of history's massive details.

With the exception of Marxist critics, they have lacked a spacious theory about the relationship of culture to social forces. When they have attempted to "relate" literature and life, they have tended to forget how "eccentric" and "dialectical" that relationship might be.[29] In the early 1970's, a powerful feminist art historian correctly warned against a blunted sense of a text as psychological realism. Linda Nochlin cautioned against:

> . . . (a) misconception of what art is . . . the naive idea that art is the direct, personal expression of individual emotional experience, a translation of personal life into visual terms. Art is almost never that, great art certainly never.[30]

Such misconceptions are but part of an unquestioning acceptance of a vulgar theory of mimesis that renders a picture a "real image of the real," a text "a real representation of the real"; that reduces a Maggie and a Nora to the status of case studies, an Eliot and an Ibsen to documentarians.[31] So erring, feminist critics (I among them) have used literature as proof simple of patriarchal squalors. To a degree, it is, in what it says and in the conditions of its production, transmission, and reception. Texts, however, also have their independence. Simultaneously, at the other extreme, feminist critics have deployed texts as narratives of the heart's desire and projected onto them the shadowy, but palpable, lineaments of dream. They have glimpsed the perfect mother, an Atlantis-like female unconscious, or a lost goddess, a sacred "gynocentric power"[32] that we can summon up through language and ritual to recreate a delightful, deliquescent tradition that will help to wash away secular horrors.

Obviously, not every feminist critic guiltily evades articulating the eccentric dialectic between history and texts. In A Literature of Their Own (1977), for example, Elaine Showalter lucidly balances them. When such errors occur, however, they strain richness from discourse. The intellectual pilgrimage of feminist criticism has been even more complicated by a theoretical question about language that matters to a sense of history: can women adopt and use the "natural language" we now have, or is that language so corrupt, so hopelessly "male," so riddled with a vain longing for a center of meaning, that women must create language anew? In a large way, a feminist critic's answer today depends on whether she subscribes to contemporary French or American feminist theory. Margaret Homans has suggested that in France language and experience are coextensive. Despite their differences, French feminist critics will then think of language as a domineering construct "whose operation depends on women's silence and absence."[33] In order to speak or to write at all, women must fly away from it. In the United States, however, language and experience seem more separable. Women, even if they wish to plant new gardens, can plow the fields of ordinary language. They need not design a linguistic *Herland*.

A feminist critic's attitude towards the legacies of natural language, whether she find them poisonous or usable, influences her politics. If a language, in and of itself, silences and marginalizes women, then transforming that language is, in and of itself, a political necessity. One must smash linguistic continuities and apocalyptically rename the world. One must revolutionize the word. One can then read Monique Wittig's *Les Guèrillères*,[34] as both prophecy and program. In that visionary, lyric, passionate book, women begin with several texts: a "great register," in which any woman may write, or read, at random; small books called "feminaries," with both blank pages on which women can write, and inscribed pages in which women can read of their sexuality and legends, of their bodies and culture. The women, however, rebel and overthrow the order of things. They burn even their own books, their own linguistic past. After their triumph, they join with men to create a new language and a novel history. Adam and Eve both speak a tongue of mutuality that Wittig refuses to imagine. If language is neutral, if grammar is really genderless, if syntax is sexless, the transformation of language itself is politically irrelevant. One can then read Sonia Johnson's autobiography as both prophecy and program. She longs for a more authentic speech, for a more egalitarian political rhetoric, but she dwells happily within the structure and conventions of English, the natural language she has inherited.

Now conjoining the argument about the gender of language is the post-structuralist question about language as a referential system, a conveyor of meaning, a medium for "truth." If language refers to little more than itself, if it conveys only itself, if it is the medium only for itself, then "woman" is little more than the Nietzschean metaphor for an impotent quest for certainty:

> And she is woman precisely because she herself does not believe in truth itself, because she does not believe in what she is, in what she is believed to be, in what she thus is not.[35]

A feminist critic's response to post-structuralism will also shape her politics. If she believes in it, she may see history and politics as but another current in the sea of language. She may forget that language does ground itself in daily relations that involve hierarchies and power. She may have a " . . . decentered vision," but it may tempt her to ignore " . . . a centered action that will not result in a renewed invisibility."[36] On the other hand, if she rejects post-structuralism, if she finds it too abstract or theoretical, she may extend reductive notions of language and literature as reliably representational.

Inevitably, for the feminist critic, the question of language becomes involved with that about sexual difference. Though thick and tousled with implication, the issue is simple enough to state baldly. If men and women have different languages, is this because we are primarily creatures of cultural and social forces (though we have some physical, natural being), or is this because we are primarily creatures of deeply structured physical, natural forces (though we have some cultural and social being)? How much has historicity built and rebuilt us? Journalism is a fun-house mirror of life. A recent journalistic account of scholars at Smith College asked this question. Answering it, the author schematizes, as if she were an allegorist, two great positions of feminist criticsm:

> Marilyn Schuster is working on the problems of narrative in French fiction by contemporary women, from Colette to Monique Wittig. She is trying to discover what is unique to women writers and what they are able to do that conventional narratives or male-dominated narratives are unable to do.
> Marilyn believes that whatever distinguishes women's voices from men's is owing to biology—to a woman's experience of herself as a physical being. Susan Van Dyne, who is studying American women poets, believes, on the other hand, that these differences are socially derived and determined. That is a question that vexes most feminists.[37]

Indeed. Even *The Second Sex* could not reconcile these apparent polarities. De Beauvoir gave both women and men existential freedom and consciousness. Yet she placed women, far more than men, under the power of the flesh, the womb, and the blood and children that wombs expel. She hung the Spanish moss of carnal fate on women's branching wills.

Feminist critics search through language for revelations of difference and for the signifiers of a femaleness that may flow beneath and below various cultures, societies, and temperaments. Their quest complements the search for an androgynous sensibility that mingles maleness and femaleness, masculinity and femininity. They seek specificity as those who sought androgyny did integration. For many now, that femaleness is located in eros, in women's capacities for a sensual pleasure at once polymorphous and clitoral.[38] Women are lively, radiant Aphrodites whose libido and body can erupt into language. A tape transcriber, once listening to me, heard my word "frisson" as "free song." She could have been musing on "l'écriture féminine."

The longing for a female language intertwines with the exploration of a special female sensibility. Such an identity may be born in women's essential selves or through more historical processes: mothering or bonding between mothers and daughters—both blends of body, brain, custom, feeling, and necessity. Whatever the source, women become more capable of affiliation, of psychic fluidity, than men. Theoreticians of a unique female psychology link it to history in contradictory ways. For some, it explains women's subordinate status. Women lack the autonomy, the greedy and tough ego, necessary for struggle in the world. For others, it explains an apparent gender difference in cultural behavior. Elizabeth Abel claims that since Austen and Dickinson women writers

> . . . have felt a particular bond with one another. This concern with collectivity mediates the desire for originality and places women writers in a different historical as well as psychological situation from their male contemporaries.[39]

For still others, women's culture is an alternative set of values that both men and women can put into practice. If they do so, they will act out and on a sense of interdependency and a competence at caring that the post-modern world, raving to devastate itself, must embody if it is to survive.

I have feared the search for a quasi-permanent, if previously repressed, "female" being, for a literature and language that spring from it, and for a criticism that hoes and waters them. I have preferred a cryptogamic to a sexualized language. Cryptogams—ferns, mosses, algae, lichen—reproduce without pistils or stamen. I have happily risked the possibility that a cryptogamic language, like cryptogams themselves, might not breed flowers. My skepticism has so many sources that it seems over-determined. History has taught us to doubt any theoretical conflation of body and performance, of physiology and one's assigned role in the world. The nineteenth-century *savants* who measured the cranium with calipers to find degrees of human nature were mindless. Moreover, such conflations traditionally rationalize hierarchal patterns of domination and submission, superior and inferior classes.

Next, I apprehend the chilly shadow of logical error, a confusion of being and doing, the presence of a superficial theory of action that insists that because one is female, one necessarily writes and speaks a female language. Next, feminist descriptions of that female language—the possibility that it might be less "linear," for example, than a male language— reconstitute regressive myths of woman as primitive, as a creature of blood and feeling, babble and fervor, eros and spreading ebullience. The belief that this language might also be politically revolutionary seems like magical thinking, a rhetorical effort to connect rhetoric as cause and vast transformations as effect. Next, to genderize language so zealously, to cast it as a binary opposition of "female" and "male" forms, is another reconstitution of an older pattern: a dualistic model of human activity that denies the dazzle, the dappledness of life. Like Mary Jacobus, I celebrate " . . . a multiplicity, joyousness, and heterogeneity which is that of textuality itself."[40] Finally, even if there were such a thing/entity/phenomenon/process as "femaleness," the difficulty of testing it is appalling. To measure what is the flesh, the natural, the humanly given, and what are the mediating forces of personality, convention, and culture is like weighing water with open hands. The "semantics of biology"[41]—the ways in which we codify, interpret, and experience our carnality, our mortality, the world of storms, stones, and chromosomes—defy any easy reading.

Given such fears, given my allusions to history throughout this essay, my suggestion for feminist criticism in the immediate future is perverse. Feminist criticism now ought to encourage the quest for a "female" writing and language; for the "female" text. It ought to interrogate women writers and artists, as part of a gynocritical tradition and in comparison to men, to see what, if anything, is as insistent a presence in and through time as DNA has been in our genes. The feminist critic herself might release her own writing, give her own language some rawness and apparent spontaneity.

Such a search will probably prove to be alchemical. We will fail, in seeking transmutations of the tongue, to find a precious essence, an all-valuable substance. Still, if this happens, if the "female" proves to be ultimately mythic and illusory, we will have scoured our consciousness. A ghostly question will cease to haunt our discourse. Moreover, in releasing our energies, we need not exhaust them. Rather, like the alchemists, we may prepare ourselves for a chemistry we did not envision, for a table of the elements we could not have set, or seen. Finally, seeking the "female" will loosen the human voice in general. The once-marginal tenants on the estate of the King's English will prise culture open.

Yet, even if feminist critics were to become such alchemists, to take typewriters and word processors as their tripods and laboratory glasses, they must hold fast to the feminist principles of feminist criticism. Feminist criticism began, in part, as an anatomy of the pain that the pressures of history had imprinted on women, as a passion to erase that pain, and as a hope, often inadequately expresed, to ally that passion with other progressive political energies. At their shrewdest, feminist critics also know that such activities must not mask a fantastic desire to regain a human paradise. To long for perpetual bliss is to behave like a consumer whose Visa accounts are never rendered, whose masters never charge.

I began with quotation. I wish to end with a difficult anecdote. I was thinking about feminist criticism one night as I was driving home from my university work. On either side the highway's twelve lanes were oil refineries, with great curved pipes and round towers. I smelled industrial fumes. I saw no green, except for paint and neon signs. Earlier that day, after a meeting, a woman colleague had told me about an experience. She had recently been raped, at knife-point, in her car, with her son watching. She was in her late twenties, her son only six. She was no Leda, the rapist no swan. To remember that story, to keep it as a fire within consciousness and the political will, is the feminism in feminist criticism. Such a memory is a base of our use of language, no matter how skeptical we might be of language's referential power, as feminist criticism annuls powerful cultural arrangements, anneals again the materials of history, and reclaims language's push of joy.

12   THE FEMALE SOCIOGRAPH:
THE THEATER OF
VIRGINIA WOOLF'S LETTERS
(1984)

The Virginia Woolf letters have come out: six volumes, nearly 4,000 individual letters. As the editors know, their survival is an accident,[1] they have depended on the habits of her receivers, not all of whom have had the retentive holding patterns of the archivist. Loss, then, necessarily salts our interpretations. Nevertheless, in the flair of the Woolf correspondence, we can read her writing and writing herself. Her letters exemplify a particular women's text, one that is neither wholly private nor wholly public. They occupy a psychological and rhetorical middle space between what she wrote for herself and what she produced for a general audience. They are a brilliant, glittering encyclopedia of the partially-said. Because of this, they probably cannot give us what Joseph Conrad's letters gave a critic like Edward W. Said: the materials for a full autobiography of consciousness, a mediation between life and work.[2] Rather, Woolf's letters inscribe a sociograph. They concern social worlds that she needed and wanted. They form an autobiography of the self with others, a citizen/denizen of relationships.

When young, teaching herself to be a writer, Woolf toyed with a quasi-Pateresque notion of the letter as a formed impression of consciousness, a shaped inscription of mind. In 1906, she informs her older friend Violet Dickinson: "A letter should be as flawless as a gem, continuous as an eggshell, and lucid as glass" (I, 264). The more she wrote, however, the more the letter became an act within, and of, the moment; less a steady mirror of the real than a dashing glimpse into, and from, its flux. Woolf need not care if language outruns sense and syntax; her perceptions a sense of

Versions of this paper were read at the Modern Language Association, Annual Meeting, December 1978, and at Hobart and William Smith colleges, May 1983. I am grateful to Louise K. Horowitz for sharing work on French criticism about letter-writing with me; to Elizabeth Wood for her comments; and to the body of Woolf criticism for its instructiveness.

decorum; response responsibility. She jauntily advises the composer Ethel Smyth: "Lets leave the letters till we're both dead. Thats my plan. I dont keep or destroy but collect miscellaneous bundles of odds and ends, and let posterity, if there is one, burn or not. Lets forget all about death and all about Posterity" (VI, 272).

Because middle space has value, Woolf guards it. Fearing that Smyth might print her letters, Woolf snaps: " . . . I dont understand the system on which your mind works, by nature. When you say for example that you are going to write something about me and publish parts of my letters—I am flabbergasted. I swear I couldn't do such a thing where you're concerned to save my life" (V, 86). Such a reaction suggests that the letters are to be read as intimate and honest expressions of the self. And yet, Woolf's voice is consistently undependable throughout the letters. It shifts, as do her allusions and strategies, depending on who her addressee/ receiver might be. An unusually introspective letter of 1929 to Gerald Brenan, on the treachery of language, concludes: "Writing to Lytton or Leonard I am quite different from writing to you" (IV, 98). For Woolf is a performer, an actress, and the letters are bravura, burnishing fragments of performance art. She creates a series of private theaters for an audience of one, each with its own script and scenery, lights and costumes. She includes precise frames of herself at the time of writing—her house is messy, she is "tipsy" from Chianti in Italy, she had some teeth pulled. They help her audience of one enter into the play. Moreover, Woolf builds her drama, in part, on the needs and nature of that audience. Each member aids in the dictation of her lines. In France with Vita Sackville-West, her lover, she reassures Leonard, her husband, of her love for him. She can be self-doubting or confident, mocking or consoling, cajoling or demanding, rebuking (especially to Smyth) or loving, sad or buoyant and mirthful. A Woolf essay says: "A good letter-writer so takes the colour of the reader at the other end, that from reading the one we can imagine the other."[3]

Clearly, Woolf's epistolary performances are generous deeds. The letter is a gift to the other based on his or her special relationship with Woolf.[4] Even her statements of personal need are flattering because they assume that her receiver has the power to gratify them. The letters also subtly adapt the manners of the good hostess. They become the text of a drawing-room conversation. This teasing deference of the performer/ hostess appears even in Woolf's earliest published letter, written in 1888, when she was six, to the poet James Russell Lowell. She pertly judges and queries the older man: "Have you been to the Adirondacks . . . You are a naughty man not to come here. Good bye" (I, 2).

In the middle space, Woolf exists both with people whom she trusts and with those with whom she has reliably limited involvements. As her language reaches out to other people, she protects herself from the loneliness, the isolation, and the blank distance between human beings she recognized and feared. Through the letter, she communicates even when the physical presence of others is unavailable or unmanageable. Like any human connection for Woolf, however, epistolary performances have their risks. They can stimulate her distrust about the steadiness of the other's presence. If written out of a sense of obligation, because of the notorious pressures of the superego, a letter might distort her. She might also deform herself if she were afraid of failing in charm. Woolf believes that all letter writing involves the donning of a mask, the creation of "a kind of unreal personality." To Jacques Raverat she muses:

> The difficulty of writing letters is, for one thing, that one has to simplify so much, and hasn't the courage to dwell on the small catastrophes which are of such huge interest to oneself; and thus has to put on a kind of unreal personality; which, when I write to you for example, whom I've not seen these 11 years, becomes inevitably jocular. I suppose joviality is a convenient mask; and then, being a writer, masks irk me: I want, in my old age, to have done with all superfluities . . . (III, 136).

Even worse, any act of language can be " . . . infinitely chancy and infinitely humbugging—so many asserverations . . . are empty, and tricks of spech . . . " (IV, 97). Finally, people, deprived of guiding gestures and intonations, might misinterpret this slippery medium. The performer cannot control the audience's response, the hostess a guest's behavior. Woolf and Sackville-West disagree about *Three Guineas*. After a flurry of letters, Woolf tells her:

> Its a lesson not to write letters. For I suppose you'll say, when you read what I've quoted from your own letter, that there's nothing to cause even a momentary irritation. And I daresay you're right. I suspect that anything written acquires meaning and both the writers mood and the reader's mood queer the pitch (VI, 257)

Scarily, misreaders can become angry, and then withhold love and praise. Two strong, linked lines in Woolf's letters are witty, incisive, acerb comments about other people and apologies for having made trouble; for having been indiscreet or acerb; for having been too little of the angel in the home. Full speech and human relations are perhaps never congruent. Even today, Woolf suffers from readers' distrust of her flamboyantly cutting tongue. One of her editors, Nigel Nicolson, says of a text:

> . . . (it is) malicious beyond the point of sanity—and perhaps for that very reason the word "malicious" is inappropriate (II, xvi).

Yet, the text is hardly dreadful. Written to Strachey, in 1915, it asks for gossip and then bursts into a fantasy about her brother-in-law Clive Bell. They will buy him a parrot, " . . . a bold primitive bird, trained of course to talk nothing but filth, and to indulge in obscene caresses . . . " (II, 61). Nicolson's distress may be indicative of what Woolf feared and guessed would happen if she were too impertinent, too vicious, too often, too directly. If so, it might explain why her rhetoric can be so appealing to her immediate recipient and so amusingly nasty about a third party—a John Middleton Murry, Ottoline Morrell, or Edward Sackville-West. She asks her receiver to share her laughter at someone outside the theater of the letter. As she sets up a conspiracy to displace hostility onto such a third party, she attempts to lull her receiver into a sense of exemption from her corrosive mordancies.

The sheer bulk of Woolf's letters is proof that their benefits outweighed these risks. In the 1930s, famous and mature, she explored a rhetorical device that might enable her to be largely angry: her admonitory, often sarcastic public letters. Some went off to magazines and journals. Another was a response to a younger generation of writers, "Letter to a Young Poet."[5] Still another was *Three Guineas*. The public letter, which concerns forces (such as the patriarchy) rather than individuals, permits Woolf to be less a gossipy friend than a commentator and prophet. The letter is less the conjuring up of a small theater than the polemical venting of her personal values in a bullying impersonal world that stomps from stupidity to murder. She could be skeptical about the form. It "seems to invite archness and playfulness" (V, 83). Yet, especially in *Three Guineas*, the public letter is a forum whose architecture itself encodes protest against restrictions. Jane Marcus remarks: "Her anger and hostility at the exclusiveness of male institutions are all the more effective because 'cabin'd and cribb'd' in limited and limiting letters. Like prison journals and letters, read while we know the author is in jail, they serve their cause not only by what they say but by the very form."[6]

Woolf's deceptively casual theory about the letter as a genre, as well as her practice, assign it to my "middle space." She suggests that the letter was once a public event that fused the functions of the newspaper and conversation. It gave a group several kinds of information on multiple channels of communication. Its high century was the "unlovable" eighteenth (II, 12). Then, because of modern technology and the media it generated, the letter lost a public role. Reduced to emotional detail, it became an "intimacy . . . on ink" (II, 22). In the essay "Modern Letters," Woolf declares:

> Only one person is written to, and the writer has some reason for wishing to write to him or her in particular. Its meaning is private, its news intimate . . . it

is a rash incriminating document . . . the art of letter writing . . . is not dead . . . but as much alive as to be quite unprintable. The best letters of our times are precisely those that can never be published.[7]

The style of the letter necessarily altered. It changed from being a carefully composed text that several readers would scrutinize to being a disheveled scrawl that one reader would consume.

If one wishes to conflate the feminine, the intimate, and the realm of feeling, Woolf's ideas about the modern letter label it a woman's art. However, one can doubt this hypothetical fusion and still see how deliberately Woolf's theory and practice feminized the genre. Although middle space is broad enough to include men and women, she believed that the letter had historically offered women a convention to manipulate when they were barred from others that men could enter. Reviewing Dorothy Osborne, she notes: "The art of letter-writing is often the art of essay-writing in disguise. But such as it was, it was an art a woman could practise without unsexing herself."[8] Because her precursors had pushed at and weakened patriarchal culture, Woolf could go beyond them. She could choose the letter as one of her arts, not as a compensation.

Her feminization of the letter is also much more. Despite the happiness of her marriage and despite the fact that Leonard is the co-author of some of her letters, they show—even to the most prudish of readers—how attracted she was to other women. The letters textualize how much women stirred her imagination and desire. Woolf writes of flirtations with women. Her style itself is flirtatious and seductive. Her profound relationships with women were, at the same time, surprisingly stable. The first, and perhaps most haunting, woman was her mother, Julia. In Cornwall, about as old as her mother was when she died, Woolf weeps. Her letters to women call for affectionate mothering and support. In 1929, she writes to Sackville-West: "Its odd how I want you when I'm ill. I think everything would be warm and happy if Vita came in" (IV, 9). Since Sackville-West is absent, Woolf will accept "long long letters" as a substitute.

Woolf writes consistently to Vanessa, who loved her but fled from her sister's demonstrativeness. The complexity of this relationship can be gauged by a letter to Clive Bell, written in 1908, where she asks him to transmit her love to Vanessa. So doing, Woolf taunts Vanessa by flaunting an attachment to Clive, a trick to arouse jealousy and attention that she would later use, more wryly, with Sackville-West. She plays a sexual game she repeats through the letters: she tells Clive how to kiss Vanessa. She becomes a voyeur who is simultaneously sister's lover; sister's daughter; brother-in-law's companion; brother-in-law's rival: "Kiss her, most passion-ately, in all *my* [italics added] private places—neck—, and arm, and eyeball, and tell her—what new thing is there to tell her? how fond I am of her husband" (I, 325)? Woolf writes to women lovers (Violet Dickinson, Sackville-West) and to serious friends (Nelly Cecil, Margaret Llewellyn Davis, Smyth). Her letters, especially to Sackville-West, can be zestful plumes of imagery, rather as *Orlando* is a rich spray of narrative. However, Woolf's initiatives toward women and responses to them are overt and free from coding. Because the letters are in middle space, they are more explicit about personal feelings than about her feminism, her public sense of women's grievances, which friends and family shrank from.[9] She bluntly tells Jacques Raverat that she "much" prefers her own sex. She places her passion before Sackville-West plainly, but not barrenly. The salutation "Dear Mrs. Nicolson" becomes "Oh you scandalous ruffian," "My dear Vita," "Dearest Creature," and "Dearest Honey." As the fire of passion became the embers of friendship, Woolf deployed a cozy metaphor to tell Smyth about Sackville-West: "Vita was here for a night. I always fall into a warm slipper relation with her instantly. Its a satisfactory relationship" (VI, 439). When she decides that Sackville-West's desire for her has vanished, Woolf writes to her baldly. In general, the prose of her letters is austere and transparent when genuine grief is near: "And do you love me? No" (V, 376).

Such directness marks her language about Vanessa's daughter, Angelica, her "adorable sprite." To be sure, Woolf did want a child early in her marriage; she envied Vanessa hers. Her letters to Angelica are fanciful and tender, cheerful and loving. She gives Angelica jokes, checks, affection, advice, news, and games—as she did to her nephews. However, her letters about Angelica that express attraction are shocking. In 1928, Woolf writes to Vanessa: " . . . I'm showing [Angelica's photographs for *Orlando*] to Vita, who doesn't want to be accused of raping the under age. My God—I shall rape Angelica one of these days . . . " (III, 497). Later, aware of how close her lesbianism and her feeling for women in her family were, she writes to Vanessa again: "This is a very dull letter, but its been so hot . . . my wits are roasting: twice I dreamt I was kissing Angelica passionately across a hedge, from which I can only deduce that incest and sapphism embrace in one breast" (V, 417). She then moves on swiftly in an epistolary gesture that makes it impossible to know if the confession was a supportable or insupportable act of speech: " . . . neither [incest nor sapphism] come within a thousand miles of me when seeing Susie Buchan or Ethyl Smyth—both of whom came here yesterday."[10]

Homosexuality is not the only subject Woolf speaks of more openly, even raucously, in her letters than in her fiction. She mentions water closets; Leonard's wet dreams; menstruation, "the usual indisposition of my sex" (II, 360); sanitary napkins; menopause; Smyth's diarrhea. So doing, taking up the body's functions, she adapts the frankness of Bloomsbury conversation to her letters and further demystifies herself as the ethereal loon of English letters. Yet the lesbianism is special. The relationship of Woolf's letters to her fiction in terms of her complex eroticism is parallel to the relationship between that eroticism and her marriage. The letters and the psychic life, which feed on each other, discreetly explore lesbianism. The fiction and the marriage, which also feed on each other, far more publicly investigate heterosexuality. That heterosexuality, not stringently homophobic, accepts lesbianism. Clarissa Dalloway remembers Sally Seton vividly. Miss LaTrobe, the lesbian artist in *Between the Acts*, is heroic. The Woolfs entertained what they called Sapphists and buggers.[11] Nevertheless, the fiction and the marriage shelter and conceal the volatile depths of Woolf's lesbian feelings.

No matter how forthcoming the letters are about the flesh, they are comparatively silent about two overwhelming forces in Woolf's life: her "madness" and her writing. Even with intimates she was reticent about the extremities of consciousness, whether the boundaries of creativity or oblivion. She muses to Dickinson:

> Now my brain I will confess, for I dont like to talk of it, floats in blue air; where there are circling clouds, soft sunbeams of elastic gold, and fairy gossamers—things that cant be cut—that must be tenderly enclosed, and expressed in a globe of exquisitely coloured words. At the mere prick of steel, they vanish (I, 320).

She could sardonically refer to being "mad," to going "insane," to headaches and an eccentric nervous system. She could say that her madness saved her from a rigid, chilly fastidiousness. She could tell appalling, funny anecdotes about her doctors and nurses. Yet such allusions and data and tales appear to disappear. They also mask her rage at her treatment. In 1925, she discusses *Mrs. Dalloway* and Septimus Smith with Gwen Raverat: "It was a subject that I have kept cooling in my mind until I felt I could touch it without bursting into flame all over. You can't think what a raging furnace it is still to me—madness and doctors and being forced" (III, 180). The metaphors of heat and fire consistently figure passion. Certain Woolf/Dickinson letters are "hot." Erotic passion is more detachable, however, more speakable, more writable, than rage at the consequences of madness. Woolf immediately adds to the Raverat letter, "But let's change the subject."

To Smyth, Woolf, in an autobiographical rush, praises her madness as a source of art:

> . . . And then I married, and then my brains went up in a shower of fireworks. As an experience, madness is terrific I can assure you, and not to be sniffed at; and in its lava I still find most of the things I write about. It shoots out of one everything shaped, final, not in more driblets, as sanity does (IV, 180).

Yet, her letters are oddly superficial for someone whose life was reading, talking, and writing; who was absorbed in her work and in her own psychology as a writer; who was prodigiously productive. She could mention her schedule and its disruptions. She could wonder nervously about a new book's reception—from family, friends, reviewers, and a public that might send her "abuse or ecstasy" (VI, 267). She could be snide, rueful, or shrewd about other writers. In the beginning of her career, she rummages through the past for models; in the middle, she implicitly compares herself, often anxiously, to contemporaries; toward the end, she both supports and describes the next generation. She could declare how much her writing needs the stimulus of the noise, chaos, and color of reality. She could wonder how she might go on with her texts. For example, after her father's death, she anguishes because she cannot tell him in writing about her sorrow. (Sir Leslie Stephen, unlike his daughter, destroyed letters to him.) Simultaneously, the father personifies a blocking force. In 1908, she writes to Clive Bell:

> I dreamt last night that I was showing father the manuscript of my novel; and he snorted, and then dropped it on to a table, and I was very melancholy, and read it this morning,and thought it bad. You dont realise the depth of modesty in to which I fall (I, 325).

Despite such utterances, Woolf's letters are not her diaries. Written to others, not to the self; written for others, as well as the self, they do not reveal Woolf in her most entangled, most diving engagement with language. Indeed, they were often a distraction that permitted her to be with language, but not with its most inexorable demands and rewards. She told Smyth that she only wrote "letters when my mind is full of bubble and foam; when I'm not aware of the niceties of the English language" (V, 396).

Woolf's volumes of letters occupy still another kind of middle space: between the "literal" and the "literary," those two frayed poles with which some stake out the territories of discourse. Her letters can be literal. Sending simple information, they communicate on a flat plane. Contemporary readers may need annotations to understand a sentence. They may have to learn who "The Nun" might be, but once annotated, the letter limits its own meaning. Lunch will start at 1 p.m. Angelica is 10. The Press will reject a manuscript. Or, then, the letters are full of gossip, that discourse of exchange of details about friends and daily life. As a gossip, Woolf is conventionally, even stereotypically, feminine, but as she gossips, elsewhere, in another space, she is struggling for the different speech her novels articulated.

Even so, to borrow Roger Duchêne's terms, Woolf is an "auteur épistolaire," not a mere "épistolier." Growing in and through language, her performance can be self-reflexive. On Christmas Day, 1922, she tells Brenan: "Never mind. I am only scribbling, more to amuse myself than you, who may never read, or understand: for I am doubtful whether people, the best disposed toward each other, are capable of more than an intermittent signal as they forge past—a sentimental metaphor . . . " (II, 598). In her texts, a lucid element becomes more and more vital. She scrawls down miniature plays, with stage directions and dialogue. She characterizes some people and transforms others into characters. Her brother Thoby, before his death, is "Milford." In an 1896 letter to him, she is "Miss Jan," a helter-skelter thing. The wind has blown her skirt over her head, and her red flannel drawers have flashed before a curate (I, 2). Many images have the strength of acid: "I have had two bloody painful encounters with Middleton Murry; we stuck together at parties like two copulating dogs; but after the first ecstasy, it was boring, disillusioning, flat" (III, 115). Frequently, her tropes traverse individual letters to become conceits that provide linguistic and emotional continuity; a recurrent backdrop for the theater; furniture for the drawing room. Especially for erotically charged relationships, they can be cozily animalistic. A kindly bestiality manages eros by domesticating it and distancing it from the human body. Dickinson is a kangaroo, who offers a pouch for Virginia, her wallaby, a dear marsupial with snout and paws. Leonard is "Mongoose" to her "Mandril." To Sackville-West, she and her sexuality are "Potto," an African lemur with features of an English housedog. To show her union with Sackville-West and their differences at once, Woolf transmutes her lover into another dog, but one more capable of opulence than shabby Virginia: " . . . Vita is a dear old rough coated sheep dog: or alternatively, hung with grapes, pink with pearls, lustrous, candle lit . . . " (III, 224).

Because of such tropes, because of her vast capacities for metaphoric fantasy, Woolf's letters swerve toward poetic fiction. Very occasionally, the letter constitutes a poetic or pathetic lie. One, in 1906, is poignant. To protect Dickinson, herself sick, Woolf (then Virginia Stephen) concealed the death of Thoby from her for a month. She sent a series of letters she might have written if Thoby had lived. On the day he dies, Woolf—in an act of defiance, denial, and charity— writes Dickinson to chat about illness, work, literature, gossip, and their feelings for each other. Then she ends with a broken cry for consolation. As syntactically jagged as the truth of that moment, it is unequivocal in its painful equation of death and love, equivocal in assigning the cause of pain: "Goodnight and God—have I a right to a God? send you sleep. Wall nuzzles in and wants love. Yr. AVS" (I, 248).

More commonly, Woolf imagines scenes self-consciously. She will send Elizabeth Bowen a tea caddy in magenta plush, embroidered with forget-me-nots in gold. She and Leonard will kiss for an hour. When she is dead, she will read Smyth's letters and have "many rights" (V, 178). As a dancer or athlete exercises the body, so Woolf trains her ability to poke and reassemble the materials of the day. As her letters use facts to construct fictions, they become a modern version of the epistolary novel. Time passes, but plot is fragmented. Characters arbitrarily pass before her. Perception and the phantoms of fantasy blur. In her unintended epistolary novel, Woolf also retains her impulse toward social satire. Her sociograph is a comedy of manners, as her first two novels were. The range of letters is a deposit for residual, as well as experimental, writing techniques.

Her last letters, though, are terrible, like Shakespeare's dark comedies, and heart-wrenching. A final unsigned note to Sackville-West, on March 22, 1941, is tough, compressed. Someone has apparently composed a letter to Sackville-West, but mailed it to Woolf. She declares, "No, I'm not you. No I don't keep budgerigars." Finally, she asks, seemingly of birds, but, in retrospect, of herself:

> If we come over . . . may I bring her a pair if any survive? Do they all die in an instant? When shall we come? Lord knows— (VI, 484)

Three of Woolf's last letters belong to the last two weeks of that same month. One is to Vanessa, the beloved woman; two to Leonard, the beloved man. They echo and repeat each other, as if Woolf were drafting the chorus for her own tragedy. They have, to a painful pitch, the generosity and gratitude that most of her letters display. They tell of her absolute love for Vanessa and Leonard, and then give reasons for the suicide she was planning and would so quickly choose. For she is hearing voices, the old sign of her illness, and she refuses to fight them again. The voices are like a letter she did not write, that she cannot control, that she must receive. They are a grotesque, cruel intrusion in a middle space of consciousness; killer buffoons at loose in a theater of mind.

 The Woolf letters are now a part of, and guide to, history. Her editors, serving as her historians, have added an appendix to the sixth volume. It includes letters found too late for inclusion in the earlier volumes to which they chronologically belong. The last text in this coda, though undated, may be from the mid-1930s. To Leonard, it tells him that Woolf has slept well, that she is about to begin writing for the day. She asks him to get her cigarettes. Then she concludes, in a throwaway life-line of language from Sussex to London, "Shall come back tomorrow for certain" (VI, 532). In the tomorrow in which we read, she has come back in the way she would have most preferred, as a writer. We do not exist in the middle space in which she wrote the pages of her letters. We are in the public space of reading. Though her ardent mind is language now for us, its smoke print on page, we are, too, the recipients of that language, its flare, its bright edges, its self-creating giving.

13 ADRIENNE RICH AND FEMINIST/LESBIAN POETRY (1985)

> . . . it is the subjects, the conversations, the facts we shy away from, which claim us in the form of writer's block, as mere rhetoric, as hysteria, insomnia, and constriction of the throat.[1]

> Four years after . . . (Adrienne Rich) published her first book, I read it in almost disbelieving wonder; someone my age was writing down my life . . . I had not known till then how much I had wanted a contemporary and a woman as a speaking voice of life. . . . [2]

"Lesbian." For many, heterosexual or homosexual, the word still constricts the throat. Those "slimy" sibilants; those "nasty" nasalities. "Lesbian" makes even "feminist" sound lissome, decent, sane. In 1975, Adrienne Rich's reputation was secure.[3] She might have eased up and toyed with honors. Yet, she was doing nothing less than seizing and caressing that word: "lesbian." She was working hard for "a whole new poetry" that was to begin in two women's "limitless desire."[4]

Few poetic things could be more difficult—even for a writer of such fire, stone, and fern. For the "intense charge of the word *lesbian*, and . . . all its deliquescences of meaning . . . ," (*LSS*, 202) necessarily provoke readings that are potent, but confused, confusing, and contradictory. Some of us read Rich with disbelieving wonder. Imagine being a mother, in court, on the stand, in the dock, during a child custody case. Your husband's lawyer asks, with brutal repetition, "When did you first kiss this woman?" Imagine, then, the gratitude and relief of hearing:

> The man is walking boundaries
> measuring   He believes in what is his

> the grass the waters underneath   the air
> the air   through which child and mother
> are running   the boy singing
> the woman   eyes sharpened in the light
> heart stumbling   making for the open
>
>   (*DCL*, p. 59)

Yet, others read with wondrous disbelief. Alicia Ostriker, my colleague, pugnaciously declared Rich's "myth" of female sexuality "too narrow":

"I find the Lesbian Imperative offensively totalitarian, and would prefer to defend human diversity as well as human liberty."[5]

To add to the mess, even some of the supporters and defenders of Rich's sexual ideology find the call for a "whole new poetry" an emblazoned naiveté. *Surely*, they whisper nervously, she must know about our post-structural awareness of the nature of the sign. *Surely*, she must realize that language is a fiction, not a transparent vehicle of truth; that signifiers are bits and bytes of an arbitrary system, not elements in a holistic union of word and idea, word and thing. *Surely*, she must now admit that this system creates the human subject, not the other way around.[6] Others grumble that Rich's theory contradicts her poetic practice. The first is new, the second old. Rhetorically, she is more like—well, Robert Lowell—than Gertrude Stein. Rich undermines her calls for action, Marjorie Perloff claims, because of her " . . . conservative rhetoric, a rhetoric indistinguishable from the Male Oppressor."[7]

This messiness is ironic—if only because Rich herself is radiantly clear. She is, of course, one of a number of outspoken lesbian poets of the last part of the American Century. She resists being laid down as the star track in what ought to be a multiple-trek tape of the language of such women as Judy Grahn, Susan Griffin, Marilyn Hacker, Audre Lorde, Susan Sherman. "To isolate what I write," she has warned, "from a context of other women writing and speaking feels like an old, painfully familiar critical strategy."[8] Yet, I want, in gratitude and relief, to spell out how she has moved from the constriction of the throat to the construction of the page.

Before the 1970s, Rich had published poems about the feelings, social relations, and mythic promise of women. "Women" (1968) sees three sisters " . . . sitting/ on rocks of black obsidian," versions of the fates. (*PSN*, 109) Deromanticizing heterosexual love, Rich had written of the strains and loneliness within marriage. Symbolically, she had put aside a 1962 poem, "For Judith, Taking Leave."[9] Here a speaker longingly memorializes another woman, Judith: " . . . a singular event . . . a beautiful thing I saw." (*PSN*, 132) The speaker praises feminist predecessors who "suffered ridicule" for them. Then, in the middle of the poem, she calls out:

Judith! that two women
in love to the nerves' limit

Only to add, as the line runs on to the next, "with two men—."

In the early 1970s, Rich riskily uncoiled the repressed sexual and psychological materials that she had once coiled and from which she had subsequently recoiled. She announces that release in "Re-forming the Crystal." Addressed to a man, it gives him his due, and discharge. The speaker first imagines what male sexuality, "desire/ centered in a cock," might feel like. However, she passes on, old identity gone. Voice at once tough and exultant, she states, "my photo on the license is not me. . . . " (PSN, 228) She will move, a key word in Rich's vocabulary of action, to " . . . the field of a poem wired with danger . . . into the cratered night of female memory. . . . " Women now live to the nerves' limit with women. Inevitably, some poems counterpoint past identity with present; tradition with radical change. "For L.G.: Unseen for Twenty Years" ruefully wonders who, and where, a male homosexual might be. He and the speaker had been boon travelling companions twenty years before, when both were turning to men.

Significantly, "Re-forming the Crystal" alternates vertical columns of "poetry" with paragraphs of "prose." For Rich was producing controversial, influential prose as well as poetry. From 1981 to 1983, she and Michelle Cliff were to edit Sinister Wisdom, a lesbian/feminist journal. Rich, a sophisticated student of the genetics of the text, coherently crossed autobiography with biography; polemic with scholarship; political theory with literary criticism.[10] In part, her transgressions of genetic conventions are the deconstructive gestures of post-modernism—without much manic play or lucid romps. In greater part, her mingling of "subjective" and "objective" genres, advocacy and argument, demonstrates her belief in their inseparability. Her style also emblemizes the position of contemporary, educated women. No longer forced to choose between public or private lives, women can lead both—at once. No longer forced to choose between writing about public or private concerns, women can take on both—at once.[11]

Rich had consistently been "a poet of ideas,"[12] of hewn arguments as well as images. Now her ideas, doubly sited, could reinforce and annotate each other. In its totality, her work is that of a kind of conceptual artist. What is disturbing and dazzling is not the familiar notion of a conceptual artist, but the content of her ideas. Rich's lesbian/feminism reveals both the steely, stubborn logic of the geometrician (or the convert) and the sinuousness of imaginative reason. Those who insist that she is the Great Generalissima of Lesbian Poetry resist granting her her habitual gift for pragmatic self-revision and subtlety. " . . . the subject of truth," she noted in

1975. "There is nothing simple or easy about this idea. There is no 'the truth,' 'a truth'—truth is not one thing, or even a system. It is an increasing complexity." (*LSS*, 187) Yet, she consistently walks out from the cultural space in which the libraries of her father and of Harvard University had enclosed her. She announces the primacy of a woman's perspective and of women as subjects. The eye of the female writing "I" fastens on the presence of a woman. The voice of the inquiring woman asks of herself and other women: " . . . how she came to be for-herself and how she identified with and was able to use women's culture, a women's tradition; and what the presence of other women meant in her life." (*LSS*, 158)

Rich, as other feminists were doing, insists upon an idea of time as a tragic process, a fall into patriarchy. However, she promises, we can reverse that process. We can outwrestle, outwit, and feminize time. Skillfully, Rich splices two mutually enhancing narratives together that dramatize her idea of time's procession. The first is that of the self. In her prose, Rich persistently tests her generalizations against her own experiences. In her poetry, she articulates experience and discovers its meaning. Though the poetic self has a vast capacity for experiences, it reveals itself, rather than develops, in time. Indeed, a measure of development is the degree of revelation. So convinced, Rich assumes the primacy of the primal self. Appropriately, then, "Natural Resources" brilliantly extends the trope of the woman miner, as both rhetorical and historical figure. The miner excavates experience to find buried strata. In other passages, Rich is a Dickinsonian surgeon, " . . . cutting away/ dead flesh, cauterizing old scars. . . . " (*DCL*, 70) She rips away the tissue that covers old wounds, old traumas, to recover the origins of self and pain.

In her narrative, Rich is a child whom two women (one white, one black) first love before they turn her over to the father. The reality of the maternal body gives way to the "charisma" of the father's " . . . assertive mind and temperament. . . . "[13] Her reward for their rejection, and her loss, is his approval and the power of language, the conviction that " . . . language, writing, those pages of print could teach me how to live, could tell me *what was possible*." (*LSS*, 200) She becomes a child-of-the-word, unable to see that those pages veil and erase the feminine. Rich is no fan of psychoanalysis, but its tales and that of her passage from the tender passions of the realm of the mother to the symbolic order of the domain of the father half-echo each other.

Educated, a published poet, her father's pride, Rich then rejects the father—to marry a man he despises. She bears three sons. As Rich knows, but never exploits, the sheer masculinity of her heterosexual experience (the husband, the long marriage, the sons) burnishes her credibility as a witness of, and for, lesbianism. That credibility challenges a popular perception that lesbians are maculately sterile—either because they are butches, imitation men, or femmes, who will never receive the sperm of real men.

Rich's second narrative is that of any child, female or male. For them, "The mother-child relationship is the essential human relationship." (*OWB*, 127) Binding the two are the sucking mouth, the milky nipple, the mutual gaze. Then, the father—his demands, commands, needs, and seductions— will pick at those bonds; pick up his children and possess them all in a "savagely fathered and unmothered world." (*PSN*, 237) Heterosexual institutions damage both sons and daughters, but, Rich insists, in the crucial axiom of feminist theory, they damage women far more than men. Those institutions embody sufficient psychological, economic, social, and legal power to *compel* heterosexuality.[14] That compulsion redirects women away from the first and most profound object of love, the mother. Rich writes: "Probably there is nothing in human nature more resonant with charges than the flow of energy between two biologically alike bodies, one of which has laid in amniotic bliss inside the other, one of which has labored to give birth to the other. The materials are here for the deepest mutuality and the most painful estrangement." (*OWB*, 225–6)

To redeem her past, and to begin her future, Rich must return to the mother's body, in memory or with other women. So must all women. Their sources are their natural resources. In a 1963 poem about marriage, Rich, in one of the crazy intuitive flashes we label the cognitive gift of poetry, describes wanting husband to be mother:

> Our words misunderstand us.
> Sometimes at night
> you are my mother:
> old detailed griefs
> twitch at my dreams, and I
> crawl against you, fighting
> for shelter, making you
> my cave.[15]

Not until she becomes a lesbian is she content; not until then can desire fulfill its needs. In *Twenty-One Love Poems*, she writes of her female lover's

> . . . strong tongue and slender fingers
> reaching where I had been waiting years for you
> in my rose-wet cave—whatever happens, this is.
>   (*DCL*, 32)

The fecundity of woman is such that she can also give birth to and mother herself. Her body can be her "crib"; she can be her own "midwife."

She can then become a matrix that mothers others, through personality or the page. Some evidence: in 1975, Nancy Milford, the writer, read through Rich's poetry. She had a dream of the person within "Diving into the Wreck." A maternal figure was walking towards, and empowering, her: " . . . naked, swaying, bending down . . . her full breasts brushing my cheek, moving toward my mouth . . . The hands of that diving woman become our own hands, reaching out, touching, holding; not in sex but in deliverance. That is the potency of her poetry. . . . "[16]

As Rich grounds women's thoughts and feelings in their bodies, she *naturalizes* them. Her poetry harvests the earth and the elements for its metaphors: the cave; trees; plants; flowers; fields; the volcano, at once peak to ascend and crater into which to descend, breast and genitals, cervix, womb. Rich, too, has absolute competence in composing a poem, in arranging implosive patterns of rhythm and sound. Because the quality of her verbal music and choreography is so assured, a reader learns to trust the palpability of a poem; its replication of the intellectual and emotional movements of experience.

Because of the pressure and magnetism of her metaphors; because of the surprising physicality of her lines; and because of her contempt for patriarchal culture, especially in its modern and urban forms, Rich may seem to be endorsing a feminized primitivism. However, she is far too intelligent a grammarian of reality to parse it into two opposing spheres of "nature" and "culture," and clamor only for the pristine ecological purities of the first. She constructs houses on her land. Rich's dream, her imaginative vision, is of an organic, but freeing, unity among body, nature, consciousness, vision, and community. Unequivocally, lyrically, she asks women to think through their maternal flesh and their own bodies, " . . . to connect what has been so cruelly disorganized—our great mental capacities, hardly used; our highly developed tactile sense; our genius for close observation; our complicated, pain-enduring, multi-pleasured physicality." (*OWB*, 284) In a leap of faith, she wants women to become the presiding geniuses of their bodies in order to create new life—biologically and culturally. Their thoughts and visions will transform politics, " . . . alter human existence," sustain a "new relationship to the universe." (*OWB*, 285–86)

The primal bonds among mothers, sisters, and daughters are the soil from which lesbianism grows. Lesbianism does mean women's erotic passion. Indeed, the most explicitly erotic lyric in *Twenty-One Love Poems* is "(The Floating Poem, Unnumbered),", as if physical passion drifts and runs like a deep current through the seas of the connection between "I" and "you" in the sequence. However, Rich declares, in a move that lesbian/feminism, but not the culture-at-large, accepts, the lesbian cannot live only in and with love. "I want to call this, life." Rich writes, "But I can't

call it life until we start to move/ beyond this secret circle of fire. . . . "
(*DCL*, 9) Moreover, a lesbianism that is more than a treasured carnality is a
synecdoche for any female sexuality. Rich, like Monique Wittig, projects
" . . . lesbian love (a)s a paradigm of female sexuality that is neither defined
by men nor exploited by a phallocentric political system."[17]

Even more than a fancily labelled metaphor, even more than a
schematized paradigm, lesbianism forms a "continuum," a range of
"woman-identified" activities that embraces eros, friendship and intensity
between women, resistance to gynephobia, and female strength. A woman
can love men, live with men, and inhabit a point on this continuum—if she
has managed some distance from patriarchal heterosexuality. For its
imprisoning institutions have ripped daughters from mothers; lobotomized
and slashed women's psychological, cultural, and political energies. As the
brief accumulates in "Compulsory Heterosexualty," Rich mourns: "The
denial of reality and visibility to women's passion for women, women's
choice of women as allies, life companions, and community; the forcing of
such relationships into dissimulation and their disintegration under intense
pressure have meant an incalculable loss to the power of all women *to
change the social relations of the sexes, to liberate ourselves and each
other.*" (657) "Transcendental Etude," a chiselled monument of a poem,
dedicated to Michelle Cliff, elegizes "rootless, dismembered" women
whose "Birth stripped our birthright from us,/ tore us from a woman, from
women, from ourselves." (*DCL*, 75)

If women are to change themselves and their social relations, if they are
to liberate themselves and each other, they must revivify that lesbianism
hidden or denied, feared or despised. Lesbianism is an imperative, not
because Rich imposes it, but because it is a wellspring of identity that must
be sprung if women are to claim any authentic identity at all. "It is the
lesbian in us who is creative, for the dutiful daughter of the fathers in us is
only a hack." (*LSS*, 201) I remember Rich giving us these words, quietly,
tautly, in a New York hotel ballroom, in 1976, at a panel at the Modern
Language Association. She leaned forward from a dais, where three other
poets were also sitting: June Jordan, Audre Lorde, Honor Moore. I was on
a chipped and gilded chair, between two scholar/critics: one a divorced
mother, heterosexual, who called herself a lesbian out of political
sympathy, a radical feminist act of the late 1960s and early 1970s; the
second a married mother, about to begin a secret love affair with a woman,
who rarely (if ever) spoke about lesbianism. "Right on," said the first.
Enigmatically, the second looked at the husband next to her. Grinning,
with the casualness of marraige, he affectionately slapped her thigh. There
we were—an imperfect, blurry shadow of Rich's continuum.

Deftly, Rich's theories of female sexuality invert the accusatory slander
that lesbianism is "unnatural." To Rich, what is "unnatural" is not the

presence, but the absence, of women's bodies, to be "homesick . . . for a woman. . . . " (DCL, 75) In the 1970s, her theories were influenced by, and influences on, the cultural feminism that was a powerful strain in feminist thinking, particularly about sexuality, culture, and identity.[18] Reconstituting and eroticizing nineteenth-century ideologies of gender, with their endorsement of "female" and "male" spheres, cultural feminism tends to divide the world into female and male; to idealize female sexuality and being, and to demonize male sexuality and doing. Ironically, some of the principles of cultural feminism gravitate toward a conservative ideology that prefers divinely authorized gender roles and "female" and "male" behaviors that fit squarely into them. However, cultural feminism's preference for women's communities, its commitment to women's self-determination, and its loathing of patriarchal heterosexuality dismay, and repel, right-wing flappers in the Eagle Forum and their ilk.

To discover that female sexuality and being, women are to nurture natural, but defaced and obliterated, capacities for nurture and for nature itself. With the help of scholars and artists, they are to unearth primal images of these capacities, and of rituals with which to celebrate them. Some of Rich's most poignant, lambent poems present the poet as a priestess in a service with lost script; in a liturgy with missing words. In "Toward the Solstice," she laments that she does not know "in what language to address/the spirits that claim a place/beneath these low and simple ceilings." (DCL, 69) She fears that she has forgotten or failed to say the "right rune"; to "perform the needed acts. . . . " (70)

Such theories were to serve neither abstract debate (a "male" activity) nor mere poetic need (a self-indulgent sport). On the contrary. They were to be designs for action and for communal life. As a result, cultural feminists have taken sides in some of the most volatile political quarrels within United States feminism. How separate from the rest of society are women's groups to be? What is the relationship of feminism to other political movements and to the New Left? What is the meaning of pornography? What, if anything, should be done to banish it? Many of Rich's poems refer immediately to those fights. The controversial "For Ethel Rosenberg," for example, speaks vocatively to "Ethel Greenglass Rosenberg":

> would you
> have marched to take back the night
> collected signatures
>
> for battered women who kill[19]

"Take back the night" is a slogan and rallying cry for the anti-pornography movement that cultural feminism has conceived and organized. The words have inspired women. They flatten Rich's poem. Their presence gives some critics permission to tsk-tsk and scold Rich for letting a political agenda master a poet's imagination. She might legitimately scorn their motives and the blatancy of the division they invent between politics and poetry. However, she, too, is warily aware of any domination of her imagination. She fears the hunters, trappers, and wardens of the mind. One of her toughest poems, "North American Time," written in the gritty style of much of *A Wild Patience*, starts:

> When my dreams showed signs
> of becoming
> politically correct
> no unruly images
> escaping beyond borders
> when walking in the street I found my
> themes cut out for me
> knew what I would not report
> for fear of enemies' usage
> then I began to wonder
>
>   (*FD*, 324)

Something hardens the difficulty of interweaving a passionate fidelity to a politics that wants to change the laws of history; to the imagination; and to the unconscious, which nourishes the imagination as mother does the child: the very terms of Rich's politics. For lesbian/feminism, the casting of the world as a duality of dominating male and damaged female carries the virus of a double threat: it reduces the world to a duality; it reduces women to a monolith. Rich distrusts the false universal, especially among women, who are to think more specifically than men. A resonant section of "Natural Resources," the 1977 revision of "Diving Into the Wreck," rejects the words "humanism" and "androgyny." They are falsely universal; therefore, universally false.

Rich has wonderfully escaped the nets she fears, the "impasse" at which some critics pin her.[20] In part, she does so because of the Jamesian (William) belief in change that has marked all her work. We must live in an Einsteinian world of flux and chance that has neither "center nor circumference."[21] We must work and wish for a world, not as it is, but as it might be. Yet, we must respond to time present as it presents and represents itself. Because errors and lapses can stain our responses, we must abandon dreams of purity, of final cures, of a process with an end.

Logically, then, responsibly, the lesbian/feminist Rich has continued to rewrite her sense of self and politics; to question what it means to "cast my lot" in the world and to be "accountable." More and more deeply, she has engaged the structures and pain of racism. She has said that the Civil

Rights Movement of the 1960s lifted her " . . . out of a sense of personal frustration and hopelessness."[22] However, the 1970s had to teach her the harsh stiffness of her own "racist blinders." Black women's response to *Of Woman Born* had to school her in her ignorance about them.[23] Rich believes that political poetry emerges from the self's encounter with the world. Her explorations of race start with her black nurse, her other mother. Necessarily, she cannot rest there. She must go on to still other structures, other pains, of domination. Racism is inseparable from still another vise and vice of modern politics: colonialism. "To understand colonization," she writes, with self-consciousness and some self-contempt, "is taking me/ years." (*WP*, 55)

Some of Rich's most ambitious lesbian/feminist poems speak for all women and mourn their suffering, affliction, and powerlessness: "From an Old House in America," "Culture and Anarchy," "For Julia in Nebraska." Like Rich's poems about her grandmothers, they offer women their history; the arts of their endurance. Because Rich fuses women with nature, especially with the land, a history of people is a pangyneric record of place as well.

However, the recognition of racism and colonialism demands that Rich issue a series of ironic, searing, yet empathetic poems about cultivated white women with the disadvantages of sex but the advantages of class and race. A tart observation, "No room for nostalgia here," opens "Turning the Wheel," an extraordinary 1981 sequence in which Rich returns to a desert landscape. (*WP*, 52–59) The wheel belongs to both a modern woman driving her car and a Native American woman creating her pottery. The speaker sees a "lesbian archaeologist," studying shards, who asks " . . . the clay all questions but her own." She imagines, too a letter that Mary Jane Colter might have written home. Colter, an architect and designer, planned buildings at the Grand Canyon for the Santa Fe Railroad. She both preserved and appropriated Native American culture. Two years later, in "Education of a Novelist," Rich calls across time to another Southern writer, Ellen Glasgow. She condemns Glasgow for not teaching her black nurse, Lizzie Jones, to read, but confesses:

> It's not enough
> using your words to damn you, Ellen:
> they could have been my own
>
> (*FD*, 317)

Lesbian/feminist politics remain, but Rich's perceptions expand upon them. She thinks, not only of male domination, but of a system of iron patterns of power that wheel and deal and work together. Pornography violently debases and exploits women, but its nauseating "objectification" of women also warns us against slavery—of anyone by anyone.[24]

Rich now wants, in women, both "difference and identity." Women share the architecture of their bodies, the humiliation and mutilation of those bodies. What "fuses my anger now . . . ," she wrote in 1978, " . . . is that we were told we were utterly different." (*LSS*, 310) Yet, as race proves, so obviously, so profoundly, women differ, too. With delicate audacity, Rich pushes at the boundaries of those differences, pushes for the specific, and particular. As she does so, she uncovers, and must enter, still another buried part of herself: her Jewishness, the faith of father, husband, and first woman lover. She circles back to Jerusalem, the original City on the Hill. *Sources*, perhaps her most fragmented but suggestive book, exhumes that past. Rich affirms her "powerful" and "womanly" choices; a "powerful, womanly lens"—in brief, the domain of the mother.[25] However, *Sources* returns to the domain of the fathers, and to their vulnerability and pain. Arnold Rich, her father, was the outwardly successful, assimilated son of a Jewish shoe merchant from Birmingham, Alabama. Powerful and arrogant patriarch though he was, he also bore "the suffering of the Jew, the alien stamp." (15) Her mother carried the cultural genes of the Christianity that would stamp Jews out.

Then, with immense dignity, Rich writes to Alfred Conrad, the husband who committed suicide. She has had " . . . a sense of protecting your existence, not using it merely as a theme for poetry or tragic musings." (32) Now, for the first time, she believes he might hear her. "No person," her elegy ends, "should have to be so alone. . . . " (33) She has passed through the moral and psychological process that some of her most magnificent poems—"The Phenomenology of Anger," "Integrity"—envision: that between wildness and patience, rage and pitying compassion, fire and water and tears. She has completed the hardest of swings between "Anger and tenderness: my selves." (*WP*, 9).[26]

That fusion of the moral and the psychological, the ethical and the emotional, marks Rich. Her writing inflects a stable vocabulary of the good that flows, as feminism itself does, from principles of the Enlightenment, radical democracy, and a redemptive domesticity: freedom; choice; truth; a lucidity as clear as water pouring over rocks; gentleness, an active charity, swabbing "the crusted stump." (*DCL*, 63) The last of *Twenty-One Love Poems* asserts:

> I choose to be a figure in that light. . . .
> . . .
> . . . I choose to walk here. And to draw this circle.
>   (*DCL*, 36)

As insistently, Rich's writing asks how to reconcile the claims of autonomy (being free, having will) and the claims of connection (being together, having unity). Connections fuse within the self, between lover and beloved, with others. "Sometimes I feel," she wrote in 1982, "I have seen too long from too many disconnected angles: white, Jewish, anti-Semite, racist, anti- racist, once-married, lesbian, middle-class, feminist, exmatriate Southerner, *split at the root*."[27] She longs, then, for wholeness, for touch, a desire the hand signifies. The hand. It holds the pen, clasps the child, finds the lover, sews the quilt, cleans the pot, dusts the house. For Rich, hands hammer nails, empty kettles, catch babies leaping from the womb, work vacuum aspirators, stroke "sweated temples" (both body and sanctuary), steer boats. (*WP*, 9) The hand also knots in anger, smashes in pain. As palms are the canvas of our life-lines, so the figure of the hand backs Rich's vision.

Before the 1960s, her lesbian/feminism was, if not inconceivable, unspeakable. Yet, if her ideas are contemporary, her sense of the poet is not. For Rich refuses to sever poetry from prophecy, those morally driven, passionately uttered visions of things unseen and foreseen, and poetry from witnessing, those morally driven, passionately uttered insights into actions seen. What she said of Dickinson she might have said of herself:

"Poetic language . . . is a concretization of the poetry of the world at large, the self, and the forces within the self . . . there is a more ancient concept of the poet (as well) . . . she is endowed to speak for those who do not have the gift of language, or to see for those who—for whatever reasons—are less conscious of what they are living through." (*LSS*, 181)[28] She is painfully aware that she cannot control what might happen to her words after she chooses them, but she is accountable for that choice, and for her accuracy.

Rich's lesbian/feminism helps to sculpt her role as prophet and witness. Because patriarchal culture has been silent about lesbians and "all women who are not defined by the men in their lives,"[29] the prophet/witness must give speech to experience for the first time. This is one meaning of writing a whole new poetry. However, patriarchal culture has not been consistently silent. Sometimes, it has lied about lesbians. The prophet/ witness must then speak truth to, and about, power. At other times, patriarchal culture has distorted or trivialized lesbians. The prophet/witness must then use and affirm " . . . a vocabulary that has been used negatively and pejoratively."[30] She must transvalue language.

Necessarily, the prophet/witness is a performer. She demands an audience, primarily of women. However, the ideology of lesbian/feminism is suspicious of star turns. Rich herself writes in "Transcendental Etude":

> "The longer I live the more I mistrust
> theatricality, the false glamour cast
> by performance, the more I know its poverty beside

the truths we are salvaging from
the splitting-open of our lives."

(*DCL*, 74)

The performing Rich—unlike Walt Whitman or Jeremiah— has more
stamina than flash; more intensity than ebullience. She is a laser rather than
an explosion of fireworks. She will speak but in "North American Time," a
grim, colloquial meditation on the poet's responsibility, she says, self-
deprecatingly:

"Sometimes, gliding at night
in a plane over New York City
I have felt like some messenger
called to enter, called to engage
this field of light and darkness.
A grandiose idea, born of flying."

(*FD*, 327)

She will also speak, if possible, to an audience of many women. She is
allusive and intricate, but rarely elusive and snobby. In part, she has the
clarity of classical poetry. In part, she has the clarity of one who wishes to
be heard.[31]

But what language will she speak? Clearly, Rich believes in the power of
language to represent ideas, feelings, and events. Although she writes
about film and photography, she is no postmodern celebrant of the visual
media. She fears that mass TV induces passivity, atrophies the literacy and
language we need to "take on the most complex, subtle, and drastic re-
evaluation ever attempted of the condition of the species." (*LSS*, 12) Her
dream of a common language is of *words*, a shared cultural frame and
thread, communal and quotidian, "hewn of the commonest living
substance" as well as "violent, arcane." (*PSN*, 232)

Yet, the lesbian/feminist poet cannot accept language that smoothly.
What is she to do with the fact that the powerful have used language to
choke and to erase her? to mystify and to disguise? Some French
theoreticians of *écriture féminine* advocate stealing, and then, flying away
with the oppressor's speech. That theft and that escape are acts of
reappropriation and control. Certainly, in her references to male poets—
yes, even to Robert Lowell, Rich shows her authority.[32] More fervently,
Rich selects female experience— the body; mothers, daughters, and
granddaughters; lesbianism; women's history—as her subject. Men, too,
have written such experiences up and down, but men, because they are
men, have been false prophets, narcissistic and perjuring witnesses.

Sadly, that selection offers little ease. For what is Rich, who believes in
poetry, to do with the fact that lesbian/feminism has naturalized female

experience? That lesbian/feminism has rooted female experience less in language than in things, objects, inarticulate but pregnant silences? Rich's poetry itself shows how craftily she handles the issue. First, she reduces the physical presence of language on the page. She wipes away diacritical marks, the busyness of syntax. Then, she alternates words with blank spaces—for breathing, for gazing. As she pushes language towards silence, she does to the verbal image what Nathalie Sarraute (or, in her way, Jane Austen) does to narrative. Yet, she refuses silence. She has words, and doubts-in-words.

Read "The Images." (*WP*, 3–5) The poem is a series of six sections, each an irregular series of staggered three- or fourline sections. The eye cautions the reader against regularities, sonorities. Two women are in bed. In the "pain of the city," the speaker turns. Her hand touches her lover "before language names in the brain." The speaker chooses touch, but not this city, where both images of women, and the looks of men, string women out and crucify them.

The speaker then recognizes that she has romanticized language, music, art, "frescoes translating/violence into patterns so powerful and pure/we continually fail to ask are they true for us." In contrast, when she now walks among "time-battered stones," she can think of her lover. She has gone to the sea, among flowering weeds, and drawn a flower. She has been "mute/innocent of grammar as the waves." There, feeling "free," she has had a vision of a woman's face and body. Her breasts gaze at the poet; the poet at her world. Rich writes:

> I wished to cry loose my soul
> into her, to become
>   free of speech   at last.

"Free of speech" is, of course, a syntactical pun. For the speaker is both free from speech, and, now, free to speak. She comes home, "starving/for images," a body in need of culture. She and her lover, as they remember each other in sleep, will "reassemble re-collect re-member" the lost images of women in the past. They will do the work of Isis, but for Isis, not Osiris. As the culture's images seek to "dismember" them, they will fight the war of the images.

The poem's last lines then recall the picture that the speaker has drawn: a thorn-leaf guarding a purple-tongued flower. Perhaps the picture represents only a flower on a beach. Perhaps not, too. For the thorn leaf can signify the lovers' vigilance in protecting the purple-tongued flower of the vulva, of their sexuality, and of their speech. The thorn is the anger that guards their tenderness, and their poetry.

Language lies. Language invents. Poetry lies. Poetry invents. Rich accepts that "truth." Writing tells stories that matter. Writing gives us images from the mind and of the body, for the relief of the body and the reconstruction of the mind. Rich accepts that "truth" as well. If some words ("lesbian") constrict the throat, say them. Open them up. Only then can we speak enough to wonder seriously if language lies, because it is language; if language invents, because it is language, or if language lies because people are liars who invent to control, rather than to dream, and justly please.

14 FEMALE INSUBORDINATION AND THE TEXT (1986)

The words *domination* and *subordination* have the complex weightiness that *sin* and *salvation* carried in more thoroughly religious periods in the West. Being dominant or subordinate is a state of being—social, political, psychological—that is as much an element of identity as bones of the body. However, modern ideologies demand that we break up ossified hierarchal structures and knit up new ones that incarnate the values of liberty, autonomy, and equality. The position of women dramatizes the tension between hierarchal practice and more individualistic, egalitarian theory. Scholars quarrel about the universality of male dominance and female subordination, but not about its presence—in past and present.[1] Yet, both men and women call out for women's freedom and independence and for gender equality. A question that inevitably emerges is how and why some women accept traditional, submissive roles while others resist them and proclaim modernity.

To answer such a query entails the ransacking of a multiplicity of materials. The ones I wish to shake out are largely literary. So doing, I feel afloat in a frail craft in a methodological swamp. Among the dank waters and hidden beasts that I fear are ahistoricity, overgeneralization, and a naive attitude toward literature that reduces it to a mirror image of reality; to mere mimesis, or to a source of role models, a set of inspirational ego ideals. I feel a dangerous closeness to that Samuel Beckett figure who murmurs, "I'll never know." Yet that same figure says, " . . . you must go on, I can't go on, I'll go on."[2] One goes on because literature can matter for the study of female subordination, that participation in an inferior class or group, that dependence upon the rank, power, and authority of others. Moreover, literature can represent the conditions of negation and revolt and the fear, at once tremulous and arrogant, of negation and revolt. In particular, modern Western texts articulate motivation, perception, desire, scenes of interpretation—the fields of feeling and consciousness.

To serve as my compass, I will borrow from an anthropologist, Peggy Sanday, and her theory about the conditions in which women escape subordination. Because of its realism about power, the theory may be less anthropology than anthropolitics. Obviously, anthropology most often concerns preliterate rather than literate cultures. For some, like Lévi-Strauss, literacy is even a tragic intrusion into, an irreparable rupture of, a preliterate society's cohesion. Nevertheless, anthropology can provoke the literary critic through suggesting relationships between symbolic structures and material realities. Sanday explores the sexual "scripts" that various societies use to rationalize and regulate gender systems and those systems themselves. So doing, she concludes that women achieve economic and political power or authority when they have economic autonomy and when men are dependent upon their activities.[3] If Sanday is right, women are lesser when they lack economic strength and a way of making men rely upon them—if only through that strength. She also pessimistically wonders if

> women as a group have not willingly faced death in violent conflict. This fact, perhaps more than any other, explains why men have sometimes become the dominating sex. (p. 211)

She offers a tragic irony: women submit to men because they are less responsive to the howling claims of Mars.

To explore texts is to study both literature and its production. Because the West has so masculinized the creation of public culture, for a woman to write at all seriously has been, in some degree, an act of defiance.[4] Though less painfully now than before, the writing woman must oppose ideological dictates and social, familial, and material pressures that would silence her. The history of modern women writers is a colletive biography of subversive self-assertion. Demonstrating Sanday's thesis, Western women could become writers, especially after the sixteenth century, because they had some access to education and to literacy. A literary education can, luckily, be partly private and auto-didactic, self-imbibed outside of formal institutions of learning. Women could then speak to an audience affluent enough to help support a publishing industry that men ran. Their circumstances granted them the possibility of some economic autonomy and some male dependence. As a critic says of Charlotte Brontë:

> For Brontë, writing was also a way of acquiring property (even if only one's own words) and thus status where most Victorian women had none.[5]

However, writing is also an unsatisfactory test of Sanday's thesis. For all modern writers tend to achieve, not economic and political power, but moral and cultural and psychological influence. Because of this, the resistance to women as writers is less than that to women as financiers or premiers. Nor is writing itself, despite such militant metaphors as "the war of ideas," violent. One might have asked of Charlotte Brontë what Stalin so crudely asked of a pope: how many divisions do you command?

In wildly disparate ways, the women who write, these limited cultural rebels, combine several characteristics. Psychologically, they are able to express, not to repress, alienation. They can articulate difference: between themselves and others, between the perceived present and the imagined future. For still enigmatic reasons, they have a compulsive attraction to language. It has an overriding, even obsessive power, like divine spirits for the mystic. A recent biographer of Aphra Behn, the first professional woman writer in English, says, though in terms too redolent of the natural and instinctual:

> Aphra seems to have been one of those naturally prolific writers for whom setting the pen to paper was instinctive; a fundamental element of temperament.[6]

Socially, the woman writer seems to have the support of at least one other person—even though it may be erratic or rough. In her poignant, lyrical novel about a tormented working-class family, Tillie Olsen has a child, Mazie, ask her mother what the word *edication,* means. As Anna answers she, too, mispronounces *education*, but differently. That lack of a common sound signifies their mutual distance from what the word represents and the distance between them that education might breed:

> "an edjication?" Mrs. Holbrook arose from amidst the shifting vapors of the washtub and, with the suds dripping from her red hands, walked over and stood impressively over Mazie. "A edjication is what you kids are going to get. It means your hands stay white and you read books and work in an office. Now get the kids and scat. But dont go too far, or I'll knock your block off."[7]

Economically, women writers are often needy. They write because they must live and because others, like the Alcott family on Louisa, depend on the daughter-author, sister-author, or mother-author for their living. They generally have greater opportunities for money, and for acceptance, if they are shrewd and self-effacing enough to enter an "empty field," a form that codifying critics may not applaud but that a consuming audience appreciates.[8]

No matter how subversive writing might be, the woman writer's life is rarely a simple history of subversion. She may have a moment of consciousness in which she overwhelmingly *sees* her place in structures of domination and submission. However, her collective history warns us against thinking of people—except in extreme moments of insight or choice—as either totally subordinate or totally insubordinate. Instead, consciously and unconsciously, out of cunning or cowardice, many women writers have devised a series of strategies that simultaneously reveal and conceal their self-assertions through language. As a whole, they have been neither rich nor confident enough to be vastly nonconformist. Some have written—but gurgling in support of the status quo. Others have adopted male names or masculinized their creative energies. Still others, as if to show that their revolt were singular rather than collective, have presented characters lesser than themselves. As Carolyn Heilbrun says:

> one *can* act, sometimes shocking oneself at one's courage, or audacity. One lives with the terror, the knowledge of mixed motives and fundamental conflicts, the guilt—but one acts. Yet women writers (and women politicians, academics, psychoanalysts) have been unable to imagine for other women, fictional or real, the self they have in fact achieved.[9]

The play between subordination and insubordination exists inevitably in women's texts as well as in their lives. Conflict structures their linguistic worlds. In English, at least four patterns of conflict have emerged. In the first, the woman writer sublimates her anger over women's condition into a protest on behalf of others. She projects a wish to change women's role by amassing evidence as to why others ought to alter theirs.[10] In the second, a reversal of the first, attacks on women's subordination accompany an inability to imagine other liberations as well. Like a great rocket that resistance inadequately fuels, the text goes up—to explode and then fall back. In *Shirley*, her historical novel published in 1849 but set in the Napoleonic Wars of 1811–1812, Charlotte Brontë deconstructs patriarchal religion, a phallic dominance of politics and the economy, constrictions on female autonomy and work, a sexual double standard, the sufferings of a displaced working class. Yet, even her hatred of deprivation,[11] even her analysis of the interlocking systems of class and gender, cannot generate a revolutionary narrative. Her leaders of class rebellion are primitive, nineteenth-century, Yorkshire Jimmy Hoffas, the contentious and corrupt leader of the Teamsters Union in the United States in the midtwentieth century. Her narrative closes in a double marriage and a brooding elegy for the nature, mystery, and magic that industrialism has erased.

A third pattern is the construction of a self-contradictory text that rejects and affirms femininity as usual. So, in the nineteenth-century sentimental novel, women both

> wrote of their domestic dream and revealed a deep discontent . . . the positive, forceful message rode and was partly generated by an undercurrent of dissatisfaction and despair.[12]

The annotators of 3,407 books about women in the United States written between 1891 and 1920 by 1,723 authors have also isolated a "hybrid" heroine. She may act heroically but be punished, resigned or remorseful in the final pages. Many of the novels (we studied) include love stories, the inclusion of which may represent a compromise with convention or a recognition of social reality.[13]

Finally, a woman writer may pile up reasons for women's rebellion, but store them in a deterministic worldview that instructs us all to submit to large, impersonal forces. Even if Lily Bart, in Edith Wharton's *House of Mirth*, were to become a reentry student and a suffragette, Wharton's Darwinistic theories of the power of heredity and environment would undercut such an unlikely personal transformation.

Fortunately, a reader of these texts—of sublimated or terminated insubordination, self-contradicition, and fatalism— need not passively submit to their imperatives. Nor need they provide spongy escapes that absorb the restless imagination and libido. Both more and less than a collapse of self and book, reading can be an active process.

In 1932, writing to his wife from prison, Gramsci made a "just and necessary" distinction between

> aesthetic enjoyment and a positive value judgment of artistic beauty, i.e. between enthusiasm for a work of and in itself and moral enthusiasm, by which I mean a willing participation in the artist's ideological world.[14]

Readers can do even more than choose between palatable art and impalatable ideology. They can select certain ideological features and abandon others. Shirley's critique of Milton in *Shirley*, but not her marriage, may be material for an enabling myth of women's power. So may Radclyffe Hall's protest against homophobia in *The Well of Loneliness*, but not her prayers to a patriarchal God that smoke up from her last pages. Readers, like Doris Lessing's Martha Quest, may wilfully assemble from literature what they need for their reconstruction of the world. If gender marks some readings, women may pick up signals about resistance that men might miss. Reading women will secretly school themselves in the tactics of disobedience.[15]

Such processes enhance, no matter how internally, a person's sense of power and freedom. Reinforcing this is the probability that reading is an indeterminate act. Because of its very nature, a text can invite us to help create its meaning. As we decide what it is all about, we are cognitively alert, responsible, fecund, capable. We gain a sense of strength. Simultaneously, we enter into what we have left of the world of the text. We vicariously experience events and personalities we might not meet in ordinary life—including dramas of insubordination. We gain, then, a sense of possibility. If we empathize with a character, we may also mitigate some crippling loneliness, a self-perception of wierd singularity. We gain, finally, a sense of community.[16]

However, women have written still another kind of text. Here they want their readers to agree with them, to be fellow partisans of change. Their narrative lines can show conflict between the forward momentum of those who desire difference and the inertia of persons and institutions that cling to stability, but the narratives rarely contradict themselves. Resolutely, cleanly, they support those going forward. Some of these texts more fiercely and unabashedly call for change than others: certain novels about the New Woman;[17] feminist Utopias;[18] and "feminist polemic," a genre that Christine de Pisan helped to originate and that proudly, defiantly asserts the rights and dignity of women against often viciously misogynistic attacks against them.[19]

Other texts, even though they confront subordination, submerge ideology more carefully. Using Western narrative conventions, they show the transactions of a central character with the self, others, society, and history. As they embed their politics in humanized passions, they are more apt to be psychological dramas than overt feminist programs. These texts are also realistic. When subordinate groups in modern Western culture are able to speak, but when they believe that their stories have not yet been adequately told, they will tend to turn to realism, the form that promises the appearance of accuracy. Because such texts can be persuasive and instructive, I wish to mention three of them, all from the United States: *Work* (1873) by Louisa May Alcott (1832–1888), the prolific and popular writer, the author of *Little Women; Burning Questions* (1978) by Alix Kates Shulman (1932–), the contemporary novelist, radical feminist, and editor of Emma Goldman; and, finally, "Sweat" (1925), by Zora Neale Hurston (1903–1960), the black writer and anthropologist, who died in poverty and obscurity.[20]

As many people know, *Work* adapts *Pilgrim's Progress* to a nineteenth-century woman's life. Christie, Alcott's Christian, is an orphan girl. Her father was the heir of urbane culture, her mother of rural strength. Christie integrates, then, the best of various American bloodlines. She leaves the provincial farm where she has been raised in order to create, for herself, a more independent and gratifying life. Having neither legacy nor husband, she must work. Systematically, Christie takes on the jobs open to women in the nineteenth-century: domestic service; the stage; being a governess, in a home with a flighty, rich mistress who has a seductive brother; companion, wife; secretary; seamstress. She also befriends a black cook, an ex-prostitute, and a laundress. Each of these jobs is demeaning, marginal, depressing. Women accept them because they have no choice, and if they survive them, it is because of their character, not because of the job. Christie's marriage is happy, but brief. Her husband dies, heroically, in the Civil War. Despite such a bleak, trying vision of the world of work and of the home, Alcott gives us a species of a happy ending. Christie, at forty, has three consolations: a daughter, whom she loves; work, with women, which satisfies her; and religious faith, which sustains her.

Burning Questions adapts, not a religious, but a political quest. A late modern secularist, Shulman rewrites the autobiographies of radical women—Emma Goldman, Louise Michel—to fit the conditions of a twentieth-century American woman's life. Zane IndiAnna is the daughter of a bourgeois, nuclear family in the Midwest. Her mother is supportive; her father supportive but strong-minded. After graduating from a junior college, at the age of eighteen, she comes to New York in 1958. She falls in among Beats and Bohemians, who exploit her sexually and mock her psychically. To earn her living, she takes on a number of secretarial jobs. Partly in order to escape from the Midwest, she marries a lawyer and has three children. She never fully represses her rebellious self. She violates some norms. She marches for civil rights; she gets arrested at an antidraft demonstration; she has an affair. Nevertheless, she largely becomes a wife and mother, who subordinates herself to the needs of others. However, she discovers the new feminism, in the late 1960s. Psychologically, she emerges. Politically, she transforms herself. Shulman, too, gives us a species of a happy ending. For Zane, nearly forty, has her consolations: her children, whom she loves; her work, with women, which satisfies her and which has made her economically self-sufficient; and her political faith, which sustains her. Her life has also personalized the Hegelian pattern of thesis, her youth; antithesis, her marriage; and synthesis, her radical feminism, which has reanimated the best parts of her youth.

Obviously, *Work* and *Burning Questions* have their differences, which, in part, reveal profound cultural shifts within America itself. If Alcott explores religious desire, Shulman explores sexual desire. If Alcott praises submission and self-sacrifice, those "stern, sad, angels," Shulman praises self-autonomy. Yet, remarkably, both sustain Sanday's analysis of the sources of female power. Both assert women's need to achieve economic and political muscle. Like Charlotte Brontë, they represent that need through showing how hard and precarious women's lives are without such strength. Both Alcott and Shulman also believe that women are better off when men are dependent upon them. Yet, their men are most dependent for love, tenderness, sex, and children. Sadly, in industrial society, these activities take place within the same home that keeps women from achieving that economic and political muscle that they ought to have. Except for little boys, men depend less upon women than upon other men with public power. Alcott's men probably need women more than Shulman's. For Shulman's take advantage of the twentieth-century loosening of sexual restraints and marital bonds. As they seek love, tenderness, sex, and paternity, they easily go from one woman to another, substitute one woman for another. They also use the supermarket and the laundromat for services the home once gave.

Neither Alcott nor Shulman wholly sustains Sanday's provocative suggestion about the relationship between male dominance and war. Nor do they refute it. Rather, they present complex, ambiguous attitudes toward war. To be sure, war is a man's game. To be sure, war exacts a terrible price—for Christie the loss of her husband and the maiming of male bodies. Yet, Alcott finds the Civil War a moral necessity that provokes its own excitement and offers its own rewards. For Christie, they include a large measure of power and esteem. As a nurse, a role in which men are dependent upon her for their comfort and their life, she finds both. Moreover, in an awful exchange, her husband's grievous death brings her the chance to do the work she ultimately finds so enabling. Shulman finds the Vietnamese War contemptible, antiwar politics chauvinistic. Yet, Zane's protest against the war is part of her process of liberation; and her feminist politics, though tactically they prefer shock to terror, are militant and often warlike.

Both Alcott and Shulman add some oddly congruent prescriptions to Sanday's analysis for the repudiation of subordination. They dramatize the features of the rebellious psyche. Both Christie and Zane have reasons to rebel: Christie a callous Uncle who makes her dependence upon him psychically intolerable; Zane a more positive radical aunt who tactfully schools her about the diseases of the world. In both cases, the rebellious personality has an element of mystery, of inexplicability. Discontent is simply there, like a gift, or talent. Christie simply says that she has more "yeast" in her composition. Zane describes herself as a "born fanatic." An element of mystery exists, too, in the conditions of their life that ultimately permit their rebellion to flourish. Chance, coincidence, helps to keep Christie from suicide during a moment of profound depression. Luck helps Zane. She broods: "Skill, will, circumstance, history in some complex mysterious balance had all combined with luck to land us here" (p. 354).

Yet, neither Alcott nor Shulman mystifies rebellion. Surrounding Christie and Zane is a culture that offers some encouragement. Christie has read the Declaration of Independence, fairy tales, and *Jane Eyre*. She knows the discourse of political equality, of fantasy, and of women's rights to dislike subordination. Zane has the example of St. Joan; *Middletown*, a socio-logical text that critically analyzes her environment; and the autobiograph-ies of women rebels. Through culture, they have a supportive context in which to place the rebellious self only half-conscious of how rebellious it might be. Finally, both become a part of a strong women's world. For Zane, that women's world, erotically charged, included a long, gratifying lesbian love affair. Each narrative closes with an image of a politicized female community that seeks to cross the barriers of race and class, a female community that transfigures domesticity into resistance. In brief, in

Work and *Burning Questions*, women who reject subordination do so in the company of other women. Together, they have a sustaining ideology and toughness. In female interdependence is female independence.

Consistently, the writing and speaking of black women in the United States has strongly affirmed the importance of a female community to the strong black woman. However, my third text, by a black woman writer, studies a rebellion executed in isolation, without the buoyant consolation of a group, culture, or education. "Sweat" tells of Delia, a black washerwoman in Florida. She has been married for fifteen years to Sykes, who has beaten her, physically and psychologically, since the beginning of their union. Audaciously unfaithful, he expresses no need for her. Nevertheless, she has stayed with him. Though the men in the local black community disapprove of Sykes, they offer Delia little support. Two other forces help her: her church, which offers the compensations and consolations of faith, and the knowledge that she owns her home, real estate she has bought with her earnings as a laundress.

Delia finally rebels—when Sykes goes too far. He touches a nerve, which no one could have seen until it responds. It tells Delia that her survival, her sense of life itself, is now threatened. The first upswelling of female insubordination is neither ideological nor predictable. Rather, it is an abrupt reaction to a suddenly intolerable pressure, to an intolerable dissonance between what is happening and what must happen if a woman is to go on. Sykes has been openly consorting with a woman to whom he promises Delia's house and land. Coming home one Sunday, he drapes a bullwhip over her shoulders as she kneels to sort out piles of laundry. He then installs a caged rattlesnake in the yard, knowing sadistically how snakes terrify her.

Delia's first rebellion is verbal. Appropriating one of his tactics, she talks back to the blustering, astonished Sykes. Then, escalating brutality to attempted murder, he secretly puts the snake in the laundry basket he thinks she will open. Though a "gibbering wreck," she escapes, to hid in the barn. There, in one evening, she passes through a psychological process of revolt. She goes from coherent thought to "cold, bloody rage," to introspection, to retrospection, to an "awful calm." At dawn, Sykes returns drunk. In the bedroom, the snake strikes, to kill him. Though sickened, Delia lets him die horribly, realizing that he has seen her see him.

With the power of deciding whether Sykes will live or die, she makes him dependent upon her—although his dependence is more a fatal vulnerability that he has created through vain presumptions of invulnerability.

Having gone to war with Sykes, turning his weapons against him, she is now free. She has not lusted for violence. Indeed, she has passively, miserably accepted it for years. When she fights, she uses more chaotic cunning than physical aggression. A snake, not a fist, is her tool. Her war is private, personal; not public, social. If Delia is an Amazon, she lacks company. Yet, only her terrified willingness to kill breaks her bruising, mutilating alliance with Sykes.

Perhaps I have derived from my texts—my anthropology and fiction—little more than common sense might have uttered if I had had the modesty, simplicity, and common sense to summon it. Certainly I have blatantly evaded the sophisticated interrogations of the labyrinthian nexus of literature, writing, and "life" that poststructural and semiotic critics have so intelligently constructed. Despite these demurrers, I do suggest that if women are to resist subordination, as women writers partially did, they must command resources and men's recognition of women's necessity. Women must, as well, be willing to risk loss. Such a statement is not meant to glorify pugnacity, to romanticize death, or to endorse heedlessly women's performance in armed forces or police departments. Even if Sanday wonders if a historical cause of male dominance has been men's willingness to fight as a group and a historical cause of female subordination has been women's unwillingness to do so, she is not prescribing that women now give up their cabbages and become captains and kings. When I speak of risking loss, I am realistically judging the capacity of authority to punish those who doubt its legitimacy, supporting the worth of self-defense, and reclaiming rituals that emblemize a passage from momentary loss to new gain, death to rebirth.

My texts also tend to assert—as a philistine common sense and a quantity-obsessed social science will not—the vitality of the relationship between cultural artifacts and the rebellious woman's consciousness. Those artifacts harrow and nurture that consciousness. Neither epiphanies nor conversions are the result of some version of the immaculate conception. They flare up after years of preparation. So a dancer splits space in a millisecond after arduous toil. The woman who resists female subordination—no matter how erratic she may be, no matter how instantaneous she believes her consciousness of the wrong of subordination to be—may have had a long engagement with some signals from her culture. In a self-praising gesture that is no less valid for being that, texts and textualizers warn us of their patience and their own sly, peculiar power.

15

A WELCOME TREATY: THE HUMANITIES IN EVERYDAY LIFE (1986)

I am an advocate of a treaty between the humanities and everyday life. However, my title is loose enough to sprawl towards the swamp of meaninglessness. It could promise to be: 1) A series of high-minded generalities about the value of the humanities for the individual and society. Unfortunately, these liturgies tend to dull the mind and glaze the eye. 2) A statement about material culture, that study of pots and pans, sheets and shards, mirrors and middens. 3) A survey of the teaching of the humanities in the everyday life of the classroom.

Being high-minded, exploring material culture, and teaching the humanities are all important.[1] Nevertheless, I wish to explore the terms of three other relationships between the humanities and the daily busyness and business of contemporary America: 1) The work of some professional contemporary humanists who look at everyday life, including, but not limited to, its material culture. 2) Some connections between the humanities and the public. 3) Some gifts of the humanities to both professionals and the public for the sake of everyday life, a point that I hope will not itself break down into dulling, glazing generalities.

My explorations begin with the solid comfort of an anecdote. It takes place in the sixth grade of a public school in the State of Washington shortly after World War II. A teacher has given a music class a choice of what to sing in a school concert. The choice is clear—even if the reasons for it are not. The class is to vote between a Handel air and a rousing popular song, "The Freedom Train," written to promote a sleek vehicle that was carrying precious national documents on a whistle stop tour of America.

I wish to thank the Council of Chief State School Officers for inviting me to give one version of this paper in April, 1984, and the Society for the Humanities of Cornell University, and its director, Jonathan Culler, for inviting me to give another in October, 1984. I a grateful to my fellow panelists at Cornell for their attention and comments: Robert Harris, Richard Lanham, Geoffrey Marshall, and Mary Beth Norton.

One girl, Kathleen, supports Handel. Her huge brown eyes brim with tears as she vows, "Handel is better music." Nearly everyone else whoops and scoffs. "'The Freedom Train' is more fun," they holler. "And besides, it's patriotic." There is, as well, a Little Waverer. She agrees with Kathleen. She has played Handel at her piano lessons. She believes Handel is finer, and more refined, music than "The Freedom Train." However, she also agrees with the rest of the class. For "The Freedom Train" is more fun, and much more patriotic.

Class rules forbid the Little Waverer from waiving the privilege of choice. She votes for "The Freedom Train." During the concert, the next week, she bellows heartily. Yet, guiltily, she watches Kathleen. For tears are now flowing down her cheeks as she mournfully sings "The Freedom Train," a sight that crimps the Little Waverer's pleasures.

I am the Little Waverer grown large. That early experience has influenced my thinking about the humanities and everyday life. It has helped teach me to suspect any dualistic theory of culture: "high culture," to be respected and feared, and taught in the humanities classroom, and "low" or "popular culture," to be ridiculed and enjoyed, and passed down outside of the classroom. For a culture is actually a complex totality that consists of many elements. Some elements may seem to work together; some elements may seem to be at odds with each other. Whether they are compatible or antagonistic, they co-exist within that culture's field of force. One of the humanist's jobs is to show their synchronic relationships; to map how they fit and move together. For example, a humanist might tell us what it means that Handel and "The Freedom Train" were alive at the same time in the Little Waverer's sixth-grade classroom, but that the Little Waverer could choose only to perform one.

Curiously, some of the people we assign to "high culture" most deftly dramatize the inseparability of culture's various elements. I think of Jane Austen, a clergyman's clever daughter. She sold her first important novel, *Northanger Abbey*, in 1803, but it was not published until 1818, the year after her death. Her heroine is another clergyman's daughter, Catherine Morland, who will eventually marry still another clergyman. Before then, Catherine must learn the difference between fiction and fact, literary romances and lived realities. The adolescent Catherine is a sweet girl, but until growing up chastens her, she does believe that the popular fiction of her time, her time's equivalent of Gothic and Harlequin novels, might be true.

However, Austen also supports the popular fiction of the day, and her fellow/sister authors. She realizes that her culture needs both Austen's moral realism and popular fiction's fun. She bursts out against sneering critics less comprehensive than she: "Let us leave it to the Reviewers to abuse such effusions of fancy at their leisure . . . to talk in threadbare strains of the trash with which the press now groans. . . . We are an injured body. Although our productions have afforded more extensive and unaffected pleasure than those of any other literary corporation in the world, no species of composition has been so much decried."[2]

I

Realistic novelists like Jane Austen make up stories about everyday life. In the last two decades, "professional humanists" have taken up everyday life as a serious, demanding subject of study. Obviously, professional humanists are continuing to support and defend the canonical legacy of the Western humanities. It would be stupid and self-destructive not to do so. However, they are also resiting that legacy in a vaster context. They are asking questions about Native American myths as well as about the Bible the Puritans carried; about the Seneca Falls Declaration of 1848 as well as about the Declaration of Independence; about slave narratives as well as those of Ishmael. So doing, they are doing, in their way, what that canonical figure, Ralph Waldo Emerson, asked the American scholar to do: to know the meaning of "The meal of the firkin; the milk in the pan; the ballad in the street; the news of the boat; the glance of the eye; the form and gait of the body. . . ."[3]

Because it sounds like jargon, I introduce the term "professional humanists," or pH factor, reluctantly. The word points to a condition of the contemporary humanities. Traditionally, they have represented the subject matter of the study of all that is distinctly human, all that distinguishes us from angels and amoebae: our history, languages, laws, customs, values, arts, thoughts, and feelings. However, in search of precision, we have tended in the last decades to narrow "the humanities" to a set of academic disciplines that organize that study. The founding legislation of the National Endowment for the Humanities implicitly did this when it defined the humanities as the study of language, both modern and classical; of linguistics; literature; history; jurisprudence; philosophy; archaeology; comparative religion; ethics; the history, criticism, and theory of the arts; and aspects of the social sciences that have humanistic content. "Professional humanists" earn their living as practicing members of those disciplines, whether they have an academic post or work as independent scholars. The humanities are their speciality—as law is for the lawyer, drugs for the pharmacologist, and the baseball bat for the designated hitter.

The broadening of the work of professional humanists to embrace everyday life is inseparable from two other cultural developments. One is the expansion, since the 1920s, of United States higher education. Colleges and universities now enroll students, and hire faculty and administrators, from groups that they once largely excluded. This development has linked teaching, research, and learning with large, varied populations. Second, and less obvious, is the collapse of aesthetic boundaries in modern and post-modern art. Mixed-media events, happenings, and performance art deliberately erase conventional distinctions between art and life and among the arts. Anything, and everything, has become fair game for any, and every, artist. This development has made the arts, and criticism about them, more fluid, more flexible. Both developments have broadened our general culture.

Like folklore and anthropology, the new social history is an example of the connecting of humanistic inquiry with everyday life. Some of the most obvious roots of the new social history are European—the "Annales" school in France between the world wars, and the labors of E.P. Thompson and others in England. In the United States, in the early 1960s, historians began to speak of doing history "from the bottom up." They wanted to know ordinary, not extraordinary lives; the powerless, not the powerful; the often illiterate and uneducated, not the literate and educated. Because such people might not have left many documents behind, the historian had to turn to different kinds of evidence: parish registers of births and marriages; markings on tombstones; census data.

Thompson's "Preface" to *The Making of the English Working Class*, published in 1963, reveals an attractive, and common, feature of the new social history. For Thompson speaks of his human material, not as raw material, but as human beings, as human subjects that he is to "rescue . . . from the enormous condescension of posterity."[4] Those words, "condescension of posterity," like the phrase "history from the bottom up," are metonymical. That is, they stand for, they show, something other than themselves—in this case, a picture of societies that are hierarchical, with condescending higher classes and damaged, but courageous, lower ones. The historian must embark upon an urgent, moral task: to "rescue" the beleaguered existence of the "lesser orders" before time obliterates their memory altogether.

Giving urgency to, and often joining with, the new social history are other scholarly forces. Think, for example, of black studies and women's studies.[5] Black studies argues correctly that we cannot understand the humanities without understanding the influence and treatment of race. Women's studies argues, as correctly, that we cannot understand the humanities without understanding the influence and treatment of gender. Most black men and women in the United States, like most women (and men) of all races, have lived without much public power and/or recognition. As a result, much of their history has been deeply involved with everyday life. The study of blacks, of women, and of everyday life necessarily, then, stimulate each other.

Everyday scholarly movement had its prophets. Among the prophets of black studies was that compelling scholar, writer, and organizer: William E.B. DuBois. In 1903, he finished *The Souls of Black Folk*, a profound study of the meaning of being black in the United States. Significantly, before each chapter, and at the end of his book, he prints a bar or a verse of the "Sorrow Songs," of black folk music. To history, sociology, anthropology, and politics, he brings the haunting sounds of everyday life, and everyday suffering. Among the prophets of women's studies was that extraordinary novelist and critic: Virginia Woolf. In 1928, in a lecture that was to become part of *A Room of One's Own*, she spoke about the need to have more data about Elizabethan women. Woolf might have been talking about all women. "What one wants," she said: " . . . is a mass of information; at what age did (an Elizabethan woman) marry; how many children had she as a rule; what was her house like; had she a room to herself; did she do the cooking; would she be likely to have a servant? All these facts lie somewhere, presumably, in parish registers and account books; the life of the average Elizabethan woman must be scattered about somewhere, could one collect it and make a book of it."[6] Then, in 1974, in her essay "In Search of Our Mothers' Gardens," Alice Walker eloquently fused a call for black studies, women's studies, and the humanities in everyday life. Where, she asks, does one search for the creative spirit of black women? High—and low, she responds. Look at the quilts black women stitched; the stories they told; the gardens they planted. There one will see survival, art, and beauty.

Still another example of the humanities' fresh responses to the "ordinary" is a deepening interest in literacy, the ability to read, write, and control texts. In part, this interest is an act of self-survival. If the humanities are in trouble today, it is not only because they seem less practical, profitable, and central than science, economics, or accounting. It is also because they are textual. They demand an engagement with written languages. No one can read George Eliot unless he or she can read hundreds of pages of narrative. No one can write about George Eliot unless he or she can construct ideas on the building lots of the page. Kids themselves know when their literacies fail. Read, and sigh over, this mocking parody of a high school humanities paper that a high school junior wrote in 1983 and showed to me:

> Many years ago Sophocles wrote a play called Oedipus Rex. Oedipus Rex is a tradgedy (sic) play which is considered to be a great Greek masterpiece. Last year in English we learnt (sic) what a tragdedy (sic) was, and Sophocles has definitely written on . . . Oedipusses situation is really depressing.

Professional humanists today are asking at least three immense questions about literacy: How do people read, and how do we teach them to do so? How do people write, and how do we teach them to do so? And, finally, what does it mean to be literate? How does it shape and change our sense of being human? Especially in a post-modern world in which the visual image seems to rival, if not to surpass, the word as a source of instruction and pleasure? In the literature about literacy is a sprightly, provocative book, *On Literacy: The Politics of the Word from Homer to the Age of Rock*, that offers one contemporary definition of everyday literacy. The author, Robert Pattison, studied classics and English literature.[7] He found a job teaching, not Virgil or Victorian prose at a research university, but composition at a community college. He confesses: "My interest in defining literacy began while teaching freshman English in community colleges around New York. Interest is too mild a word. Freshman writing is a barrage of intellectual and social challenges masquerading as prose. (p. v)" He might have been speaking of any writing class.

For Pattison, literacy is more than a set of skills labeled reading, writing, and speaking. It is, as well, the ability to know how language works in the world. However, that relationship—between language and the world—will vary wildly from culture to culture. For the Romans, for example, the literate man could speak more finely than other men. He was a stronger rhetorician and orator. Yet, as Pattison knows, no culture is ever wholly unique. History dislikes the total anomaly. He suggests that the United States today is like the Middle Ages, especialy the Carolingian period. Now, and then, two literacies existed—one official, one vernacular. Our official language is not Latin, but a formal, codified English that such "prissy grammarians" as Edwin Newman and John Simon defend. Our vernacular is not an emerging Romance language, but the sung and/or spoken word. In brief, we have the literacy of the schools, and the literacy of common life. No kid, Pattison says wryly, misspells Led Zeppelin. Our task, as humanists and educators, is to recognize reality and grant both literacies legitimacy. Students must know Standard English, because they will need it. Students must know vernacular English, because it is the poetry of the present. Our epic poet of the future, a Milton yet unborn, will fuse them together.

No one wishes the humanities to explore and teach only the culture of everyday lives. Their sum and substance is bigger even than that. Nevertheless, the movement to have the humanities include everyday lives has provoked a debate that now wells up during discussions about curriculum, tenure, grants and fellowships, and what the word "humanities" really means. Again and again, I hear two, overlapping arguments against humanists who study everyday life.

The first argument, which echoes a cry against cultural disorder heard since the beginning of the modern period in the seventeenth century, asserts that new approaches are fragmenting the humanities. Instead of coherence, we have disintegration. Instead of culture, we have anarchy. Our task now is to restore some saving, graceful order. In August, 1984, the National Endowment for the Humanities publicized, with some fanfare, the results of a survey it had conducted as one way of performing that task. The Endowment asked what books every high school student ought to have read. The "Top Ten" were two Shakespearean tragedies; American historical documents; Twain; the Bible; Homer; Dickens; Plato; Steinbeck; Hawthorne; and Sophocles, the same *Oedipus Rex* that my high school junior flippantly analyzed.[8] The "Top Thirty" flowed from a similar vein. All its writers were white Westerners, although two were women (Jane Austen and Emily Dickinson) and one was a Communist (Karl Marx).

I read, and respect, Chaucer and Milton, Faulkner and Frost. How could I not? Nevertheless, I believe that such lists have a desperate quality. For they are at once standard and artificial; unimaginative and unreal, "conventional" in a broad sense of the word. They represent what people think they *ought* to read, and therefore what they ought to ask other people to read. Too often, they derive their sense of "oughtness" from some hazy memory of what some cultural authority proclaimed in the past. Their literary preferences are not dictated immediately after an engagement with the texts themselves. I would be as surprised to learn that everyone who responded to the Endowment survey had read the "Top Ten" authors in the past five years, let alone the "Top Thirty", as I would be to learn that each habitually whistled Handel as he or she mowed the lawn, or cleaned the house. If the adults do not read, why should the kids?

Actually, of course, the United States has created a culture that its citizens do share. That common store of experiences and values derives, not from religion or the humanities, but from our consumer society. Here, most adults read very little. Our group references are not to books, but to television, the movies, popular music, fashion, a few political figures that the media has publicized, sports, and advertising. We share Clavin Klein, not John Calvin. Although most professional humanists do not write about these galaxies of Americana, some do. All of us—humanists or not—travel in and among them every day.

A second argument against studying the humanities and everyday life is that such an enterprise deflects the humanities from their real task: to recuperate the burden of Matthew Arnold and cultivate the best that humanity has thought, and said. The *Eighteenth Annual Report* of the National Endowment for the Humanities outlines this job lucidly. Geoffrey Marshall writes of guidelines for the Division of General Programs: "The new guidelines are built upon three main goals: the interpretation and appreciation of the great influential texts of our culture; the illumination of major historical ideas, figures, and events; and increased understanding of the methods and content of the disciplines of the humanities."[9]

These two arguments are troublesome for several reasons, particularly to a Little Waverer grown large. First, adding new materials to the humanities is not a drop into chaos. Instead, it lifts us—to a place where we can recognize how heterogeneous culture is, how multiplicitous, how drenched with diversity. The real problem with new materials is the difficulty of expanding the curriculum while classroom time stands still. The teacher can be an Alice in Wonderland and choose to go faster; or to be a butcher and cut some older materials; or, preferably, to act as an archivist, with reservoirs of materials, who tells students why the syllabi is as it is, why a curriculum is as it is, why some things are in and others out, and where the "outs" are in the archives.

Next, when we speak, as Marshall does, of "great influential texts" and "major" ideas, we often talk as if greatness simply fell from the air; as if majors got promotions because of merit alone. However, as a teacher draws up a classroom plan, so a culture, through an intricate series of processes, determines what texts will influence it; what ideas will shape it. As we think about cultural "greatness," we must dissect those processes.[10] As we read Shakespeare, we must understand why he leads the "Top Ten," and how we have canonized him. If we are to have touchstones, we must map the quarry from which we cut the stones.

Next, most of us are persistently guilty of binary, or polar, or dualistic, thinking. That is, we look at the world and divide everything into one or two opposing sets: left or right, right or wrong, good or bad, the humanities of "great" works or the humanities of "everyday life." We then persuade ourselves that we must choose one set or another. We must be left or right; we must read "great" works or "everyday" ones. However, we need not indulge in such mental habits. We can shift from "either/or" to "both/and" thinking. We can support the "great" and the "everyday" lives. Like Jane Austen, we can enjoy both the great and the common works.

Boldly conceived, the humanities are the way in which we understand history, the past. They also provoke moral questions and the moral imagination. They often suggest that we ground the moral imagination in a belief in the absolute worth of the individual human person. To be sure, in the West, we have often taken a chain saw to the link between a belief in the humanities and in human rights. The figure of the Nazi officer playing Schubert in a concentration camp is a terrible symbol of the slashing of that connection. Moreover, many humanistic texts either dramatize or endorse hierarchical cosmologies or societies, in which some people seem better than others. Despite this, the humanities, like the Bill of Rights, are a moral vault in which we store, and from which we can draw, our sense of human preciousness. However, the humanities will give us neither accurate history nor a richly-grounded moral imagination unless they represent the realities and culture of everyday life. ˙

II

As the humanistic study of everyday life has grown, so have the spans between the humanities and people outside of the conventional classroom. These bridges rise up from at least three bedrock facts. First, mass higher education, surely one of the noblest of American dreams, is successful. The United States has a large group of citizens, often the first in their families to go to college, who seek culture after their formal schooling ends. For example, they visit museums. Between 1975 and 1979, visits to art museums rose about twenty percent, from 42 million to nearly 50 million people.[11] Cultural institutions have, in turn, welcomed larger publics. Joking about this, the New Yorker published a cartoon that pictured a grand museum. To enter it, people must toil up a wide staircase and pass between two stalwart columns. Hanging between the columns is a banner reading:

ART

. . . And Plenty of It![12]

Next, adult and continuing education programs enable non-traditional learners to seek out the humanities. Unfortunately, in 1981, perhaps less than 10 percent of adult education courses were in the humanities. Of these, over 25 percent were in composition and speech. Such courses also attracted more adults with less than a high-school diploma and more members of "marginal" groups—like women, members of ethnic and racial minorities, the unemployed, or senior citizens.[13] Pessimistic responses to such figures might be mournful statements about the humanities' inability, or unwillingness, to appeal to the self-interest of students in adult education, about students' inability, or unwillingness, to see that the humanities are as important to them as business, health, or engineering. More optimistic responses are also possible. We might survey students imaginatively and ask if, and why, they resist the humanities. We might also experiment with courses in the humanities *and* business, or health, or engineering.

Third, movies and television are omnipresent. They present history, political science, and anthropology in documentaries. I think, for example, of Daniel Walkowitz, who practices the new social history. He both wrote a monograph about the workers in an upstate New York town and then went out and raised money to make a documentary about them.[14] Less happily, the media · play at history, political science, and anthropology in the "docudrama," which lavishly and cynically mingles speculation, fact, and commercials. The media dramatize literature through *Masterpiece*

Theater—although they often cosmetize the realities of mass culture rather as business ethics courses do the market place. The media can also explore poetry, religion, art, dance, and music as scrupulously as any academic setting.

The cultural presences of mass higher education, adult education, and the media in our culture are familiar. Less well-known are a unique conjunction of learning and democracy: the state humanities councils, a gallant set of organizations that embodies, as mass education does, a vision of a widely-informed citizenry. Organized during the early 1970s, through the National Endowment for the Humanities, the councils now exist in every state, Puerto Rico, the Virgin Islands, and the District of Columbia. Although independent state-wide committees direct each council, they continue to receive supervision and funding from NEH itself. In 1976, Congress mandated that the councils should receive a minimum of 20 per cent of the program funds in the NEH budget. Indeed, the interest of legislators, primarily but not exclusively that of Representative Sidney Yates and Senator Claiborne Pell, has strengthened the councils vigorously.[15]

Originally, the councils were to show how the humanities might help us discuss questions of public policy, from local land use to foreign affairs. Daniel Callahan, the founder of the Hastings Center, argues convincingly that the humanities can serve three realms: that of "public policy . . . the aggregate collection of those actions undertaken by government . . . to advance the welfare of its citizens . . . and its national interests . . . "; that of "public policy analysis . . . an analytical and disciplined effort to articulate the practical alternatives open to government in implementing public policy commitments . . . "; and that of "public policymaking . . . the actual act of making a policy choice, or implementing a policy option. . . ."[16] Whatever the realm, the humanities were to have a place and purpose in the everyday world of public events and decisions. The humanities were to encourage the presence of an alert, informed, judicious citizenry.

In 1977, this mandate loosened and grew. The councils became freer to support a variety of programs, by professional humanists and citizens, about the humanities: exhibits about local history, reading groups about aging in nursing homes, conferences on women's literature, discussion of Hispanic culture in America, institutes for high school teachers, seminars on nuclear war. In 1983, more than 25,000,000 Americans took part in such events, among them 15,000 scholars.[17]

In September, 1983, for example, I spoke in the parish house of an Episcopal Church in Essex, New York, a town of about 500 people on the western shores of Lake Champlain. My theme was rural isolation; my text Emily Brontë's *Wuthering Heights*. My audience, from the community, consisted of English professors and people who had not completed high school. We discussed that nineteenth-century English novel together. I had but one disappointment: I thought I might speak in the Grange Hall. But my lecture conflicted with Bingo night, and I gave way to its superior force.

Like libraries, museums, historical societies, zoos, and public broadcasting, the state councils make culture and learning accessible away from both the formal classroom and the home. They occupy a middle space between school and family. Their learners are neither enrolled students nor children, but sensible adults in quest of facts, ideas, images. That much ballyhooed report, *A Nation At Risk: The Imperative for Educational Reform*, urged America to create a "Learning Society." It would reflect a " . . . commitment to a set of values and to a system of education that affords all members the opportunity to stretch their minds to full capacity, from childhood through adulthood. . . ."[18] But America *has* created a set of institutions to sustain a "Learning Society." Our amazing task now is to nurture them.

Despite their maturing promise, the state councils have three difficulties that grow from the nature of the humanities in the United States today. Although they are innovative, the councils can no more escape from the humanities in general than a grange hall can escape from the weather. First, most practicing humanists are now professionals, largely employed in schools, colleges, and universities. There, they are central to their own departments, but often peripheral to the social sciences, the natural sciences, the professional schools, and society-at-large.

The results are predictable. Too many humanists are hermetic, capable of speaking only to other specialists. Inseparable from their professional identities can be one of two defensive responses to their marginality: an inflated sense of their own importance, or, at the other extreme, an ironic and ultimately paralyzing self-deprecation. When they go outside of the academy, they are aware that the reward system of the profession, and their peers, will not recognize their efforts. Unwittingly, these efforts can often be incoherent, or condescending. The humanists behave like fumbling missionaries—although they carry the teachings of culture rather than those of a church.[19]

For their part, non-specialists assume that the humanities are the province of the specialist's classroom or its surrogate. They act as if they were temporarily returning to the role of student, rather than creating the role of co-investigator of arts and letters. If they become a public representative to a state council, they can judge projects as their own college professors might have some years ago.

Next, professional and non-professional humanists alike have different theories about what the humanities ought to do. For some the humanities are subversive. They strip away illusions, complacency, and provincialism. They are " . . . instruments of discovery and melioration, and inevitably radical politics." For others, the humanities support, rather than subvert, established things. They " . . . undergird the moral authority necessary to political order." History, for example, " . . . contains the cumulative evidence for the legitimacy of traditional economic, social, and communal institutions."[20] For still others, the humanities are a balance against the realities of a competitive, hard-nosed, tough world. Like good women, they provide a softer sphere, a respite, from masculine toil, strife, ambition, and game plans for success. This notion also appeared in *A Nation At Risk*.[21] It claims that we need the humanities, because they " . . . enrich daily life, help maintain civility, and develop a sense of community." (p. 10) Finally, for still others, the humanities are simply there as objects to be studied. We ought not to expect them to do *anything*.

A third difficulty for the state councils is the serious national quarrel about the purpose of federal funding for culture. Like a bad fairy, the quarrel was present at the birth of the National Endowment for the Humanities. In 1965, bipartisan Congressional support, which scholarly organizations such as the American Council for Learned Societies had encouraged, created both NEH and the National Endowment for the Arts under the rubric of the "National Foundation for the Arts and Humanities." NEH irrevocably joined schools, colleges, universities, and some found-ations and other philanthropies as the major sources of support for the humanities.

Some thought that NEH ought to be like NEA. Strongly rooted in various communities, NEH would seek to diffuse the experience of the humanities. In brief, it would be extensive. The state councils, like other public programs, embodied this vision. In 1981, perhaps one-half of NEH's budget went to public programs. However, others thought that NEH ought to be like the National Science Foundation. Strongly rooted in the academy, it would push at the borders of knowledge. In brief, it would be intensive. The tension between the two visions of NEH often reductively appeared, and consistently appears, as a series of quarrels between two polarities: between "excellence" and "equity," or between the intrinsic "merit" of various proposals and the "representation" of the experiences and perspectives of sectarian constituencies. Unfortunately, commentators who cannot escape from binary thinking often unfairly castigate scholarship about and for everyday life as "equity" programming, more attentive to the needs of thosse constituencies than genuine research.[22]

One difficulty with these difficulties is that they unnecessarily weaken the humanities about, for, and within everyday life. In theory, professional humanists ought to be able to speak outside of the sanctuary of the classrooms of higher education, and the academy ought to be able to praise them for it. To earn a Ph.D., or to grant a Ph.D. ought not to doom one to a monogamous form of teaching, or learning. Nor should people believe that only the credential of a Ph.D. renders one fit for discourse about the humanities. Does one need to be an M.D. to care about healing?

A J.D. to care about justice? An M.B.A. to care about money?

Moreover, the state councils need not rummage among and then act on but one of the several competing theories about the purpose of the humanities. Their job is to illuminate the competition itself; to reveal the choices that people have in saying what the humanities are and what they mean. Surely, in a pluralistic democracy, the idea of a one-party culture, which everyone's taxes support, is absurd. So doing, the state councils can also avoid having the trap of binary thinking snap shut on them, the trap that forces them to believe that they must stand up for "excellence" or "equity," for "merit" or for "representation." These are compatible values, which we render incompatible only because we think in terms of dualizing the world, and then divorcing the dualities from each other, rather than in terms of harmonizing and reconciling many messages and signals. Teaching and learning often begin in simple needs, and end in the revelation of simplicities, but between the beginning and the end, where most teaching and learning go on, we endure and celebrate complexities.

III

I have argued for humanistic scholarship about everyday life, and for structures that connect all the humanities to everyday life. Let me offer a final proposition: the humanities—these texts, pictures, scores, records, sounds, languages, signs— represent people in action. They show thought in action, the imagination in action, societies in action, beliefs in action, the body in action. Humanistic scholarship codifies, organizes, these representations of people in action. If we really bring the humanities into everyday life, and not just into the classroom or an occasional seminar, their calls, and our responses, might nurture several necessary capacities for action within us.

The humanities, then, can work *for* everyday life. The world is now ambiguous, hard to decipher, full of jokesters, con artists, deceivers, and self-deceivers. We have to know how to interpret it, how to think critically about it. Reading the humanities, and listening to them, can breed such a talent. To understand the humanities, one has to have the stamina and curiosity of the investigative reporter, or the detective. We need these logical, subtle skills to grasp the realities of everyday.

Our world is also as socially and culturally varied as the messages our eyes carry to our brain during a walk down an ordinary street. In the United States alone, children are born into homes that speak languages from Asia, Africa, Europe, and Latin America—as well as that amalgam of Latin, German, Celt, French, and Anglo-Saxon we call English. By 1990, the groups we now label as "minorities" may be a third of our youth. In Texas and California, nearly half of the high school graduates may be members of "minority" groups. For our humane survival, we must know what we share, and what separates us. Fortunately, the humanities show us both ourselves and the otherness of others: Krishna as well as Christ; Mencius as well as Aristotle; the beliefs of Yorubas as well as Romans; the labor of a village woman as well as that of an industrialist's wife. As flight simulators train pilots and astronauts, so the experience of the humanities, generously taught, can prepare us for sympathy with diversity.[23]

I wish to conclude as I began: with an anecdote. It concerns the humanities in everyday life. It shows how possible it is to incorporate them into that everyday life and increase our capacities for interpretation and empathy. A few months ago, I returned to the same town where the Little Waverer voted to sing "The Freedom Train." On a family errand, I found myself in the basement of a Baptist Church. A community choir was singing Bloch's "Sacred Music," in Hebrew.

To join the choir, the singers had to audition for a choirmaster on the faculty of a local community college. They respected, and needed, his specialized skills. He respected, and wanted, their enthusiasm and talent. Their rehearsal was now happening in the early evening—after the singers had put in a day as bakers, or parents, or secretaries, or sales-persons, or doctors. They were sitting on tin chairs, holding their music, wearing the clothes of ordinary Americans. Yet, that night, they were basses and altos, tenors and sopranos, singing in Hebrew, struggling and soaring. They were there because of the music, because of their common need to understand and to perform. They were, and are, the humanities in and for everyday life.

16 NANCY REAGAN WEARS A HAT: FEMINISM AND ITS CULTURAL CONSENSUS (1987)

Like every great word, "representation/s" is a stew. A scrambled menu, it serves up several meanings at once. For a representation can be an image—visual, verbal, or aural. Think of a picture of a hat. A representation can also be a narrative, a sequence of images and ideas. Think of the sentence, "Nancy Reagan wore a hat when she visited a detoxification clinic in Florida." Or, a representation can be the product of ideology, that vast scheme for showing forth the world and justifying its dealings. Think of the sentence, "Nancy Reagan, in her hat, is a proper woman." In the past twenty years, feminist thinking about representation has broken apart. This fracture is both cause and symptom of the larger collapse of a feminist cultural consensus. Some of the rights have been thematic. What is to be represented? Others have been theoretical. What is the nature of representation itself? I wish to map these rifts, especially those in the United States, and to wonder about the logic of a new cultural consensus.

In the late 1960s, feminists began to share a cultural consensus about the representation of women and gender. Few who built up that consensus were village idiots. Even without being semioticians, everyone more or less knew that the marriages between the signifier and the signified in that odd couple, the sign, were ones of convenience. Everyone more or less knew that the marriages between the sign and the referent, that hubbub out there, or somewhere, were also ones of convenience. Some survived.

I gave earlier versions of this paper at the Barnard College Scholar and the Feminist Conference, March 1986; the fourteenth annual University of Alabama Symposium on English and American Literature, October 1986; and the Seminar on Sex, Gender, and Consumerism, New York University Institute for the Humanities, October 1986. My thanks to the participants in those events for their responses, and to Elizabeth Meese, Alice Parker, and Elizabeth Helsinger for their comments. A companion essay, "Woolf's *Room*, Our Project: Feminist Criticism Today," will appear in *Frontiers of Criticism*, ed. Ralph Cohen, forthcoming.

Others were obsolete, cold, hostile, ending in separation or divorce. Everyone more or less knew that when I exclaimed, "Nancy Reagan wears a hat," it was easier for a fellow citizen of my linguistic community to understand me than for a stranger to do so. Nevertheless, the consensus offered a rough, general theory of representation that extolled the possibility of a fit between "reality" and its "description" or "image".

Such a general theory framed the five terms of the feminist cultural consensus. In brief, these terms were:

1. The dominant, and dominating, representations of women are misrepresentations. Often viciously misogynistic, such misrepresentations shoot and pop up in literature, the media, and the arts; history; philosophy; psychology and sociology; science; law; medicine; myth and religion; and everyday speech. These bad pictures of women are acts of both commission and omission. They overtly lie, fabricate, and simply erase great realities, such as the presence of women of color. One reason why misrepresentations exist is the fact that men have created and maintained them on the wholesale/holesale and retail/retale level. Having done so, men, like voyeuristic gods, like to gaze at their handiwork. Women then have a limited repertoire of responses. They can believe that they live in order to be gazed upon, in order to be an appearance, in life or in art. Femmes may arrange their chapeaus, for a walk or for a painting. At the same time, women gaze upon themselves in order to make sure they are keeping up appearances. As John Berger, the art critic, wrote in 1972, women must come to consider themselves both "the surveyor and the surveyed."[1]

2. One of the tasks of feminism—at once ethical, aesthetic, and educational—is to confront these misrepresentations. As the emotions of confrontation raced back and forth between cool disdain and hot anger, feminists were to engage in lots of activities: (a) *Exposing* the mechanisms of misrepresentation. One of the reasons for the appeal of *The Second Sex* was the power of Simone de Beauvoir's explanation of this machinery: men's desire for the Female Other. (b) *Restoring* the past, writing an accurate history of work, play, homes, arts, crafts, costumes. As the Sears Roebuck case was so painfully to prove, a new history was no mere "academic matter." Feminist historians could disagree, and a trial judge, in a court of law, could use the word of one, and not the other, in his decisions. (c) *Generating* accurate representations for the present. Replace "male" lies with women's truth. Secular feminists would rewrite the body, self, intimacy, social relationships, and history. Theological feminists would re-represent the divine, using the materials of either traditional mono-theisms or of unorthodox religions: witches, saints, spirits, or the black goddesses that Audre Lorde was to evoke in her poetry. (d) *Projecting* the

future. Through science fiction, utopias, and dystopias, feminists would render visible the invisibilities of times that might come. Samuel R. Delaney, for example, in *Stars in My Pocket Like Grains of Sand* (1984), imagines a universe of galaxies that contain about 6,200 inhabited worlds. Despite a vast competition between kinship and sign systems, some of the worlds are domains of congenial diversity. A homosexual space traveler, Marc Dyeth, is the product of a rich "nurture stream." His genetic ancestry, which includes both humans and aliens, reconciles differences.

3. The representation of women had to become far, far more diverse if it was to be real.[2] Slowly, grudgingly, a picture of woman gave way to pictures of differences among women that the body, sexuality, age, race, class, ethnicity, tribalities, and nationalities had forged. These pictures did more than provide a rich variety of experiences and narratives. Far more painfully, they revealed women dominating other women; women using women as the Other; women finding other women revolting. Moreover, agreement about feminist issues did not insure agreement about other public issues. In 1970, Lorde frankly, ruefully, sardonically, articulated that combination of unity and division. Her poem, "Who Said It Was Simple," was about a black feminist, in Nedicks, listening to the white feminists with whom she was to march talk about race. Later, in Alaska, a Tlingit woman, devoted to subsistence culture, wrote, in "Genocide," about another woman devoted to *her* ecological vision:

> Picketing the Eskimo
> Whaling Commission
> an over-fed English girl
> stands with a sign
> "Let the Whales Live."[3]

4. Feminists had a way of judging the legitimacy, accuracy, and cogency of the representations of women. Did they seem true to a woman's experience? Could a woman, would a woman, serve as a witness to their validity? If she could, the representation was acceptable; if not, not. Significantly, the title of an early, influential collection of literary essays was *The Authority of Experience: Essays in Feminist Criticism*.[4] The trust in women's experience in North American feminist writing has been as common and as pervasive as city noise. To cite but one recent example. In January of 1986, PEN held an international congress in New York City on the theme of "The Writer and the State." The PEN president was that vortex of brilliance, adrenaline, and daffiness: Norman Mailer, never a man to duck out of his masculinity. During the course of the Congress, women protested the lack of women on its panels: only 2 of 24 panelists on a Monday; 6 of 28 panelists on a Tuesday. A seasoned group, the protestors

included Margaret Atwood, Betty Friedan, Elizabeth Janeway, Cynthia Macdonald, and Grace Paley. Reporting on the event, Miriam Schneir commented: "There is no substitute for experience, and most of us had gone through all-too-similar experiences, all-too-many times before."[5]

Inseparable from such powerful strains in American culture as Protestantism and pragmatism, this term of feminism's cultural consensus praised the narratives of the personal event (the diary, letters, auto-biography, self-portraiture, confession, biography) in writing, filmmaking, and art. Experience generated more than art; it was a source of political engagement as well. By 1972, the "roots of gender politics" were planted. Both men and women were to water them, but experience meant that those roots were stronger for women than for men. Ethel Klein, the political scientist, has concluded: "For women, feminism is part of their personal identity or consciousness. For men, feminism is an abstract issue of rights and obligations. Since both men and women come to feminism from different paths—personal experience in one case and ideology in the other—feminist views are likely to have a greater influence on women's political views than on men's."[6]

5. As feminists were to insist on the connections between the private and the public, the domestic and the political, the reproductive and the productive, so they were to see the buzzing inseparability of culture and politics. To be sure, the powerful tended to get the culture they wanted. A Mailer was the president of PEN. However, powerlessness need not be synonymous with passivity. The powerless have a culture of resistance, which works through code; through the direct statement of polemic; and through the indirection of irony and parody. An "Unofficial White House Photograph," which feminists like to send each other, shows Nancy and Ronald Reagan standing in front of a window with thick, blue curtains. Facing the camera directly, the First Couple smiles eagerly, ingratiatingly. Beyond the window looms the Washington Monument, a pointed phallic column. However, the column looks foggy, misty. Nancy's head (hatless) is placed on Ronnie's torso, clad in a business suit. Ronnie's head (hatless) is placed on Nancy's body, in beruffled blouse and skirt. Decapitation and transposition drain gender of their power—as a guillotine drains a head of blood and oxygen.

Happily, cultural work can change politics, particularly political attitudes, even if that change seems marginal and unpredictable. A recent study found that college students in an introductory course in Women's and Men's Studies (in California) "scored . . . lower in sexist attitudes towards woman . . . at the end of the course" in comparison to a control group and in comparison to their own sexism at the beginning of the semester.[7] The victory may seem small, but no victory is to small to dismiss.

In the late 1960s, United States feminists were developing a political as well as a cultural consensus. The political definition of "representation" differs from its cultural one. In politics, the word "representation" tends to mean not a picture of the world but the active presence of a person who can legitimately draw a picture of the world of one group of constituents for other groups. Such a "representative" then speaks for his or her constituency and acts on its behalf. Despite this wee semantic shift, the terms of the political consensus were often similar in kind to those of the cultural consensus. First, feminists believed in the possibility of just representations of "reality," even though political theory since Aristotle and political practice since Adam had unjustly misrepresented women through mistreatment and exclusion. Moreover, women could and should be political participants. So doing, they could and should represent themselves and others. A woman could cast exemplary and surrogate votes. Finally, there was a cluster of women's issues that politics had to handle; that politics had to get a handle on. Feminism spoke for a set of legitimate political concerns. The National Women's Conferences, held in Houston in November, 1977, articulated them. Months of raw politicking preceded the conference, between social conservatives and feminists and among feminists. Only that politicking wrote a statement in support of women's studies. Only that politicking produced feminist unity in support of lesbianism. Still, the pressure cooker of the conference did end with an agenda for feminist politics.[8] Moreover, the state, the federal government, supported the Conference. Washington and Houston served each other.

Like a contract, a consensus manages agreements. Of course, any consensus leaves some opinions out. The United States feminist political consensus omitted or feared certain ideological stances: Marxism and socialism, those demons of American politics; anarchism; the wilder poetries of radical cultural feminism, including the wimmyn's lyrics of lesbian separatism; and social conservatism, the only stance rigidly opposed to feminism. In Houston, *its* few believers in some state delegations stolidly refused to support even the blandest measures, such as equal access to credit. Since these excluded nonmiddles were mutually contradictory, they could not reach, or even imagine, an oppositional consensus, an agreement among outsiders. Moreover, even though the feminist political consensus did not fully incorporate every strain of feminism, such as the intellectually vigorous socialist feminism, most strains stayed alive. As a result, feminist strategies were mutually inconsistent. No single representation of feminism could emerge. Contrast two images of feminists who care about peace. One is of the Committee on National Security. Formed in 1982, it has a large advisory board of prominent women. It organizes conferences on defense issues, with female and male speakers, in hotels in Washington, D.C. The second is of a demonstration in March, 1980. A group, the "Spinsters," weaves a symbolic web, "with thousands of yards of colored yarns, threads and strings," around the Vermont Yankee Nuclear Power Plant in Vernon, Vermont.[9] Media images of feminism boiled up the representational pot even more prettily.

The feminist cultural consensus was more spacious, more receptive to Marxism, socialism, and lesbianism, than the political consensus. For the shapers of the cultural consensus were more aloof from the inhibitions of electoral politics, freer from its discipline. However, its looseness helped to make the cultural consensus more vulnerable to centrifugal flights. During the 1970s, forces, two explicitly feminist, pulled away from each other: (1) revivified feminist interest in the specifically female, which lesbian separatists expressed most radically; (2) rambunctious right-wing conservatism; (3) neoconservatism (the N-Cs); (4) neoliberalism (the N-Ls); and (5) in the mid- and late 1970s, feminist postmodernism, which distrusted the concepts of a center and of a monolithic consensus themselves.

Without any planning, the first four forces agreed with each other and the disappearing consensus about the relationship of representation to reality. Variously, each burnished the idea of the "maternal" as well. Motherhood was a natural gift; a source of identity; a subject; a literally vital social role. Together, then, these four forces endorsed a doubled set of ancient beliefs: in the mimetic power of languages to reproduce the world and in the mimetic power of the female to reproduce the species. The appeal of these beliefs was strong enough to attract groups whose ideology and style was otherwise fervently different. For some, Nancy Reagan was a glamorous heroine; for others, an expensively clad creep.

The fifth challenge, feminist postmodernism, had a sweeping theoretical interest in the presence and/or absence of the maternal in phallocentric discourse. However, postmodernism was skeptical about the possibility of any reality beyond the discourse of representation. Here the fun began. Among the provocative critics of the theory that representations could give us a picture of reality, could be "realistic," were feminist film critics and filmmakers. They subverted the belief that film documentaries could ever tell us the truth (whatever *that* word meant) about women, even if feminists directed those documentaries. For the very promise of the documentary— that it was a window on reality, that it showed us "real people"—was a lie. The job of the filmmaker, then, was to produce avant-garde films that would reveal both the lies of the patriarchy and of the realistic, representational genres that both patriarchs and women had practiced.[10]

Let me foreground, in turn, each of these five forces:

1. The feminist cultural consensus had tended to play down sex and gender differences, naturalized binary oppositions between female and male. Ethically, the consensus asked its practitioners to stop playing them

out. The recognition of the amazing maze of differences among women, of the endless diversity of women's experience as historical agent and as signifier, helped to undermine the idea of a single and singular femaleness. If the woman reader was not the English daughter of the British empire, Jane Eyre was far less apt to be the Exemplary Female Subject.

However, that wilder poetry of radical cultural feminism, spinning away in be/witching campsites at the margins of the consensus, sang of the female. Such music could appeal to many lesbian and heterosexual woman alike. For the lesbian, the "female" was an erotic and psychological necessity; for the heterosexual woman, the "female" was a psychological core that might sustain her in a patriarchal society that constantly threatened to ream out real women. The most responsible of the theoreticians of the female insisted that a political will accompany sexual and psychological freedom. In 1977, in "Natural Resources," Adrienne Rich rewrote one of her earlier poems, "Diving into the Wreck." Mourning the loss of the dream of man as brother; attacking the reality of man as killer, as "blood-compelled exemplar"; celebrating women and their capacity to transform scraps into patchwork, Rich ends:

> I have cast my lot with those
> who age after age, perversely,
> with no extraordinary power,
> reconstitute the world.[11]

A focus on *women as women* spread out luxuriously. It prepared the nonfeminist public for Carol Gilligan's *In A Different Voice* in 1982. After Gerda Lerner and her adaptations of Mary Beard (*Black Women in White America*, 1972; *The Female Experience*, 1977); after Alice Walker ("In Search of Our Mothers' Gardens," 1974), people could ask about a women's historical tradition. After Jean Baker Miller (*Toward a New Psychology of Women*, 1976), people could ask if women had not developed a different, and precious, set of values. After Jessie Bernard (*The Future of Motherhood*, 1975), Adrienne Rich (*Of Women Born*, 1976), or Nancy Chodorow (*The Reproduction of Mothering*, 1978), people could ask about the place and representation of the mother. They helped to supplement the obsession of psychoanalysis with fathers and sons with an interest in mothers and daughters; Laius and Oedipus with Demeter and Persephone.[12] After Hélène Cixous, Julia Kristeva, Luce Irigaray and other French writers, in their limited United States translations, people could ask about a female language, that notable "écriture féminine."

French theory helped, too, to conjoin the female with pleasure. It replaced the image of the well-dressed lady with that of the laughing Medusa of Cixous. A woman no longer hid her hair beneath her hat and clothes. Her locks flowed out, like stars strewn across the sky. A woman's lips were no longer pinned shut. They were open; the cries that poured forth were joyous, bliss-ridden. However, in her United States versions, Cixous could be tricky. For she seemed to inscribe two possibilities, two promises: a "female" language, from the body, that only women might write, in the white ink of the mother's milk, and a "feminine" language, from a place in the symbolic contract, that both men and women might exude.

2. Right-wing conservatism was inseparable from the career of Phyllis Shlafley. Women were wives and mothers; men were their husbands and benign rulers. In 1972, she formed STOP-ERA, one of several groups like Happiness of Motherhood Eternal (HOME) or Humanitarians Opposed To Degrading Our Girls (HOTDOG). Right-wing conservatism was potent because it could summon up, separately or together, a number of forces. It could call on the institutional power and psychological authority of monotheistic religions, particularly of Christianity. Conservative Christianity proclaimed both that the family man's word was law and that the Word was Law. Reassuringly connecting language and moral absolutes, it provided an iron, but never ironic, stability. Despite the solace that feminist theology provided to many women, the pervasive secularism of the feminist cultural consensus prevented it from sufficiently offering that theology as a counter-practice, and counterweight, to patriarchal beliefs. Right-wing conservatism could also appeal to fears: to the fears of women that they would be vulnerable and helpless if men did not protect them economically; to the fears of men that they would be vulnerable and helpless if women did not submit to them; and to the fears of both men and women that the world would be wholly cruel, wholly pitiless, wholly formless, if it had neither havening homes nor nurturing mother figures. Finally, right-wing conservatism benefited from defense mechanisms against any unconventional or impermissible sexual desires, including a severing of femininity and maternity.

3. In 1972, too, Midge Decter published a feisty, yet snivelling, little polemic: *The New Chastity and Other Arguments Against Women's Liberation*, a founding text of neoconservative thinking about women (the N-Cs). Decter likes some women. She dedicates her book to her mother, "who made being a woman seem such a worthy adventure"; to Sherry, who made the best jokes; and to Jacqueline, "who scatters blessings," an unwitting prophet of postmodernism. For Decter, these women are all that feminists are not: familial; happy and cheerful; giving and generous. *The New Chastity* begins with a sarcastic paraphrase of *The Feminine Mystique*. Intellectually, Decter's feminists, symptoms of the parlous condition of the American mind, refuse to see several truths: the truth that nature wants women to be heterosexual mothers; the truth that sex is harder for men than for women; the truth that women already have equality and justice; the truth that marriage is not misery and "shitwork," but women's desire.

Decter states firmly, "the plain unvarnished fact is that every woman wants to marry."[13] Emotionally, Decter's feminists are timid boobies, fearful of the struggle that public success entails, self-pitying and self-hating. Feminists are "little girls." Thank no heavens for little girls.

Decter has been the Grand Mummy for a corps of younger female N-Cs. More urban and urbane than right-wing conservatives, Decter's Daughters are less dependent on the Bible as a sacred text. They are also more accepting of women in the public labor force and in intellectual circles. Decter's Daughters publish in *Public Interest*, *Commentary*, and *The New Criterion*. There, they display three interlocking disagreements with feminists. First, these N-Cs trust the market far more than feminism usually does. They distrust any shackling of the market's invisible hand, a shackling that they believe advocates of comparable worth dangerously desire. As a result, N-Cs attribute women's economic position to a historical, and rational, alliance between market forces and women's choices, not to discriminatory practices. Second, NC-s are suspicious of any analysis that speaks of the "patriarchy," "male hegemony," "male dominance," or "gender inequity." Often bland and casual about men's power over women, the N-Cs find feminism grim and paranoid about the social relations of the sexes. Finally, the N-Cs believe that the word "family" applies only to those clusters of intimacy that blood or law creates. Far less cordial to different forms of the family and of intimacy than the feminist cultural consensus was, N-Cs valorize bourgeois family forms and their construction of the maternal role.

Vigorously, Decter's Daughters scrub away at Decter's Feminists. In an article about comparative worth, Rachel Flick admits that feminists have at last recognized that sexual differences do exist. But now they want the market to be "nice," to conform to feminine values. They are incapable of accepting the reality that the market has to be "efficient," to act on masculine values.[14] In a review of an anthology of essays of feminist criticism by Elaine Showalter, Carol Iannone excoriates her subject. Feminists, obsessed with women's weakness, have "an extraordinarily withered view of feminine history." They are too perverse even to realize that literature can transcend "the ordinary life of their times" and address that Mr. Chips of metaphysics, "universal truths." Feminists violate "common sense and scholarly standards." Why, then, have their representations of women become a part of the academy? Because weak-kneed, weak-willed administrators have "capitulated" to feminist critics. In effect, feminist critics have, yes, castrated our educators.[15]

4. In 1983, Judith Stacey incisively isolated a complicated class of ideas that she called "conservative feminism."[16] She located its origins in the late 1970s in the work of Alice Rossi, Betty Friedan, and Jean Bethke Elshtain. Although Stacey praised "conservative feminism" for forcing feminists to

think again about intimacy, equality, child development, and hetero-sexuality, she found the turn towards timidity dangerous. For "conservative feminism" repudiates the sexual politics of the 1960s and 1970s that called for the reconstruction of both sex and gender. Instead, "conservative feminism" celebrates the family and biological motherhood. It scolds feminists for struggling against male domination and deflecting our attention from other questions.

Neo-liberal thinkers about women (the N-Ls) are the partners and descendants of such conservative feminists. The N-Ls attempt to mediate among all feminists, rightwing conservatives, and the N-Cs. Frightened by the difficulties of the feminist political consensus, such as the 1982 defeat of the ERA, the N-Ls position themselves in what they hope will be a new political center. Unlike the N-Cs, the N-Ls do not sneer at feminism. Instead, their responses are ambivalent. On the one hand, the N-Ls can call themselves feminists; can associate themselves with the movement; can announce feminist credentials. They are more supportive of abortion rights than right-wing or neoconservatives. I have more in common with them than I would with a Decter Daughter. On the other hand, the N-Ls disapprove of much of the movement to which they give some loyalty. Although they dislike right-wing conservatism, the N-Ls tend to attribute its rise, in part, to the strategic errors of feminism.

The N-Ls now have at least two tactics for distancing themselves. First, they proclaim their sorrow that feminism has gone astray. If women of color had to correct an obvious racism in the feminist cultural and political consensus, the N-Ls point to a far less obvious indifference to ordinary women, especially to heterosexual mothers. If women of color want feminism to be more progressive, the N-Ls want it to be more "realistic" about the "average woman's" daily life. This means realizing that the average woman (that sturdy fiction) wants to belong to a "conventional" family (another sturdy fiction)—even if she is a part of the public labor force. To help her, the N-Ls call for "protective legislation" for mothers and (heterosexual) families. Presenting themselves as the friend of the married working girl, the N-Ls, who lack a rigorous analysis of race and class, reconstitute a white middle-class ideology of domestic life.

The second N-L strategy is to ignore much of what feminism has actually done. Seeking both originality and the publicity that feeds on originality, the N-Ls erase the complexities and accomplishments of the movement they half-embrace. They act as if they were among the first to discover the values of pay equity, or decent child-care policies, or that old war horse, flexi-time. Calling for realism, the N-Ls deal in half-truths.[17]

5. In 1974, Juliet Mitchell, in *Psychoanalysis and Feminism*, signaled the redemption of psychoanalysis as, at the very least, a tool for the exploration of the unconscious and as an explanation of the construction of

subjectivity and a subject's sense of sex and gender. Could we, for example, see Nancy Reagan, in her hat, as a phallic mother? During the 1970s, too, European thinking about ideology, language, and interpretation began to intersect with strains of United States feminist theorizing. It became a matter for meaning that Roland Barthes had published "The Death of the Author" and Mary Ellmann *Thinking About Women* in the same year (1968). In 1979, a Barnard College Scholar and the Feminist Conference, "The Future of Difference," inventively presented this swirling confluence of revisionary psychoanalysis, European post-structuralism, and feminism: feminist postmodernism.

Though more radically than the consensus, feminist postmodernism doubted the "naturalness" of any sex differences. Sex and gender were a linguistic affair. In 1970s, feminists seriously, if inadequately, began the labor of confronting a triad of differences: those that race, class, and gender had manufactured on history's assembly line of pain. Feminist postmodernism supplemented this essential work by asking what might be positively charged about differences, at least of perspective; what might be invigorating about rifts, at least in the landscapes of thought. Though less insistently than the consensus, often alarmingly so, feminist postmodernism asked what politics its theories might entail. If a particular theory seemed persuasive, what practice would it demand? In brief, what might an idea mean for feminism? For an end to social, cultural, psychological, and sexual structures of domination?[18]

Despite these mutualities, the feminist postmodernists stirred and troubled the feminist cultural consensus. Adding to the discomfort were the difficulties of the feminist political consensus: the vitriol and viciousness of anti-abortion forces; the 1980 loss of the support of the presidency; the defeat of the Equal Rights Amendment; the inability to stop the obscene increase in the pauperization of women and children. To a member of the feminist cultural consensus, postmodernists liked really strange, far-out cultural events. They preferred Gertrude Stein to Charlotte Brontë, Mary Kelly to Georgia O'Keeffe. In a feedback loop with this aesthetic preference were the questions that postmodernists were asking about representational codes; their often abstract interrogations of signifying practices as the matrix of meaning and subjecthood; and their fascinated gaze, at once unblinking and ironically winking, at that old boy network; the phallus. Describing her project, Lisa Tickner writes:

> It was psychoanalysis that permitted an understanding of the psycho-social constructions of sexual differences in the conscious/unconscious subject. The result was a shift in emphasis from equal rights struggles in the sexual division of labor and a cultural feminism founded on the reevaluation of an existing biological or social femininity to a recognition of the processes of sexual *differentiation*, the instability of gender positions, and the hopelessness of

excavating a free or original femininity beneath the layers of patriarchal oppression.[19]

The theory that representational machineries were reality's synonyms, not a window (often cracked) onto reality, eroded the immediate security of another lovely gift to Western humanism: the belief in a conscious self that generates texts, meaning, and a substantial identity; a notion that a recent Koren cartoon wistfully parodies. The scene is a birthday party. Like all of Koren's people, the partygoers have pop eyes, armadillo noses, and spiky hair (except for men going bald). Balloons litter the ceiling, presents the floor. Around a table sit eight little girls, some in paper hats, staring at a happy Birthday Girl and her cake with six candles. Smiling watchfully and sweetly, Mother holds the back of Birthday Girl's chair. Holding a tray full of glasses and bowls of ice cream, Dad stands at attention. Ah, sighs the Birthday Princess, "I'm about to experience the totality of who I am!"[20]

Poor Birthday Princess! For what if her identity were not such a piece of cake? What if Western humanistic notions of the self were a snaring delusion? What if we are inextricably caught under the net of our own language, our own concepts? What if we thrash within the "hermeneutic circle?" As a result, we may never be aware enough of our own perspectives to use them to interpret anything reliably. Moreover, what if the unconscious writes our scripts? If so, is it not vain and silly to think that we know what the "self" is? And why do we insist on an integrated self that is the center of the world? What if we are fragmented, decentered? Can we not be postmodern enough to accept, even to enjoy, this?

One example of the move from the feminist cultural consensus to postmodernism: In Western thought, the metaphor of the "cave" in Plato's *Republic* (book 7) is an influential trope for the ascent to reason. In the cave, we see only shadows. Freed from the prison of the cave, we can stagger outside and see the sun of truth. However, an alternative myth of the cave also exists, that of the crevice in which the Cumaean Sybil dwells and exhales prophetic speech.

In the Romantic period, in 1818, Mary Shelley visited Italy with Percy Shelley. They visited Naples and the landscape of the Sybil. In 1826, a widow, Mary Shelley wrote her novel, *The Last Man*. In an introduction, her narrator elaborates on that autobiographical fact. She tells of going to Naples in 1818 on a beautiful December day with a companion. They enter the Sybil's cave. They go deeper and deeper until they grope their way into a room with a stone bench. Its floor is strewn with leaves and bits of bark. The narrator's companion sees that writing, ancient and modern, covers them. From time to time, the two return to the cave to read the inscriptions. After her companion's death, the narrator forms her story from those inscriptions. She adds to, adapts, and translates them.[21]

Next, in the New Feminist period, in 1979, the critics Sandra M. Gilbert and Susan Gubar took on the metaphor of the cave. Powerful shapers of the feminist cultural consensus, they saw the cave as a representation of women in patriarchy. Her "cave-shaped anatomy is her destiny." However, women can alter that destiny. Sadly, Mary Shelley only partly realizes the power that might have been hers. Anxious about entering culture, she lets her male companion identify the writing on the leaves. Yet, to her glory, she stitches together the "dismembered, dis-remembered, disintegrated" pieces of her "precursor's art."[22]

Then, in 1985, Toril Moi approached Gilbert and Gubar, among others. Moi is a smart, hard-edged intellect. Why, she asks sardonically, do Gilbert and Gubar insist that the woman artist *gather up* the Sibyl's leaves? Why do they want a "whole text"? An organic representation? Is this, ironically, not a phallic desire? Why can't Gilbert and Gubar approve of disconnections? The post-structuralist adds, "Parallel to the wholeness of the text is the wholeness of the woman's self: the integrated humanist individual is the essence of all creativity. A fragmented conception of self or consciousness would seem to Gilbert and Gubar the same as a sick or diseased self."[2] Heel, feminist physicians, and heal thyselves.

The feminist cultural consensus, that contract about opinions, is beyond restoration. Its practitioners are too numerous, too dissimilar in situation, for one agreement to accommodate all the theories, ideas, and perceptions by and about women in the postmodern world. The question is not how to paste and staple a consensus together again but rather how to live culturally and politically with fragmentation. Happily, United States public opinion routinely, if casually, supports feminist issues. For example, a recent profile of college undergraduates claimed that about 92 % presented themselves as liberal, middle of the road, or only moderately conservative. Over 75 % thought a woman should have "freedom of choice" about abortion. A majority of men, about 60 %, but a minority of women, 40 %, thought that "pornographic materials should be legally available to adults." Such agreement may give feminists a chance, despite right-wing and neoconservative rantings, despite neoliberal pressures, to think things through. (Sadly, the number of undergraduates who wanted to go on to graduate or professional education in women's studies, like the number who wished to do so in botany, geography, or the foundations of education, was too small to be measured.)[24]

At and in this moment, two responses to fragmentation are unacceptable. The first is to imitate the great male modernists and lament fragmentation; to speak, as Hardy did, of the "ache of modernism"; to grieve, as Yeats did, that "the center will not hold"; to picture, as Eliot did, the world as a wasteland, as heaps of filthy shards, chips with neither fish nor mister. The second unacceptable response is to howl, not at the fathers, but at the daughters; to accuse the feminist postmodernists of burrowing up to male intellectual masters, of betraying feminist political commitments, of writing obscurely, of being ungrateful.

For the feminist postmodernists have gifts for the parties that remain after the ripping apart of the feminist cultural consensus. Obviously, postmodern writing urgently asks for sophisticated new ways of thinking about the subject and her society. As obviously, it breaks open spaces within cultures, including feminist cultures. The winds that blow through these spaces dash at conformity; repetitions of outworn ideas; jejune, if seemingly satisfactory, assumptions about the reflectiveness of our representations of the world; presumptions about the value of monolithic generalizations about the female; and assumptions that "feminism" is a stronger word than "feminisms."

A keener postmodern sensibility might have helped feminists avoid some of the dug-in ideas in two contemporary political and cultural fights. Their public settings have been legislatures and courts. There lawmakers and lawgivers get to choose among representations of women that competing groups of feminists offer. For the most part, these legislators, judges, and juries are neither accountable to nor much interested in feminism. The more serious, and continuing, struggle has been over pornography and over laws that would enable women to declare a pornographic image a violation of her civil rights. In this, I have opposed such laws and supported the Feminist Anti-Censorship Task Force (FACT). I signed on to the 8 April 1985 "Amici Curiae" brief in the Indianapolis case (*American Booksellers Association, Inc.* v. *William H. Hudnut III*).[25] Like other FACTionalists, I have abhorred both the representations of violence against women and a struggle within feminism about pornography that has distracted our attention from the issues of "real equality, real power—strengthened civil rights legislation, affirmative action to achieve economic parity, improved education, access to public office, better services for victims of violence and abuse."[26]

In part, this feminist disagreement has been about the nature of the representation of female sexuality. Should feminists picture women's bodies only as exploited, at risk, which they are, or should feminists "put forward a politics that resists deprivation and supports pleasure"?[27] Simultaneously, are women to be pictured as wholly exploitable, delicate, wholly at danger, or are they capable of resistance and strength? In part, the struggle has been about the relationship of the state to the production of images. When can the state, whether an individual citizen sets it in motion or not, control that production? In part, the struggle has been about the ways in which we read, in which we interpret imagery. Can the law spot a representation of "sexual subordination"? Can one image be extracted from a narrative as a whole? A tag from a syntagmatic process? In part, the disagreement has concerned the relationship of images to behavior and about the ability of a positivist social science to graph that relationship? Does an image directly influence behavior? If so, how? Or, as the "Amici Curiae" brief stated, correctly:

"Sexual imagery is not so simple to assess. In the sexual realm, perhaps more so than any other, messages and their impact on the viewer or reader are often multiple, contradictory, layered and highly contextual."[28]

Finally, in part, the struggle has been about the ability of one woman to speak for all women; for one woman to become a common voice; for the deep structure of one throat. On January 2, 1986, Andrea Dworkin testified at the New York City Hearings of the Attorney General's Commission on Pornography. Like Catharine A. MacKinnon, Dworkin has defined and passionately supported anti-pornography legislation. Dworkin's speech was well-crafted and rhetorically shrewd. Identifying herself with all women; picturing women as tortured and men as torturers and rapists, she summoned the Commission to listen to women, to believe them, and to relieve them of their gags and bonds. She was, as well, a voice for other victims who could not be heard.[29] Other commissioners, accepting the truth of that self-representation, then expressed a debt to her for inspiring them to battle, as if her voice, at once individual and collective, had caused them to march out, like French soldiers behind St. Joan.

My second case is the Ginny Foat trial. Let me admit that I wrote a skeptical review of Never Guilty, Never Free, her autobiography.[30] Born into an Italian, working-class family, Foat ultimately became president of California NOW. In 1983, she was charged with murder. Apparently, another NOW member helped to arouse the charging legal authorities. The only evidence was the "word" of a brutal, alcoholic exhusband, Jack Sidote. Reasonably, a jury found her innocent. For feminists, the Foat case involved a survivability of two Utopian representations of women: that they are essentially innocent, essentially good, and that they are, like the women in violent pornography, essentially victims, an image that the image of innocence makes logically necessary.

In the media, in court, and in her autobiography, Foat incorporates these representations into her self-dramatization. Submerging her will, willfulness, and strength, she asks other feminists to believe her because life and Sidote have battered her. Yet, the gaps in her narrative are holes into which doubt must flow. Nevertheless, like Dworkin, she claims the right to speak for all women. The jurors who freed her apparently did so, not because she had suffered under patriarchy, but because they found "reasonable doubt" about her guilt, a patriarchal legal standard. Yet, after her trial, Foat declared the verdict a victory for all women. "Well," a female juror said, "I didn't elect her to speak for me."[31]

Unfortunately, feminism lacks any organization (a sweetly old-fashioned word) within which to test, refine, and revise the ideas of feminist post-modernisms. Instead, feminism has a number of cultural committees, organizations, caucusses, and disciplines. In the same way, although feminisms together represent a national movement, they have no national party. A consensus for political action emerges haphazardly. We badly need a group that would call together, but not dictate to, members of these committees, organizations, caucusses, and disciplines. I am aware of at least three weaknesses in such a proposal: the utopianism of my faith in the ability of people to deal with the mutual suspicions that swirl around any meeting room, any gymnasium and symposium, be it spatial or electronic; next, the inadequacy of any cultural theory that fails to ask how it might influence television, the most powerful machinery of representation in the West; and finally, the limits of any cultural theory that has no accompanying social theory, no real connections between culture and society. Weak though it is, my proposal imagines how players (of all genders) might juxtapose points of view to lace together new, perpetually provisional feminist cultural treaties.

As Donna Haraway suggests, such a group would be chary of any theory of a group's essential unity. Instead of a consensus, it would set up coalitions. It would search for affinities, not for a common identity.[32] Equally chary of a dominant discourse, such a group would trust oppositional viewpoints, like those of women of color. Adapting the legacy of the postmodernist Virginia Woolf of *Three Guineas* and her Society of Outsiders, Haraway fictionalizes a Sister Outsider. With her other sisters, she speaks an "infidel heteroglossia."[33] Given its multiplicity of oppositional voices, such a group would, I suggest, have to develop an ethics of correction; an ethics that delights, not in the imposition of "right," but in charity of response, clarity of speech, and self-consciousness about principle and practices.

With such an ethics, my group might dwell within theoretical questions that affect our daily lives, as quantum waves do space. If we cannot represent women as total victims, how do we represent pain without blaming the victim? If postmodernism has erased the humanistic picture of the coherent, individual self, what will justify an ethics of respect for the individual person? Without believing in totalities again, can we have communal ties other than a joy in opposition? Can an ethics of correction permit both feminists and right-wing conservatives to speak together? The last such experiment, between some radical feminists and some social conservatives, did end up with that antipornography legislation.

Despite that coalition, feminists might have a special aptitude for such an "infidel heteroglossia." This is not because of some "female" talent for balancing marginality and affiliation, but because of the moral and strategic necessities that have forced feminists to practice what I call "herterogeneity."

Feminists have begun with the obvious acknowledgment of some sexual difference between female and male, of some difference between the penis and the vagina. They have recognized gender differences between feminine and masculine.[34] However, with the challenges of feminist postmodernism, they have begun to graph how pervasively the structures of discourse have boxed up sexual difference and jockeyed to create gender difference. Because, too, feminists are dwelling with differences among women, among the many interpretations of "her," they have instructed themselves in living among differences, among many genes and genera. Such lessons have warned feminists of both monolithic and dualistic thinking; of too great a trust in the article "the" and the conjunctions "either" and "or." Herterogeneous thinking prefers the article "a" and the conjunctions "both/and."

The need even to imagine such a conference center for the practice of a new feminist cultural treaty, of herterogeneity, marks a period in which few boundaries, as they dissolve, can be full stops. The turmoil over the older feminist cultural consensus is a synecdoche as well for a larger cultural moment in which old, often dear borders are going, going, but not quite gone. Indeed, the radical conservatives, the N-Cs, and, to a degree, the N-Ls, are hammering in supports for shaky fence posts and stakes. Harsh conflicts about the "appropriate" representations of gender, that boundary between female and male, abound. A county in Tennessee adopts a first-grade textbook. It shows a girl named Pat and a boy named Jim reading *and* cooking raisin pudding, ham, and tomato on toast. Jim cooks before Pat, earlier than Pat *and* in front of Pat. Appalled, Robert B. Mozert, Jr. and his colleagues in COBS (Citizens Organized for Better Schools) sue the schools. The image of Jim cooking before Pat shows first-graders an absence of God-given roles for the two sexes. Mozert, Jr. and COBS feel the schools are promoting a religion: secular humanism. So doing, they are running amok and amuck.[35]

Contradictions within representations of gender also exert themselves. I call the appearance of such contradictions the "Cagney and Lacey" syndrome. In the TV show, Cagney and Lacey are friends. They have earned jobs in that citadel of masculinity, the police station. However, both women are white. Moreover, they work among men. Other than Cagney and Lacey, the show has very few women.[36] Cagney is single; Lacey is married. Though coupled at work, they practice marginal and traditional alternatives after work.[37]

As the mass media seek to contain contradictions, feminists both profit from and deconstruct them. What, a feminist might ask, would Cagney and Lacey be like if they were active lesbians? If only one of them were an active lesbian? What if she were to leave the precinct and drop by what was once the Duchess Bar in Sheridan Square in New York for a beer or a soda? However, simply because such analytic feminist activity can happen, it neither exempts feminisms, nor renders them immune, from internalizing the contradictions that pulsate around us. Nor does such explosive activity keep feminists like me from having to manage still another contradiction: believing in the worth of the hurlyburly competitive marketplace of ideas even while calling for representative groupings and troopings that would soothe that competition through a conversation that would button up the homicidal thrusts of competition.

Eventually, though, our conversations must end in action; our remonstrations, no matter how deliciously in parts and partial, in demonstrations, and not simply the demonstrations of logical proof. Finally, we need a feminist switching point when we must move from cultural explorations to explicit political practice. Our tone might become less ironic, less allusive, less playful. It might become blunter, angrier. We might have to conjoin our awareness of the construction of "history" and ideology with a deed. I believe that we reach such a switching point when we confront daily survival issues for women and children, for almost any woman, and certainly for any child. Survival issues are food, water, shelter, health, education, and protection from any domestic or state violence. In *The Brothers Karamazov*, Ivan declares that he cannot believe in God because he sees children being beaten on earth; because he has watched parents force a 5-year-old girl to eat shit. Both cultural and political feminism began in the refusal to acept women's pain, the sound of "hurt" in "herterogeneity." Now, a refashioned cultural and political feminist agreement might see a switching point between speech and act in the arduous toil for survival of women and children.

Would Nancy Reagan doff her hat in the direction of this representation of rectitude?

Notes

Introduction

1. Poem 258, *The Poems of Emily Dickinson*, Vol. I, ed. Thomas H. Johnson (Cambridge: Belknap Press of Harvard University Press, 1951, 1955, 4th printing 1968), p. 185.

2. Maurice Sendak, *Where the Wild Things Are* (New York: Harper and Row, Publishers, 1963), unpaginated.

3. Matthew Arnold, "On the Modern Element in Literature," *On The Classical Tradition*, ed. R.H. Super, *The Complete Prose Works of Matthew Arnold*, I (Ann Arbor, Michigan: University of Michigan Press, 1960), p. 20.

4. Many groups have sustained me, among them the friends of feminism at Barnard College; my colleagues at Rutgers University; the University of Chicago Press and my co-editors at *Signs: Journal of Women in Culture and Society*, where I served as founding editor from 1974–80; *Ms. Magazine*; the New York Council for the Humanities; and various programs for studying women and gender.

5. This volume does not include any of the editorials from *Signs*, one of which first used the phrase "new scholarship about women," nor any of the on-going reports about women's studies that I issue periodically. Too many of them seemed like portraits of a particular moment in time. This book also excludes essays and reviews about single figures (e.g. Margaret Atwood, Joan Didion, Charles Olsen, John Sayles) if they seemed too focussed on that figure or one aspect of that figure; much of my more journalistic or more bureaucratic work; some material over which newer writing has poured dust; and my studies of Gertrude Stein, which will appear in a book from the University of Chicago Press.

6. The second essay, "'Thy Neighbor's Wife'," is also marred. Since 1971, the scholarship about my subject, the relationship of black movements and women's movements, has refined my conclusions. My language, which frequently sets up a binary opposition between "blacks" and "women," can read as if all blacks were men, all women white. So doing, it leaves out black women. Bell Hooks, *Ain't I A Woman: Black Women and Feminism* (Boston: South End Press, 1981), pp. 139, 143–45, corrects me. Finally, I use the term "feminism" ahistorically when I apply it to the 19th century. "Feminism" did not become part of our political and cultural vocabularies until the 20th century, as Nancy Cott proves in *The Grounding of Modern Feminism* (New Haven and London: Yale University Press, 1987).

7. *The Poems of Gerard Manley Hopkins*, 4th ed., ed. by W.H. Gardner and N.H. MacKenzie (London: Oxford University Press, 1967), p. 98.

1. BLACK CULTURE/WHITE TEACHER

1. Bone is an erudite, sympathetic, and helpful critic. However, he shows not only a white tendency toward *ex cathedra* pronouncements but also the way in which whites have been preferred to blacks as critics of black literature. His book, *The Negro Novel in America*, printed in 1958, was reprinted and revised in 1965. By 1968 it had gone through five printings. In contrast, Sterling Brown's encyclopedic *The Negro in American Fiction*, issued in 1937, languished until 1968, when the small Kennikat Press in Port Washington, New York, reissued it.

2. From "Back With the Wind," in *William Styron's Nat Turner: Ten Black Writers Respond*, edited by John Hendrik Clarke. Copyright © 1968 by Beacon Press.

3. "We Walk the Way of the New World" by Don L. Lee, in *Negro Digest*, September 1969. Reprinted with permission.

2. "THY NEIGHBOR'S WIFE, THY NEIGHBOR'S SERVANTS": WOMEN'S LIBERATION AND BLACK CIVIL RIGHTS

1. Gunnar Myrdal, Appendix 5, "A Parallel to the Negro Problem," *An American Dilemma* (New York: Harper and Brothers, 1944), p. 1077.

2. W.E.B. DuBois, "The Damnation of Women," *Darkwater* (New York: Schocken Books, 1969), p. 164.

3. Gilbert H. Barnes and Dwight L. Dumond, eds., *Letters of Theodore Dwight Weld, Angelina Grimké Weld, and Sarah Grimké 1822–1844* (New York: D. Appleton-Century Company, 1934), 2: 842.

4. *The History of Woman Suffrage*, I: 60–61. *History of Woman Suffrage* is the unique history of American feminism from its origins until the ratification of the Nineteenth Amendment. Elizabeth Cady Stanton, Susan B. Anthony, and Matilda Joslyn Gage edited the first three volumes; Susan B. Anthony and Ida Husted Harper the fourth; and Mrs. Harper the fifth and sixth. My citations from the first three volumes will be from the second edition (Rochester: Charles Mann, 1889); from the fourth volume (Rochester: Susan B. Anthony, 1902); from the last volumes (New York: The National American Woman Suffrage Association, 1922).

5. Catharine A. Beecher, *Essay on Slavery and Abolitionism, with Reference to the Duty of American Females* (Philadelphia: Henry Perkins, 1837), p. 99.

6. Frederick Douglass, *Life and Times of Frederick Douglass, Written by Himself*, (1892) (New York: Collier, 1962), p. 469. Good accounts of Douglass' work for women's rights are Benjamin Quarles, "Frederick Douglass and the Woman's Rights Movement," *Journal of Negro History* 25 (January 1940): 39–44, and *Life and Writings of Frederick Douglass*, ed. Philip S. Foner, 4 volumes (New York: International Publishers, 1950).

7. Frederick Engels, *The Origin of the Family, Private Property, and the State* (New York: International Publishers, 1942), p. 65.

8. Harriet Martineau, *Society in America* (London: Saunders and Otley, 1837), 2: 118. Martineau's chapter, "The Political Non-Existence of Women," is acute and acerb.

9. *History of Woman Suffrage*, 1:222.

10. *Ibid.*, pp. 680–681.

11. *Ibid.*, p. 471.

12. *Ibid.*, p. 854.

13. Beecher, *op cit.*, p. 144.

14. *History of Woman Suffrage*, 1:469.

15. *Ibid.*, p. 528.

16. *Ibid.*, p. 52.

17. Angelina Grimké, *Letters to Catherine E. Beecher* (Boston: Isaac Knapp, 1838), p. 114. A harassed, exhausted Miss Grimké answered *An Essay on Slavery*.

18. *Weld-Grimké Letters*, 1:403.

19. *History of Woman Suffrage*, 1:40.

20. In Catherine H. Birney, *The Grimké Sisters* (Boston: Lee and Shepard Publishers, 1885), p. 204.

21. *Weld-Grimké Letters*, 1:428.

22. In Birney, op. cit., pp. 202–203.

23. *History of Woman Suffrage*, 1:53–62.

24. *Ibid.*, 2:58.

25. *Ibid.*, p. 60.

26. *Ibid.*

27. *Ibid.*, pp. 60–61.

28. Susan B. Anthony did try to vote in 1872. A nineteenth-century forerunner of Chicago Judge Julius J. Hoffman found her guilty for such heresy.

29. *History of Woman Suffrage*, 2:193.

30. Douglass, *Life and Writings*, IV, 212–13.

31. *History of Woman Suffrage*, 2:216.

32. *Ibid.*, p. 382.

33. *Ibid.*, pp. 391–392.

34. *Ibid.*, 3:792·793.

35. *Ibid.*, 2:415.

36. *Ibid.*, p. 94.

37. *Ibid.*, p. 353.

38. *Ibid.*, 3:14.

39. *Ibid.*, 2:311.

40. A text of Blackwell's letter is in *ibid.*, pp. 929–931.

41. An excellent, full account of this is Aileen Kraditor, *The Ideas of the Woman Suffrage Movement 1890–1920* (New York: Columbia University Press, 1965).

42. The National American Woman Suffrage Association was the result of a merger in 1890 between the two older woman suffrage groups.

43. *History of Woman Suffrage*, 5:60.

44. *Ibid.*, p. 59.

45. *Ibid.*, p. 83.

46. *Ibid.*

47. *Ibid.*, p. 105.

48. *Ibid.*, p. 106.

49. Eleanor Flexner, *Century of Struggle: The Woman's Rights Movement in the United States* (New York: Atheneum, 1968), p. 129. Miss Flexner's book remains the most lucid survey of the origins of feminism in America. An unpublished doctoral dissertation, K.E. Melder, "The Beginnings of the Women's Rights Movement 1800–1840" (Ann Arbor: University Microfilms, 1964), is also very useful.

50. Lillian Smith, *Killers of the Dream*, rev. (New York: W.W. Norton, 1961), p. 141.

51. Carol Hanisch, "Hard Knocks: Working for Women's Liberation in a Mixed (Male-Female) Movement Group," Shulamith Firestone and Anne Koedt, eds. *Notes from the Second Year: Women's Liberation* (New York, 1970), p. 60. Other white women veterans of the civil rights movement have less unhappy accounts of what happened, particularly in the South. They accuse some women of themselves using sex in order to gain power. They say that at least in the beginning women were influential. A white woman was the first administrator of the Student Non-Violent Co-ordinating Committee office in Atlanta. Jobs were given out on the basis of competence. Women could not have some simply because it would have been stupid and dangerous to have a white woman appear in public with a black man.

52. "The Negro Family: the Case for National Action," in Leon Friedman, ed., *The Civil Rights Reader* (New York: Walker and Company, 1967), p. 291.

53. The memo, written for private circulation, is dated November 18, 1965. It was later printed in *Liberation*, 11 (April 1966): 35–36. *Liberation*, 11 (December 1966) went on to print four more articles about the same problem, which gave some programs for women's liberation and which drew parallels between being a black and being a woman in America.

54. Roxanne Dunbar, "Female Liberation as the Basis for Social Revolution," Firestone and Koedt, *op. cit.*, p. 48. Dunbar says the Vietnamese have also done this.

55. The Honorable Shirley Chisholm discusses separatism: " . . . because of the bizarre aspects of their roles and the influence that nontraditional contact among them has on the general society, blacks and whites, males and females, must operate independently of each other in order to escape from quicksands of psychological slavery." Her essay, "Racism and Anti-Feminism," *Black Scholar*, 1 (January–February 1970): 40–45 is a lucid account of the new feminism by an admirable black woman.

56. Beverly Jones and Judith Brown, "Toward a Female Liberation Movement" (Boston: New England Free Press, n.d.).

57. It should be noted that when many contemporary feminists compare themselves to slaves, they are speaking of historical slavery, not of black American chattel slavery of which they have no personal knowledge. They are influenced not only by Engels but by John Stuart Mill's *The Subjection of Women* (1869).

58. Harry Reasoner, CBS early evening news, June 25, 1970. Reasoner was commenting on a court decision permitting women to enter McSorley's, a New York Bar.

59. Joel Kovel, *White Racism: A Psychohistory* (New York: Pantheon, 1970) p. 193, gives a brilliant analysis of the way in which biology, economics, and cultural assumptions may have come together to breed American racism. He says that while the South enjoyed the black body and the North made it taboo, for both regions it was:

> the very incarnation of that fecal substance with which the whole world had been smeared by the repressed coprophilia of the bourgeois order. Here was the central forbidden pleasure that had become generalized into the pursuit of world mastery: the playing with, the reincorporation of lost bodily contents, the restoration of the

narcissistic body of infancy, the denial of separation and the selfhood that had been painfully wrung from history. Here was the excremental body that had been hated, repressed, spread over the universe, but which was still loved with the infant's wish to fuse with the maternal image.

However, Kovel writes as if "man" meant both "man" and "woman," there being no difference between them, or as if writing about "man" were enough.

60. Such attitudes, once clandestine, are now much discussed in many places. Among them are Eldridge Cleaver, *Soul on Ice* (New York: Dell Publishing Co., Delta Book, 1968); E. Franklin Frazier, *The Negro Family in the United States*, rev. and abrd. ed. (Chicago: University of Chicago Press, 1966); Frantz Fanon, *Black Skin, White Masks*, trans. Charles Lam Markman (New York: Grove Press, 1967); Calvin C. Hernton, *Sex and Racism in America* (New York: Grove Press, 1966); Theodore R. Hudson, "In the Eye of the Beholder," *Negro Digest* (December 1969): 43–48; LeRoi Jones, *Dutchman and The Slave: Two Plays* (New York: William Morrow, Apollo Edition, 1964); LeRoi Jones, "American Sexual Reference: black male," *Home* (New York: William Morrow, Apollo Edition, 1966).

One of the most interesting studies of white women and black women is Archibald E. Grimké, "The Sex Question and Race Segregation," *Papers of the American Negro Academy* (Washington, D.C., December 1915). Grimké, a lawyer, writer, publicist, and diplomat, was asking white women to help create legal equality for blacks and to end the double standard which had so victimized black women. Yet he was dubious about the possibility of sexual solidarity because of the resentment white women felt toward black women. Grimké, born in 1849, was the illegitimate son of Henry Grimké, Angelina and Sarah's brother, and Nancy Weston, a family slave. After the Civil War, he left the South to educate ihimself in the North. His aunt Sarah, who accidentally discovered his existence and then deliberately discovered his blood relationship to her, helped him to go on to Harvard.

61. *Black Scholar* 1 (January–February 1970): 29.

62. Robert Staples, "The Myth of the Black Matriarchy," *Black Scholar* 1 (January–February 1970): 15. Staples, who thinks the black woman more aggressive, independent, and self-reliant than the proto-typical white woman, finds the myth of the black matriarchy a "cruel hoax," which the white ruling class has imposed in order to create internal dissensions within the black community.

63. Perhaps a transcendent ideal of modern socialism may unite elements of the two movements. However, I think that for the moment new feminism's allegiance to abolishing sexism and black liberation's allegiance to blackness are both too strong for that.

64. Barbara Deming, *Prison Notes* (Boston: Beacon, 1970), pp. 119–120.

3. WHAT MATTER MIND: A THEORY ABOUT THE PRACTICE OF WOMEN'S STUDIES

1. I am grateful to the many people who have helped me to work out my ideas, especially to the participants at United States Office of Education Affirmative Action Institutes at the University of Florida and at the University of Tennessee in June, 1972; Lila Karp: and to my colleagues and students at Barnard College.

Two papers, which I read in unpublished form, touch on several of the points I mention. They are Sheila Tobias, "Women's liberation phase two," and Konnilyn G. Feig, "Myths of women's liberation: The feminist movement revisited."

2. Elaine Showalter, in "Introduction: Teaching about women, 1971," *Female Studies IV* (Pittsburgh: KNOW Press, Inc., 1971), recalls that in 1969 she was the only faculty member at a workshop about higher education at a conference about women who was actually teaching a course about women. Showalter's essay is a thorough, competent survey of Women's Studies programs and the literature about the. My count of courses comes from the KNOW Press *Female Studies* Series, available from KNOW, Inc., P.O. Box 86031, Pittsburgh, Pennsylvania 15221. In a letter to me, dated 26 July, 1972, Bernice Sandler, Executive Associate, Association of American Colleges, says she estimates there might be around 700 courses, having come "across courses that were not listed" in *Female Studies*.

3. The women's colleges have, however, been comparatively slow to initiate Women's Studies. See Caroline Bird, "Women's lib. and the women's colleges," *Change*, 4, 30 (April, 1972), 60–65.

4. See Joreen, "The tyranny of structurelessness," *Second Wave*, 2, 1 (1972), 20–25, 42, for general comment about elitism, the star system, and international democracy.

5. Florence Howe, "A report on women and the profession," *College English*, 32, 8 (May, 1971), 850. The paper was read as an introduction to the M.L.A. Forum on Women in the Profession, December, 1970.

6. My informant, whose anonymity is kept for obvious reasons, was responding to a questionnaire circulated in the spring of 1972 by the Barnard Women's Center to solicit entries for a bibliography *Women's Work and Women's Studies* 1971.

7. *Vindication of the Rights of Women* (New York: W.W. Norton and Co., Inc., 1967), 49.

8. *Middlemarch* (New York: New American Library, Signet edition 1964), 11–12.

9. *Politics*, Book I, Chapter 12. My edition is Richard McKeon (Ed.), *Introduction to Aristotle* (New York: Random House Modern Library, 1947), 574.

10. Three brilliant essays—Cynthia Ozick, "Women and creativity: the demise of the dancing dog"; Elaine Showalter, "Women writers and the double standard"; and Linda Nochlin, "Why are there no great women artists?"—expose this corollary. See Vivian Gornick and Barbara K. Moran (Eds.), *Woman in Sexist Society* (New York: Basic Books, 1971), 307–366. Signet Books issued a paperback edition in 1972. Other incisive comment includes Mary Ellmann, *Thinking About Women* (New York: Harcourt, Brace, Jovanovich, 1968); Eva Figes, *Patriarchal Attitudes* (New York: Fawcett, 1971, copyright 1970), esp. Chapters IV and V; and Florence Howe, "The education of women," *Liberation Now!* (New York: Dell Laurel Book, 1971), 293–305. Cf. Eldridge Cleaver, *Soul On Ice*, still the most provocative analysis of the way in which the formula men/mind, but women/matter has been transformed into white man/mind, all blacks/matter.

11. *Emile*, trans. Barbara Foxley (London: J.M. Dent and Sons, Ltd., Everyman's Library, 1950), 306. Wollstonecraft wrote her *Vindication of the Rights of Women* in part to refute Rousseau's theories of women's intellect and their education.

12. School enrollment figures also show how much we have institutionalized our belief that men are rational and women not. In 1969, 91.6 percent of all boys between the ages of 16 and 17 were in some kind of school. So were 87.7 percent of the girls. 59.4 percent of all boys between the ages of 18 and 19 were still in school. Only 41.8 percent of the girls were. We educate women, but not that highly.

Kenneth A. Simon and W. Vance Grant, Table 4, *Digest of Educational Statistics* (Washington, D.C.: U.S. Government Printing Office, 1970), 4. I have assumed that the gap between 16/17 and 18/19 represents, for the most part, the gap between high school and more advanced work.

13. The influence of the research of Matina Horner has been wide and widely noted. Horner concluded that women wish to avoid success; they fear it will have negative consequences, especially if achieved in competition with men. See "Sex differences in achievement, motivation and performance in competitive and non-competitive situations," a doctoral thesis completed at the University of Michigan in 1968, reported in *Dissertation Abstracts* (1969), *30* (1-B), 407. Dr. Susan M. Robison, Psychology Department, Ohio University, Lancaster, Ohio, is doing work that appears to confirm and to extend Horner's findings.

14. Federal funding of women's programs is possible. On 18 April, 1972, the Honorable Patsy Mink introduced a bill, the Women's Education Act of 1972, "to authorize the Secretary of Health, Education, and Welfare to make grants to conduct special educational programs and activities concerning women, and for other related educational purposes." (92nd Congress, 2nd Session, H.R. 14451). The bill was referred to the Committee on Education and Labor.

4. THE ANDROGYNE AND THE HOMOSEXUAL

1. A version of this paper was read at Yale University, February, 1974. Some of its ideas were first published in my review of Carolyn G. Heilbrun, *Toward A Recognition of Androgyny, in Nation, 217,* 18 (November 26, 1973), 566–569.

2. See C.G. Jung, *Psychology and Alchemy,* in *Collected Works,* Vol. 12, 2nd ed., Bollingen Series XX (Princeton: Princeton University Press, 1968,) 581 pp., and Marie Delcourt, *Hermaphrodite: Myths and Rites of the Bisexual Figure in Classical Antiquity,* trans. Jennifer Nicholson (London: Studio Books, 1961, first published 1956), 109 pp.

3. (New York: Harcourt, Brace & World, Inc., Harbinger edition, first copyright taken out 1929), 102.

4. *Beyond God The Father: Toward A Philosophy of Women's Liberation* (Boston: Beacon Press, 1973), 26.

5. Nigel Nicolson, *Portrait of a Marriage* (New York: Atheneum, 1973), 106.

6. For a sense of that variety, see Clellan S. Ford and Frank A. Beach. Chap. VII, *Patterns of Sexual Behavior* (New York: Harper and Brothers and Paul B. Hoeber, 1951), 125–143; Wainwright Churchill, *Homosexual Behavior Among Males: A Cross-Cultural and Cross-Species Investigation* (Englewood Cliffs, New Jersey: Prentice-Hall, Prism paperback edition, 1971), 347 pp. and "Appendix III" of the *Wolfenden Report.*

7. *The Second Sex,* trans. and ed. H.M. Parshley (New York: Bantam edition, 1961), 398–399. If one is seeking a symbol of flexibility in character structure, one might recall that the expression "Lesbian rule" denotes a lead mason's rule that could be bent to fit the curves of a moulding. In Book V, *Nicomachean Ethics,* Aristotle uses it as a metaphor to picture his theory that in some cases laws must adapt themselves to facts. To be fair, the lesbian rule later became a metaphor to picture pandering to popular opinion and for tawdry permissiveness.

8. A cursory, tentative look at histories of homosexuality provokes the thought that there may often be a coincidence between a formal disapproval of homosexuality in a society and a social, political movement towards equality for women. There may often be a

coincidence between an acceptance of homosexuality and a lack of social, political status for women. *If*, and I cannot emphasize that "if" firmly enough, an approval of homosexuality and a disapproval of equality for women work together, and *vice versa*, then an ideology that grounds gay liberation and women's liberation together in a larger, general ideology of human rights and civil liberties will help to relieve the polarization between male homosexuals and women.

9. *The Development of Sex Differences*, ed. Maccoby (Stanford: Stanford University Press, 1966), 35. Maccoby then mentions "a few exceptions in the literature to this generalization."

10. For a philosophical analysis of the terms "feminine" and "masculine" see Sue Larson, "What Befits a Woman," a paper first read at Vassar College, April, 1974.

11. I am grateful to Professor Barbara Gelpi for her work in studying that bias.

12. "The Poet as Woman," *Southern Review*, *II*, 4 (Spring 1937), 784. Ransom was reviewing Elizabeth Atkins, *Edna St. Vincent Millay and Her Times*. The essay is also a good example of the bad habit of thinking that the feminine is as much a part of the natural world as the female; that the masculine is as much a part of the natural world as the male, though a characteristic of the masculine is the intellectual transcendence of the natural.

13. (New York: Ace Books, 1969), 90.

14. I Corinthians, 13, 1–7, *New English Bible*.

6. TILLIE OLSEN: WITNESS AS SERVANT

1. For comment, see Ellen Moers, *Literary Women: The Great Writers* (Garden City, New York: Doubleday and Co., 1976), pp. 13–41; Elaine Showalter, *A Literature of Their Own: British Women Novelists From Bronte to Lessing* (Princeton: Princeton University Press, 1977), pp. 28–9.

2. See Showalter, pp. 29–31; 182–239. For an interesting study of what might be covert protest, see Helen Waite Papashvily, *All the Happy Endings* (New York: Harper and Brothers, 1956).

3. For a preliminary account of other examples of the literature of synthesis, see Nan Bauer Maglin, "Discovering Women's Activist Fiction," *University of Michigan Papers in Women's Studies, 11, 2* (1976), pp. 96–104.

4. The phrase is from Gayle Rubin, "The Traffic in Women: Notes on the 'Political Economy' of Sex," *Toward an Anthropology of Women*, ed. Rayna R. Reiter (New York: Monthly Review Press, 1975), pp. 157–210.

5. "Biographical Interpretation," in Rebecca Harding Davis, *Life in the Iron Mills, or the Korl Woman* (Old Westbury, New York: Feminist Press, 1972), p. 156. Olsen praises Davis for having written the first novel in America that shows the destructive effects of industrialism on laborers, but she regrets Davis' inability to see the destructive effects of middle-class sex roles on her own life and imaginative powers.

6. *Yonnondio: From the Thirties* (New York: Delacorte Press, Seymour Lawrence, 1974), p. 191. Italics author's.

7. *Harper's Magazine*, 231 (October 1965), 153–161.

8. *Tell Me a Riddle* (New York: Delta Book, 1961), p. 75.

9. "One Out of Twelve: Women Who Are Writers in Our Century" (A Talk to College

Teachers of Literature, 1971), in *Working It Out*, ed. Sara Ruddick and Pamela Daniels (New York: Pantheon Books, 1977). Since I read the article in galleys. I have no exact page reference.

10. *Tell Me a Riddle*, p. 12. The story, "I Stand Here Ironing," begins with one of Olsen's most famous lines, "I stand here ironing, and what you asked me moves tormented back and forth with the iron." The line expresses the interweaving of psychological need and the rhythms of toil within the fabric of the home.

11. "Biographical Interpretation," p. 78.

12. "One Out of Twelve."

13. "Biographical Interpretation," p. 84.

14. See Walter Rideout, *The Radical Novel in the United States* 1900–1954: *Some Interrelations of Literature and Society* (Cambridge: Harvard University Press, 1956), p. 10.

15. See *Women's Studies Newsletter* (Old Westbury, New York: Feminist Press) 2 (Winter 1972); 3 (Spring 1973); 4 (Summer 1973), for Olsen's long, detailed reading lists about women's experiences.

7. Shakespeare and the Soil of Rape

1. *The Rape of Lucrece*, lines 1259–60. All quotations are from *The Complete Works of Shakespeare*, ed. by George Lyman Kittredge (Boston: Ginn, 1936).

2. Marvin Spevack, *A Complete and Systematic Concordance to the Works of Shakespeare*, V (Hildesheim: Georg Olms, 1970), 2713–14, 2718.

3. David Wilbern, "Rape and Revenge in *Titus Andronicus,*" *English Literary Renaissance*, 8 (1978), 164.

4. In contrast, the deceiving of Angelo in the matter of the bedtrick, though underhanded, is not comparable to rape. Angelo is neither forced into something against his will nor conscious of pain and humiliation during the sexual act.

5. Leo C. Curran, "Rape and Rape Victims in the Metamorphoses," *Arethusa*, II, Nos. 1/2 (1978), 223, also points out that rape is "perceived primarily as an offense against the property or honor of men." In brief, rape in a shame culture makes women guilty.

6. Because husbands perceive rape as a form of infidelity, their psychic response to the raped wife has similarities to the attitude toward a possibly unfaithful wife: a disruptive suspicion, confusion, anger, and sense of loss, conveyed metaphorically through references to the sheets of the marriage bed that no longer seem white.

7. Sherrin Marshall Wyntjes, "Women in the Reformation Era," *Becoming Visible: Women in European History*, ed. Renate Bridenthal and Claudia Koonz (Boston: Houghton Mifflin, 1977), p. 187. See, too, in the same volume, Joan Kelly-Gadol, "Did Women Have a Renaissance?" pp. 137–64, and Richard T. Vann, "Toward a New Lifestyle: Women in Preindustrial Capitalism," pp. 192–216.

8. Lawrence Stone, *The Family, Sex and Marriage in England, 1500–1800* (New York: Harper & Row, 1977), p. 7. Others have likewise claimed that the junction of the sixteenth and seventeenth centuries was "an important crisis in the historic development of Englishwomen." I quote from Alice Clark, *Working Life of Women in the Seventeenth Century* (New York: Harcourt, Brace and Howe, 1920), p. 2. Stone, though he realizes that women were important economic assets, denies the view "that the economic

contribution of the wife to the family budget necessarily gave her higher status and greater power, and that her progressive removal from the labour force as capitalism spread prosperity slowly downward was the cause of her social degradation" (p. 200). Clark supports such a theory.

9. Coppélia Kahn, "The Rape in Shakespeare's *Lucrece*," *Shakespeare Studies*, 9 (1976), 68. After giving the first version of this paper, I read in manuscript Kahn's essay which explores several of the same issues with admirable depth, subtlety, and persuasiveness.

8. AD/D FEMINAM: WOMEN, LITERATURE, AND SOCIETY

1. A coherent defense of such a position is Joan Kelly-Gadol, "The Social Relation of the Sexes: Methodological Implications of Women's History," *Signs: Journal of Women in Culture and Society*, 1, no. 4 (Summer 1976): 809–23. A cogent assessment of the positions from which the permanence of "feminine" and "masculine" traits have been argued is Anne Dickason, "The Feminine As a Universal," in *Feminism and Philosophy*, ed. Mary Vetterling-Braggin, Federick A. Elliston, and Jane English (Totowa, N.J.: Littlefield, Adams, 1977), pp. 79–100. Texts that give historical solidity to some of my concerns include Alison Adburgham, *Women in Print* (London: George Allen and Unwin, 1972); Germaine Brée, *Women Writers in France* (New Brunswick, N.J.: Rutgers University Press, 1973); Ellen Moers, *Literary Women: The Great Writers* (Garden City, N.Y.: Doubleday, 1976); Ann Douglas, *The Feminization of American Culture* (New York: Alfred A. Knopf, 1977); Elaine Showalter, *A Literature of Their Own* (Princeton, N.J.: Princeton University press, 1977).

2. Carolyn C. Lougee, in *Le Paradis des Femmes: Women, Salons, and Social Stratification in Seventeenth-Century France* (Princeton, N.J.: Princeton University Press, 1976), persuasively points out relationships among women as writers; women as cultural arbiters; the argument about the nature of women; and a revision of the French social structure.

3. Gaye Tuchman and Nina Fortin, Department of Sociology, Graduate School and University Center, City University of New York, "Men, Women and the Novel: Submissions to Macmillan and Company, 1866–1887," p. 4. Tuchman and Fortin have analyzed the submissions of men and women to the English publishers. They are careful not to conclude too much from their material, but their findings have parallels elsewhere.

4. A brilliant interpretation of that tradition is Sandra M. Gilbert, "Patriarchal Poetry and Women Readers: Reflections on Milton's Bogey," *PMLA* 93, no. 3 (May 1978):368–82. I have also discussed this problem in "Sex, Gender, and American Culture," in *Women and Men: Changing Roles*, ed. Libby A. Cater, Anne Firor Scott, Wendy Martyna (New York: Aspen Institute for Humanistic Studies, 1976), pp. 201–44. Praeger reprinted the book in 1977.

5. My thanks to Robert D. Cottrell for his succinct labeling of that tradition in "Colette's Literary Reputation in the Twenties," a paper read at the Rutgers Conference on "Women, the Arts, and the 1920s in Paris and New York," April 1978.

6. *Mary, A Fiction*, ed. Gary Kelly (London: Oxford University Press, 1976), p. 52.

7. *Aurora Leigh and Other Poems*, intro. by Cora Kaplan (London: The Women's Press, 1978), p. 38. As they have done for subversive and avant-garde movements in general, small presses now transmit much of the contemporary women's writing and reprint valuable, out-of-print books.

8. For a recent defense of women's literature as historical, see Lillian S. Robinson, *Sex, Class and Culture* (Bloomington: Indiana University Press, 1978). Robinson argues that the proper female text calls for both gender and class revolution.

9. In terms of comprehensiveness, no one has probably yet surpassed Simone de Beauvoir's analysis of men's writing about women in *The Second Sex*. Among the more valuable recent explorations are Froma I. Zeitlin, "The Dynamics of Misogyny: Myth and Mythmaking in the *Oresteia*," *Arethusa II*, nos. 1–2 (Spring-Fall 1978): 149–84; John Goode, "Women and the Literary Text," *Rights and Wrongs of Women*, ed. Juliet Mitchell and Ann Oakley (Harmondsworth, Middlesex, England: Penguin, 1976), pp. 217–55; Annette Kolodny, *The Lay of the Land* (Chapel Hill: University of North Carolina Press, 1975).

10. Though good critics no longer repeat that slur, it persists informally and in some academic circles. See, for example, an article assessing children in day care centers that had male teachers: Bryan E. Robinson˜nd Helen Canaday, "Sex-Role Behaviors and Personality Traits of Male Day Care Teachers," *Sex Roles: A Journal of Research* 4, no. 6 (December 1978): 857. Robinson and Canaday list under "masculine behaviors" such actions as "ride trikes" and "build blocks, build structures, set up farms and villages." Under "feminine behavior" they have, among other things, "paint," and "artwork, cutting, pasting, drawing with crayons or chalk."

11. *A Room of One's Own* (New York: Harcourt Brace and World, Harbinger Book, 1967), p. 51. To interpret the lack of an author's name as a sign of deprivation is, of course, historically conditioned, not a necessary act.

12. Anne Bradstreet, "The Prologue," in *The Works of Anne Bradstreet*, ed. Jeannine Hensley, forward by Adrienne Rich (Cambridge: Belknap Press of Harvard University Press, 1967), pp. 15–16. Unfortunately, the question of a special female poetics is beyond the scope of this essay, but such a poetics, when codified, could easily be compatible with my suggestions about women's literature here.

13. In *The Bostonians*, Matthias Pardon tells Olive Chancellor that he suffers "from the competition of 'lady-writers.' . . . They certainly made lovely correspondents . . . you had to be lively if you wanted to get there first. Of course, they were naturally more chatty; and that was the style of literature that seemed to take most today." (London: John Lehmann, 1952), p. 116.

14. *Ladies Home Journal* 95, no. 11 (November 1978): 197. All quotes are from this number. An excellent collection of essays about women and the mass media is Gaye Tuchman, Arlene Kaplan Daniels, and James Benet, *Hearth and Home: Images of Women in the Mass Media* (New York: Oxford University Press, 1978), esp. pp. 93–221. For a reanalysis of some of its points, see Tuchman's "Review Essay: Women's Depiction in the Mass Media," *Signs: Journal of Women in Culture and Society* 4, no. 3 (Spring 1979): 528–42.

15. Commentators on such contradictions are indebted to Roland Barthes, *Mythologies*, trans. Annette Lavers (New York: Hill and Wang, 1972), pp. 50–52.

16. Doris Lessing, *The Golden Notebook* (New York: Bantam Books, 1977), p. 61.

17. *A Room of One's Own*, p. 35. The mirror image is shifting in current women's writing, from the polished surface in which men reflect themselves or women their putative narcissism, to a speculum with which women explore their bodies and themselves.

18. *Diving into the Wreck: Poems, 1971–1972* (New York: W.W. Norton, 1973). In 1971, Rich gave the lecture "When We Dead Awaken: Writing as Re-Vision," a prose equivalent of many of these poems. Published in 1972, it was republished in *Adrienne*

Rich's Poetry, selected and edited by Barbara Charlesworth Gelpi and Albert Gelpi (New York: W.W. Norton, Norton Critical Edition, 1975), pp. 90–98. Rich's work after *Diving into the Wreck* has explored a female world in far more radical ways.

19. I am using the Keith Cohen and Paula Cohen translation of "Le Rire de la Méduse," *Signs* 1, no. 4 (Summer 1976): 875–93. For Cixous's place in the movement, *écriture féminine*, see Elaine Marks, "Women and Literature in France," *Signs* 3, no. 4 (Summer 1978): 832–42; Carolyn Greenstein Burke, "Report from Paris: Women's Writing and the Women's Movement," *Signs* 3, no. 4 (summer 1978): 843–55; and Georgiana Colvile, "The Future of Ecriture: Cixous," given at the meeting of Section 472, "Theories of 'Feminine Writing' among French Writers," Modern Language Association, 29 December 1978.

9. Zero Deviancy: The Lesbian Novel in English

1. The number of texts about lesbians, by lesbians and non-lesbians, is unclear. There are about twenty-three hundred entries in Gene Damon and Lee Stuart's *The Lesbian in Literature: A Bibliography* (San Francisco, 1967) and about nineteen hundred entries in the revised edition by Damon, Jan Watson, and Robin Jordan (Reno. Nev., 1975). While this second edition has more nonfiction entries and has been updated, the compilers have also cut over a thousand entries from the first edition because they referred to "trash" men had written for male readers (p. 26). The pioneering survey of the figure of the lesbian in Western literature remains Jeannette H. Foster's *Sex Variant Women in Literature: A Historical and Quantitative Survey* (London, 1958), but adding to it now is Lillian Faderman's valuable *Surpassing the Love of Men* (New York, 1981).

2. For a study of the French literary tradition, see Elaine Marks, "Lesbian Intertextuality," in *Homosexualities and French Literature*, ed. George Stambolian and Marks (Ithaca, N.Y., 1979), pp. 353–77. Several of the articles on female sexuality which were collected in *Women—Sex and Sexuality*, ed. Stimpson and Ethel Spector Person (Chicago, 1980), have insights into modern lesbianism.

3. Roland Barthes, *Writing Degree Zero*, trans. Annette Lavers and Colin Smith (Boston, 1970), pp. 76–77. Barthes has claimed that a recent novel, Renaud Camus' *Tricks* trans. Richard Howard (New York, 1981), which I read in manuscript, exemplifies homosexual writing at the degree zero. In his preface, Barthes says that homosexuality is " . . . still at that stage of excitation where it provokes what might be called feats of discourse," but "Camus' narratives are neutral, they do not participate in the game of interpretation." I suggest that *Tricks* does interpret a pattern of male homosexual activity as a fascinating, intense, limited, and only apparently permissible form of experience.

4. Gayle Rubin, introduction to Renee Vivien's *A Woman Appeared to Me*, trans. Jeannette H. Foster (Reno, Nev., 1976), p. v.

5. See Vern L. Bullough and Martha Voght, "Homosexuality and Its Confusion with the 'Secret Sin' in Pre-Freudian America," *Journal of the History of Medicine and Allied Sciences* (Spring 1973): 143–55; rpt. in Bullough, *Sex, Society, and History* (New York, 1976), pp. 112–24. My thanks to Mari Jo Buhle for bringing this article to my attention.

6. See Bullough, *Sexual Variance in Society and History* (New York, 1976), p. 605.

7. Linda Gordon, *Woman's Body, Woman's Right: A Social History of Birth Control in America* (New York, 1976), p. 164.

8. Rictor Norton, "The Homosexual Literary Tradition," *College English* 35, no. 6 (March 1974): 677; see also *College English* 36, no. 3 (November 1974), "The Homosexual Imagination" ed. Norton and Louis Crew. For an enthusiastic survey of lesbian writing,

see *Margins* 23 (August 1975), "Focus: Lesbian Feminist Writing and Publishing," ed. Beth Hodges, esp. Julia P. Stanley, "Uninhabited Angels: Metaphors for Love" (pp. 7–10), which makes several points similar to mine here. For critical studies of the literature about male homosexuals, see Roger Austen, *Playing the Game: The Homosexual Novel in America* (Indianapolis, 1977), and Robert K. Martin, *The Homosexual Tradition in American Poetry* (Austin, Tex., 1979).

9. June Arnold, *Sister Gin* (Plainfield Vt., 1975), p. 82. For an account of a facade that a lesbian community kept up, see Vern and Bonnie Bullough, "Lesbianism in the 1920s and 1930s: A Newfound Study," *Signs* 2, no. 4 (Summer 1977): 895–904.

10. I have written about coding by those who consider themselves sexual anomalies in "The Mind, the Body, and Gertrude Stein," *Critical Inquiry* 3, no. 3 (Spring 1977): 489–506. Detailed work on Stein's codes includes: Richard Bridgman, *Gertrude Stein in Pieces* (New York, 1970); Linda Simon, *Biography of Alice B. Toklas* (Garden City, N.Y., 1977); William Gass, *World within the Word* (New York, 1978), pp. 63–123; and Elizabeth Fifer, "Is Flesh Advisable: The Interior Theater of Gertrude Stein," *Signs* 4, no. 3 (Spring 1979): 472–83.

11. See Nina Auerbach, *Communities of Women: An Idea in Fiction* (Cambridge, Mass., 1978), pp. 186–87, for more comment on the "O".

12. See Blanche Wiesen Cook, "'Women Alone Stir My Imagination': Lesbianism and the Cultural Tradition," *Signs* 4, no. 4 (Summer 1979): 718, and Lillian Faderman, "Love between Women in 1928" (paper delivered at the Berkshire Conference, Vassar College, Poughkeepsie, N.Y., 18 June 1981).

13. Wyndham Lewis, *The Apes of God* (New York, 1932), p. 222.

14. My comments footnote Sandra M. Gilbert's "Costumes of the Mind: Transvestism as Metaphor in Modern Literature," *Critical Inquiry* 7, no. 2 (Winter 1980): 391–417.

15. Havelock Ellis, "Sexual Inversion," *Studies in the Psychology of Sex*, 2 vols. (1901; New York, 1936), 1:1, 122.

16. Erving Gottman's *Stigma: Notes on the Management of Spoiled Identity* (Englewood Cliffs, N.J., 1963), pp. 8–9, has influenced my analysis here.

17. Radclyffe Hall, *The Well of Loneliness* (1928: New York, 1950), p. 437; all further references to this work will be included in the text.

18. Cook, "'Women Alone,'" p. 719.

19. Though Hall's father deserted her mother around the time of Hall's birth, he left the child a generous inheritance. She was one of several aesthetic lesbians whose incomes permitted them to do more or less as they pleased. Class cannot abolish the stigma of homosexuality, but it can mitigate some of the more painful impressions.

20. As late as 1974, when the American Psychoanalytic Association voted to declassify homosexuality as a mental illness, lesbian writers were still dipping into the reservoir of such romantic tropes, as in Kate Millett's *Flying* (New York, 1974): "Taste of salt. Catching it in my mouth. A thirst to suckle it. . . . Very small thing. Pain of tenderness. . . . Fire. The vulva a sun setting behind trees" (p. 536).

21. I am gratefully adapting these terms from Victor Turner's "Passages, Margins, and Poverty," *Dramas, Fields, and Metaphors: Symbolic Action in Human Society* (Ithaca, N.Y., 1974), p. 233.

22. Alfred C. Kinsey et al., *Sexual Behavior in the Human Female* (1953: New York, 1965), p. 477. I am sure that this secondary consciousness will appear in autobiographical texts that scholars have previously ignored or been ignorant of. See, e.g., Elsa Gidlow, "Memoirs," *Feminist Studies* 6, no. 1 (Spring 1980): 103–27.

23. See Rubin, introduction to Vivien's *A Woman Appeared to Me*, and George Wickes, *The Amazon of Letters: The Life and Loves of Natalie·Barney* (New York, 1976).

24. A more ironic and subtle English equivalent is Elizabeth Bowen's *The Hotel* (New York, 1928). Patricia Highsmith's ("Claire Morgan") *The Price of Salt* (New York, 1952), like *Labyrinth*, is about the family and the lesbian's need to leave it even if she is a mother.

25. Bertha Harris (personal interview, New York, 3 August 1977); unless otherwise indicated, all further quotations from Harris are from this interview. See also Lois Gould, "Creating a Women's World," *New York Times Magazine*, 2 January 1977, pp. 34, 36–38.

26. I am indebted for this concept to Paul Robinson's *The Modernization of Sex* (New York, 1976). I have written in more detail about the relationship of the women's movement to American culture in "Women and American Culture," *Dissent* 27, no. 3 (Summer 1980): 299–307.

27. Ann Allen Shockley has suggested that the taboo on such a lesbian voice has been stronger in the black community than in the white, but even there the gags have loosened; see Shockley, "The Black Lesbian in American Literature: An Overview," in *Conditions Five, The Black Women's Issue*, ed. Lorraine Bethel and Barbara Smith (1979): 133–42. The entire issue is courageous and important. See also J.R. Roberts, *Black Lesbians: An Annotated Bibliography* (Tallahassee, 1981), with a foreword by Smith.

28. Elana Nachman, *Riverfinger Woman* (Plainfield, Vt., 1974), p. 13.

29. Jill Johnston, *Lesbian Nation: The Feminist Solution* (New York, 1973), p. 97.

30. For example, in Linda Crawford's *A Class by Herself* (New York, 1976), pills and booze compel a far greater renunciatory attention than does the stigma of lesbianism.

31. Alma Routsong ("Isabel Miller"), interview in Jonathan Katz, *Gay American History: Lesbians and Gay Men in the U.S.A.* (New York, 1976), p. 442. The career of one professional novelist replicates the historical shift from a stress on the stigmatized text to its rejection. As "Ann Aldrich," Marijane Meaker wrote widely read novels about the romances and difficulties of the lesbian subculture. Then under her own name she published *Shockproof Sydney Skate* (New York, 1972). Profitable, well received, it is about a triangle consisting of a woman, the younger woman with whom she has an affair, and her son, who is in love with the younger woman as well. The lesbian circles are little more absurd than any other subject of a comedy of manners.

32. Nachman, *Riverfinger Woman*, p. 13.

33. For a scrupulous exploration of lesbianism and women's worlds in the poetry of the 1960s and 1970s, see Mary Carruthers, "Imagining Women: Notes Towards a Feminist Poetic," *Massachusetts Review* 20, no. 2 (Summer 1979): 281–407.

34. See, e.g. Joan Winthrop, *Underwater* (New York, 1974), p. 256. Winthrop has her central character indulge in a good deal of masculine role playing, which occurs with a certain *esprit* but is only one aspect of personality, not a controlling force as it is in *The Well of Loneliness*. That the role playing takes place after a radical mastectomy is a point Winthrop does not explore. She does, however, say that her heroine's fantasies of being male were the product of years of her own "repression" (personal interview, Sag Harbor, N.Y., 28 July 1976).

35. A notable example is Barnes' *Ladies Almanack: Written and Illustrated by a Lady of Fashion* (1928; New York, 1972) A dazzling analysis of this work is Susan Snaider Lanser's "Speaking in Tongues: *Ladies Almanack* and the Language of Celebration," *Frontiers* 4, no. 3 (Fall 1979): 39–46. The issue devotes itself to lesbian history and culture.

36. Harris, "The More Profound Nationality of Their Lesbianism: Lesbian Society in Paris in the 1920s," in *Amazon Expedition: A Lesbian Feminist Anthology*, ed. Harris et al. (Washington, N.J., 1973), p. 88; see also "What We Mean to Say: Notes Toward defining the Nature of Lesbian Literature," *Heresies* 3 (Fall 1977): 5–8, an issue of exceptional interest.

10. THE COMPANY OF CHILDREN

1. Jane Flax, "The Family in Contemporary Feminist Thought: A Critical Review," in the *Family in Political Thought*, ed. Jean Bethke Elshtain (University of Massachusetts Press, 1982), offers a much more sophisticated analysis of the family's links to production, reproduction, and the construction of internal world.

2. Andrew Hacker, "Farewell to the Family?", *New York Review of Books* XXIX, 4 (March 18, 1982), helpfully summarizes recent family developments.

3. Barbara Ehrenreich, "Family Feud on the Left," *Nation*, 234, 10 (March 13, 1982).

11. FEMINISM AND FEMINIST CRITICISM

1. Poem 276, *The Poems of Emily Dickinson*, Vol. 1, ed. Thomas H. Johnson (Cambridge: Belknap Press of Harvard University Press, 1955, 1968 printing), p. 197.

2. Patrocinio Schweickart, "Response," *Signs: Journal of Women in Culture and Society*, 8, 1 (Autumn 1982), 175. Schweickart's response is one of several to Myra Jehlen, "Archimedes and the Paradox of Feminist Criticism," *Signs*, 6, 4 (Summer 1981), 575–601, which has stimulated and influenced me. My comments now also extend my pieces, "On Feminist Criticism," *What Is Criticism?*, ed. Paul Hernadi (Bloomington: Indiana University Press, 1981), pp. 230–41, and "Ad/d Feminam: Women, Literature, and Society," *Literature and Society, Selected Papers from the English Institute*, 1978, New Series, no. 3, ed. Edward W. Said (Baltimore: Johns Hopkins Press, 1980), pp. 174–92.

3. Elaine Showalter, "Feminist Criticism in the Wilderness," *Critical Inquiry*, 2, 2 (Winter 1981), 179–205, is a splendid overview of contemporary feminist criticism. The essay is reprinted in *Writing and Sexual Difference*, ed. Elizabeth Abel (Chicago: University of Chicago Press, 1982), 9–35.

4. Nina Baym, "Melodramas of Beset Manhood: How Theories of American Fiction Exclude Women Authors," *American Quarterly*, 33, 2 (Summer 1981), 123–39.

5. *New York Times* (September 5, 1982), F-19. The next page shows another replay of antique images. The headline for a story about the rise in the stock market reads "The Running of the Bulls." In the foreground are two brokers, both young white men. Grinning, triumphant, they hold drinks. In the background are women: some customers, more of them waitresses.

6. Susan Griffin, "Thoughts on Writing a Diary," *The Writer on Her Work*, ed. with intro. by Janet Sternburg (New York: W.W. Norton, 1980), p. 110.

7. *Yale Gertrude Stein*, ed. Richard Kostelanetz (New Haven: Yale University Press, 1980), p. 111. Stein then adds: "Not as if it was tried." The phrase has at least two meanings: no one has really done this before; if you are going to do this, do it as if no one really had before, i.e., begin again.

8. Antonio Gramsci, *Letters from Prison*, selected, translated from the Italian and

introduced by Lynne Lawner (New York: Harper and Row, Colophon edition, 1975), p. 245.

9. To raise money for a tenure battle at the University of California/Santa Cruz, supporters of the beleaguered professor, Nancy Shaw, sold bright T-shirts with the slogan, "This Scholar is No Gentleman," stamped on in stark lettering.

10. See Rachel Blau DuPlessis and Members of Workshop 9, "For the Etuscans: Sexual Difference and Artistic Production—The Debate Over a Female Aesthetic," *The Future of Difference*, ed. Hester Eisenstein and Alice Jardine (Boston: G.K. Hall, 1980), pp. 128–56.

11. See the work of Sally McConnell-Ginet in *Women and Language in Literature and Society*, ed. Sally McConnell-Ginet, Ruth Borker, and Nelly Furman (New York: Praeger, 1980), pp. 3–25, and in *The Future of Difference*, pp. 157–66.

12. An example is Marie Shear, "Solving the Great Pronoun Problem: Twelve Ways to Avoid the Sexist Singular," *Perspectives: The Civil Rights Quarterly* (Spring 1981), 18–24. The fact that this article appears in a civil rights journal shows an awareness of the connection between a bias-free speech and a climate of civil equity.

13. Nancy K. Miller, "Emphasis Added: Plots and Plausibilities in Women's Fiction," *PMLA*, 96, 1 (January 1981), 36–48.

14. Annette Kolodny, "Honing a Habitable Landscape: Women's Images for the New World Frontiers," *Women and Language in Literature and Society*, pp. 188–204.

15. "On Being Female, Black, and Free," *The Writer On Her Work*, p. 96.

16. Anne K. Mellor, "On Feminist Utopias," *Women's Studies*, 9, 3 (1982), 243.

17. I have changed the names in this letter, the donor of which prefers to be anonymous.

18. Susan Harding, "Women and Words in a Spanish Village," *Toward an Anthropology of Women*, ed. Rayna R. Reiter (New York: Monthly Review Press, 1975), pp. 283–308, is a brilliant analysis of women's language, including gossip.

19. The phrase "feminist polemic" is from Moira Ferguson. See, too, Joan Kelly, "Early Feminist Theory and the *Querrelle des Femmes*," *Signs: Journal of Women in Culture and Society*, 8, 1 (Autumn 1982), 4–28. Jean Bethke Elshtain, "Feminist Discourse and Its Discontents: Language, Power, and Meaning," *Signs*, 7, 3 (Spring 1982), 603–21 offers another analysis of the relationship of language to patterns of domination. Virginia Woolf's writing as a whole reveals every one of the relationships between language user and audience I have just outlined.

20. Mona Van Duyn, "Leda and Leda Reconsidered," *No More Masks!*, ed. Florence Howe and Ellen Bass (Garden City, New York: Doubleday Anchor Books, 1973), pp. 129–32. For a discussion of these poems that is similar to mine, see Elizabeth Janeway, *Cross-Sections* (New York: William Morrow, 1982), pp. 212–13.

21. Adrienne Rich, "Rape," *Diving Into the Wreck* (New York: W.W. Norton, 1972), pp. 44–45.

22. Sonia Johnson, *From Housewife to Heretic: One Woman's Struggle for Equal Rights and Her Excommunication from the Mormon Church* (Garden City, New York: Doubleday Anchor Press, 1983).

23. Peggy Reeves Sanday, *Female Power and Male Dominance* (New York, Cambridge University Press, 1981), esp. pp. 15–51.

24. Susan G. Cole, "Could Greek Women Read and Write?", *Women's Studies: Special Issue About Antiquity*, ed. Helene Foley, 8, 1/2 (1981), 129–55.

25. Linda K. Kerber, *Women of the Republic: Intellect and Ideology in Revolutionary America* (Chapel Hill: University of North Carolina Press, 1980).

26. In a superb essay that warns against severing criticism from interpretations of social and political worlds, Edward W. Said speaks of " . . . opening the culture to experiences of the Other which have remained 'outside' (and have been repressed or framed in a context of confrontational hostility) the norms manufactured by 'insiders.'" "Opponents, Audiences, Constituencies, and Community," *Critical Inquiry*, 9, 1 (September 1982), 25.

27. In *Midnight Birds*, ed. Mary Helen Washington (Garden City, New York: Doubleday Anchor Books, 1980), pp. 195–248.

28. "Natural Resources," *The Dream of a Common Language* (New York: W.W. Norton, 1978), p. 67.

29. I borrow the terms from Edward W. Said, "The Text, The World, The Critic," *Textual Strategies*, ed. Josue W. Harai (Ithaca: Cornell University Press, 1979), p. 184.

30. Linda Nochlin, "Why Are There No Great Women Artists?" *Woman in Sexist Society*, ed. Vivian Gornick and B.K. Moran (New York: New American Library, 1972, originally published 1971), pp. 482–83.

31. See, for example, Carol Gilligan, though a brilliant and sensitive psychologist, in "In a Different Voice," *Future of Difference*, pp. 282–83.

32. The phrase is from Gloria Orenstein, "The Goddess as Symbol: A Gynocentric Vision in Modern Women's Literature," p. 21 in 1981 manuscript.

33. Margaret Homans, "The Ambiguities of Representation in Recent Women's Fiction; Testing the Franco-American Alliance," 1982, manuscript page 1.

34. *Les Guérillères*, trans. David LeVay (New York: The Viking Press, 1971, French edition 1969).

35. Jacques Derrida, *Spurs*, trans. by Barbara Harlow (Chicago: University of Chicago Press, 1979), p. 53.

36. I am adopting phrases of Nancy K. Miller, "The Text's Heroine: A Feminist Critic and Her Fictions," *Diacritics* (Summer 1982), 53. Miller is in dialogue with Peggy Kamuf, "Replacing Feminist Criticism," 42–47. Together, they offer a witty statement of the argument I have outlined.

37. Barbara Grizzuti Harrison, "What Do Women Want?", *Harper's* (October 1981), 47. In conversation, April, 1982, Schuster told me that article misrepresented her.

38. See, for example, Gayatri Chakravorty Spivak, "French Feminism in an International Frame," special issue of *Yale French Studies*, 62 (1981), 154–84. Three articles in *Feminist Studies*, 7, 2 (Summer 1981) are relevant to this question: Ann Rosalind Jones, "Writing the body toward an Understanding of L'Écriture Feminine," 247–63; Hélène Vivienne Wenzel. "The Text as Body Politics/An Appreciation of Monique Wittig's Writings in Context," 264–87; Carolyn Burke, "Irigaray Through the Looking Glass," 288–306.

39. Elizabeth Abel, "(E)merging identities: The Dynamics of Female Friendship in Contemporary Fiction by Women," *Signs*, 6, 3 (Spring 1981), 434.

40. "The Difference of View," *Women Writing and Writing About Women*, ed. Mary Jacobus (New York: Barnes and Noble, 1979), p. 12.

41. Kirsten Hastrup, "The Semantics of Biology: Virginity," *Defining Females: The Nature of Women in Society*, ed. Shirley Ardener (New York: John Wiley, 1978), p. 49.

12.   THE FEMALE SOCIOGRAPH:
THE THEATER OF VIRGINIA WOOLF'S LETTERS

1. I will use the United States edition of the Woolf letters, all edited by Nigel Nicolson and Joanne Trautman: *The Letters of Virginia Woolf*, I, 1888–1912 (New York: Harcourt Brace Jovanovich, 1975); II, 1912–1922 (New York: Harcourt Brace Jovanovich, 1976); 1923–1928 (New York: Harcourt Brace Jovanovich, 1978); IV, 1929–1931 (New York: Harcourt Brace Jovanovich, 1981); V, 1932–1935 (New York: Harcourt Brace Jovanovich, 1982); VI, 1936–1941 (New York: Harcourt Brace Jovanovich, 1982). In quoting from this edition, idiosyncracies of Woolf's spelling have been maintained.

2. Edward W. Said, *Joseph Conrad and the Fiction of Autobiography* (Cambridge: Harvard Univ. Press, 1966). My concept of "middle space" for Woolf's letters is not dissimilar to Barbara Hernnstein Smith's theory about the status of letters in *On the Margins of Discourse* (Chicago: Univ. of Chicago Press, 1978, paper 1983), but I am less concerned with the status of the letter as interpretable object.

3. "Dorothy Osborne's *Letters*," *Collected Essays*, III (London: Hogarth Press, 1967), p. 63. She makes a related point in "Lord Chesterfield's Letters to His Son," *ibid.*, p. 84. A voracious reader, Woolf liked memoirs, biographies, and letters—in brief, the texts of self. For example, the Flaubert/Sand correspondence delighted her.

4. In "Woolf as Letter-Writer: A Reflection of the Other Person," given at the Modern Language Association, December 1978, Joanne Trautman analyzes the influences of G.E. Moore's ideal of friendship, the recognition "with precision what are the qualities of our friends," on Woolf's practice. Ms. p. 9.

5. *Letter to a Young Poet* (1932) was No. 8 in the Hogarth Press Letter Series. Dismaying a generation of poets who had considered Woolf a friendly precursor, it was answered by Peter Quennell, *A Letter to Mrs. Virginia Woolf* (Leonard and Virginia Woolf, Hogarth Press, 1932), No. 12 in the Hogarth Series. The fact that both letters were issued by the same press shows how friendship still walled in disagreement. For more detail, see John Lehmann, *Thrown to the Woolves* (London: Weidenfeld and Nicolson, 1978), pp. 29–31. The letter series was not financially successful.

6. Jane Marcus, "'No More Horses': Woolf on Art and Propaganda," *Women's Studies*, 4, 2–3 (1977), 274.

7. *Collected Essays*, II (London: Hogarth Press, 1966), pp. 261–62. Woolf's letters frequently close with orders to her addressee to burn the page, to hide its message, and so forth.

8. "Dorothy Osborne's *Letters*," III, p. 60.

9. Although the editing of Woolf's letters is scrupulous, Nigel Nicolson's discomfort at Woolf's feminism betrays him into error. Introducing Volume V, he writes that Leonard Woolf was silent in his autobigraphy about *Three Guineas*, which "may be indicative of what he thought at the time" (V, xvii). However, Leonard did mention *Three Guineas* in his autobiography, saying that both it and *A Room of One's Own* were political pamphlets in the tradition of Mary Wollstonecraft's *A Vindication of the Rights of Women*. See *Downhill All the Way* (London: Hogarth Press, 1967), p. 27.

10. Woolf usually called lesbianism "sapphism," but Ethyl Smyth provoked her into using the more modern "lesbianism." A recent account of the Sackville-West relationship is Louise A. DeSalvo's "Lighting the Cave: The Relationship between Vita Sackville-West and Virginia Woolf," *Signs: Journal of Women in Culture and Society*, 8, 2 (Winter: 1982),

195–214. See also *The Letters of Vita Sackville-West to Virginia Woolf*, ed. Louise DeSalvo and Mitchell A. Leaska (New York: William Morrow and Co., Inc., 1984).

11. The vocabulary of sapphists and buggers—like Woolf's racism, anti-Semitism, and cracks about the lower order— reflects undeniably, albeit unhappily, the ugly, myopic aspect of her vision.

13. ADRIENNE RICH AND LESBIAN/FEMINIST POETRY

1. Adrienne Rich, "It Is the Lesbian in Us . . . ," *On Lies, Secrets, and Silence*, hereafter *LSS*, (New York: W.W. Norton and Co., 1979), p. 201.

2. Helen Vendler, "Ghostlier Demarcations, Keener Sounds," *Adrienne Rich's Poetry*, ed. Barbara Charlesworth Gelpi and Albert Gelpi, hereafter *ARP*, (New York: W.W. Norton and Co., Norton Critical Edition, 1975), p. 160. Vendler's essay was originally published in *Parnassus*, II, 1 (Fall/Winter 1973). As Marjorie Perloff has pointed out to me in conversation, Rich is the only living poet who is the subject of a Norton critical anthology.

3. In 1975, when *ARP* appeared, Rich also published *Poems Selected and New, 1950–1974*, hereafter *PSN*, (New York: W.W. Norton and Co.). Mark that the first poem is "Storm Warnings", the last "From an Old House in America," which ends, "Any woman's death diminishes me."

4. Adrienne Rich, *The Dream of a Common Language: Poems 1974–1977*, hereafter *DCL* (New York: W.W. Norton and Co., 1978), p. 76.

5. *Writing Like a Woman* (Ann Arbor: University of Michigan Press, 1983), p. 121.

6. Rachel Blau DuPlessis, *Writing beyond the Ending: Narrative Strategies of Twentieth-Century Women Writers* (Bloomington: Indiana University Press, 1985), pp. 138–9, expresses this position most sympathetically, in an elegant exegesis of Rich, which discusses the poetics of her lesbian/feminism.

7. Marjorie Perloff, "Private Lives/Public Images," *Michigan Quarterly Review*, 22 (January 1983), 132. My essay, "Curing: Some Comments on the Women's Movement and the Avant-Garde," compares Stein and Rich. Manuscript read at the University of Houston, March, 1985, and at the University of California/Irvine, May, 1985, forthcoming in a collection of essays about the avant-garde, edited by Sandy Friedan and Richard Spuler, Munich: Fink (sic).

8. Adrienne Rich, "'Comment' on Susan Stanford Friedman," *Signs: Journal of Women in Culture and Society*, 9, 4 (Summer 1984), 737. Friedman's article, "'I go where I love': An Intertextual Study of H.D. and Adrienne Rich," appeared in *Signs*, 9, 2 (Winter 1983), 228–245. Elly Bulkin, "'Kissing/ Against the Light': A Look at Lesbian Poetry," *Lesbian Studies: Present and Future*, ed. Margaret Cruikshank (Old Westbury, New York: Feminist Press, 1982), 32–54, is a solid survey. For analyses of other genres, see Bonnie Zimmerman, "The Politics of Transliteration: Lesbian Personal Narratives," *Signs*, 9, 4 (Summer 1984), 663–682, and my "Zero Degree Deviancy: The Lesbian Novel in English," *Critical Inquiry*, Special Issue, "Writing and Sexual Difference," ed. Elizabeth Abel, 8, 2 (Winter 1981), 363–379.

9. See, too, Bulkin, 45–46.

10. Marilyn R. Farwell, "Adrienne Rich and Organic Feminist Criticism," *College English*, 39, 2 (October 1977), 191–203, analyzes Rich's literary criticism.

11. I have adapted this idea from one of the most competent studies of Rich, her

development, and relationship to Anne Bradstreet and Emily Dickinson as Puritan American women writers: Wendy Martin, *An American Triptych* (Chapel Hill: University of North Carolina Press, 1984), p. 5.

12. Ostriker, *Writing Like A Woman*, p. 102.

13. Adrienne Rich, *Of Woman Born: Motherhood as Experience and Institution*, hereafter *OWB* (New York: W.W. Norton and Co., 1976), p. 219.

14. Rich writes of this most fully in "Compulsory Heterosexuality and Lesbian Existence," hereafter *CH*, *Signs: Journal of Women in Culture and Society*, 5, 4 (Summer 1980), 631–660. The founding editor of *Signs*, I had asked Rich, over a white tablecloth at lunch in a Chinese restaurant on the Upper West Side of New York City, if she would be generous enough to contribute. I respected, and feared, her intellectual purity. I hoped she would not find me an academic muddle. Yes, she said, she had an article, about heterosexuality and lesbianism. The essay was one of the most famous *Signs* published. For extended comment, read "Viewpoint," by Ann Ferguson, Jacquelyn N. Zita, and Kathryn Pyne Adelosn, *Signs*, 7, 1 (Autumn 1981), 158–199.

15. "Like This Together," *The Fact of a Doorframe: Poems Selected and New 1950–1984*, hereafter *FD* (New York: W.W. Norton and Co., 1984), pp. 62–63.

16. "This Woman's Movement," *ARP*, p. 202.

17. Martin, p. 211.

18. Alice Echols, "The New Feminism of Yin and Yang," *Powers of Desire: The Politics of Sexuality*, ed. Ann Snitow, Christine Stansell, and Sharon Thompson (New York: Monthly Review Press, 1983), pp. 439–459, gives an informed, if not throbbingly sympathetic, account of 1970s cultural feminism. She has published a version in "The Taming of the Id: Feminist Sexual Politics, 1968–1983," *Pleasure and Danger: Exploring Female Sexuality*, ed. Carole S. Vance (Boston: Routledge and Kegan Paul, 1984), pp. 50–72. Together, the books represent new directions in the feminist debate about female sexuality in the 1980s, largely toward a theory of female sexuality as a source of pleasure, fantasy, delight. Elizabeth Wilson, "Forbidden Love," *Feminist Studies*, 10, 2 (Summer 1984), 213–226, is an intriguing English parallel.

19. "For Ethel Rosenberg," *A Wild Patience Has Taken Me This Far*, hereafter *WP* (New York: W.W. Norton and Co., 1981), p. 29.

20. Perloff, 136, for one.

21. Martin, p. 9.

22. "Split at the Root," *Nice Jewish Girls: A Lesbian Anthology*, ed. Evelyn Torton Beck (Watertown: Persephone Press, 1982), p. 81. Rich notes the extent of her debt to her friendship with Audre Lorde and her life with Michelle Cliff for her understanding of racism, and of "passing."

23. "Response," *Sinister Wisdom* 14 (Summer 1980), 104–05. Rich thanks Elly Bulkin, who helped open a public debate in lesbian/feminism about racism and Mary Daly's work.

24. Adrienne Rich, "Afterword," *Take Back the Night*, ed. Laura Lederer (New York: William Morrow and Co., 1980), p. 314.

25. *Sources*, hereafter *S* (Woodside, California: The Heyeck Press, 1983).

26. I suggest that Rich has refined a poetics of anger and tenderness in a line that begins with the two stresses of the spondee, or, occasionally, a trochee, and then relaxes into her controlled, but flexible, iambic feet. Look at the phrase "Anger and tenderness" itself.

27. "Split at the Root," p. 83. Rich's work is evidence for Alicia Ostriker's typology of

women's poetry: " . . . the quest for autonomous self-definition; the intimate treatment of the body; the release of anger; and . . . for want of a better name, the contact imperative." The latter craves unity, mutuality, continuity, connection, touch. "The Nerves of a Midwife: Contemporary American Women's Poetry," *Parnassus*, 6, 1 (Fall/Winter 1977), 73 82–83.

28. Albert Gelpi, "Adrienne Rich: The Poetics of Change," *ARP*, p. 148, persuasively casts Rich as prophet and scapegoat.

29. "Three Conversations," *ARP*, p. 112.

30. "An Interview: Audre Lorde and Adrienne Rich," in Audre Lorde, *Sister Outsider* (Trumansburg, New York: The Crossing Press, 1984), p. 112.

31. Several critics comment on Rich's clarity, e.g. Martin, p. 169; Suzanne Juhasz, *Naked and Fiery Forms, Modern American Poetry by Women: A New Tradition* (New York: Harper Colophon Books, 1976), pp. 178–180, 202.
　　In her memoir of Rich as teacher, a sort of performance, Joyce Greenberg says: " . . . there was nothing of the actress, nothing of the performer about her." "By Woman Taught," *Parnassus*, 7, 2 (Spring/Summer 1979), 91.

32. Joanne Feit Diehl, "'Cartographies of Silence': Rich's *Common Language* and the Woman Writer," *Feminist Studies*, 6, 3 (Fall 1980), 545, confronts the issue of Lowell and Rich. My comments about Rich and language owe much to this essay.

14. FEMALE INSUBORDINATION AND THE TEXT

1. A recent endorsement of the universality of male dominance is Michelle Zimbalist Rosaldo, "The Use and Abuse of Anthropology," *Signs: Journal of Women in Culture and Society* 5:3 (Spring 1980): 389–417. For counterarguments, see Eleanor Leacock, *Myths of Male Dominance: Collected Articles on Women Cross-Culturally* (New York: Monthly Review Press, 1981), and Carol MacCormick and Marilyn Strathern, eds., *Nature, Culture and Gender* (New York: Cambridge University Press, 1980).

2. Samuel Beckett, "The Unnamable,". *Three Novels* (New York: Grove Press, Evergreen 1965), 414.

3. Peggy Reeves Sanday, *Female Power and Male Dominance: On the Origins of Sexual Inequality* (Cambridge and New York: Cambridge University Press, 1981), 114.

4. For more details, see my article, "Sex, Gender, and American Culture," *Women and Men: Changing Roles, Relationships, and Perceptions*, ed. Libby A. Cater and Anne Firor Scott, with Wendy Martyna (New York: Aspen Institute for Humanistic Studies, 1976), 201–44; my article "Ad/d Feminiam: Women, Literature, and Society," *Literature and Society: Selected Papers from the English Institute, 1978*, ed. Edward Said (Baltimore: Johns Hopkins Press, 1980), 174–92; Sandra M. Gilbert and Susan Gubar, *The Madwoman in the Attic* (New Haven: Yale University Press, 1979); Tillie Olsen, *Silences* (New York: Delacorte Pres, Seymour Lawrence, 1978), 306.

5. Helen Taylor, "Class and Gender in Charlotte Brontë's *Shirley*," *Feminist Review* 1 (1979): 90.

6. Angeline Goreau, *Reconstructing Aphra* (New York: Dial Press, 1980), 117.

7. Tillie Olsen, *Yonnondio: From the Thirties* (New York: Delacorte Press, Seymour Lawrence, 1974), 4.

8. For a study of women novelists in Victorian England who exemplify the empty-field phenomenon, see Gaye Tuchman and Nina Fortin, "Edging Women Out: Some

Suggestions About the Structure of Opportunities and the Victorian Novel," *Signs: A Journal of Women in Culture and Society* 6:2 (Winter 1980): 308–25. Obvious examples include mysteries, children's literature, popular-advice manuals, contemporary Gothic romances, early "soap operas."

9. Carolyn Heilbrun, *Reinventing Womanhood* (New York: W.W. Norton and Co., 1979), 72.

10. Ellen Moers, *Literary Women: The Great Writers* (Garden City, New York: Doubleday and Co., 1976), esp. 13–41.

11. For a fine analysis of this, see Carol Ohmann, "Historical Reality and 'Divine Appointment' in Charlotte Brontë's Fiction," *Signs* 2:4 (Summer 1977): 757–78.

12. Mary Kelley, "The Sentimentalists: Promise and Betrayal in the Home," *Signs: Journal of Women in Culture and Society* 4:3 (Spring 1979): 436–37.

13. Diva Daims, "Toward a Feminist Tradition," with Janet Grimes, Computer Print-Out, State University of New York/ Albany (April 6, 1982), lines 119–23.

14. Antonio Gramsci, *Letters from Prison*, selected, translated from the Italian, and introduced by Lynne Lawner (New York: Harper and Row, Harper Colophon Book, 1975, copyright 1973), 245.

15. For an exploration of female and male ways of reading, see Annette Kolodny, "A Map for Rereading: Or, Gender and the Interpretation of Literary Texts," *New Literary History* 11:3 (Spring 1980): 451–67.

16. I am, I hope with reasonable justice, taking this argument from Wolfgang Iser, "Indeterminacy and the Reader's Response in Prose Fiction," *Aspects of Narrative: Selected Papers from the English Institute*, ed. J. Hillis Miller (New York: Columbia University Press, 1971), 1–45. For a synthesis of feminist and reader response criticism, see Judith Fetterly, *The Resisting Reader* (Bloomington: Indiana University Press, 1978).

17. For helpful comments about the New Woman and recent studies of the literature about her, see Nina Auerbach, "Feminist Criticism Reviewed," *Gender and Literary Voice*, ed. Janet Todd (New York: Holmes and Meier Publishers, Inc., 1980), 258–68. See, too, Elaine Showalter, *A Literature of Their Own* (Princeton: Princeton University press, 1977), 182–87.

18. The best-known feminist Utopia is Charlotte Perkins Gilman, *Herland*, first published in 1915 and reissued in 1979 (New York: Pantheon Press), with an introduction by Ann J. Lane.

19. The phrase *feminist polemic* is from Moira Ferguson, Department of English, University of Nebraska/Lincoln. See, too, Joan Kelly, *Women, History and Theory* (Chicago: University of Chicago Press, 1984), 65–109.

20. Hurston is almost the coeval of Richard Wright (1908–1960), an observation that I am grateful to W.W. Cook for making. I will be quoting from the following texts: Louisa May Alcott, *Work*, introduction by Sarah Elbert (New York: Schocken Books, 1977), 125. Jean Fagan Yellin, "From *Success to Experience*: Louisa May Alcott's *Work*," *Massachusetts Review* 21:3 (Fall 1980): 527–39 (a good exegesis); Alix Kates Shulman, *Burning Questions* (New York: Alfred A. Knopf, 1978), 14; "Sweat," *I Love Myself When I'm Laughing . . . And Then Again When I Am Looking Mean and Impressive: A Zora Neale Hurston Reader*, ed. Alice Walker (Old Westbury, N.Y.: Feminist Press, 1979), 197–207.

15. A Welcome Treaty: The Humanities in Everyday Life

1. *Against Mediocrity: The Humanities in America's High Schools*, ed. Chester E. Finn, Jr., Diane Ravitch, and Robert T. Fancher (New York: Holmes and Meier, 1984), is a recent collection about humanities in the classroom. See, too, *Priorities for the Humanities: A Report*, from the National Humanities Alliance (September, 1984), which recommends "maintaining and enlarging N(ational) E(ndowment) for the H(umanities) programs of elementary and secondary education. . . " (p. 5). Occasionally, this subject has its own mind-dulling, eyeglazing earnestness. I once, for example, read about Project THUMP, i.e. "Teaching the Humanities Using Multi-Cultural Perspectives," in which high-mindedness and Disney seemed to meet.

2. Jane Austen, *Northanger Abbey* (New York: Penguin Books, 1972), p. 58.

3. Ralph Waldo Emerson, "The American Scholar" in Joseph L. Blau, ed., *American Philosophical Addresses, 1700–1900* (New York: Columbia University Press, 1946), p. 168.

4. E.P. Thompson, *The Making of the English Working Class* (New York: Vintage Edition, 1966), p. 12. *Ordinary People and Everyday Life: Perspectives on the New Social History*, ed. James B. Gardner and George Rollie Adams (Nashville, Tennessee: American Association for State and Local History, 1983), is an excellent introductory text.

5. For a skeptical response, by a historian of women, see Hilda L. Smith, "Women's History and Social History: An Untimely Alliance," *OAH Newsletter* (November 1984), 4–6. OAH is the Organization of American Historians.

6. Virginia Woolf, *A Room of One's Own* (New York: Harcourt, Brace and World, Harbinger edition, 1929), p. 47.

7. Robert L. Pattison, *On Literacy: The Politics of the Word from Homer to the Age of Rock* (New York: Oxford, 1982). In "Critics as Connoisseurs of Chaos," Geoffrey Hartman speaks of the tension between standard prose and "linguistic inventiveness" in ways that surprisingly parallel Pattison (in *Innovation/Renovation: New Perspectives on the Humanities*, ed. Ihab Hassan and Sally Hassan, Madison: University of Wisconsin Press, 1983, pp. 105–6).

8. National Endowment for the Humanities, *Insight* (September 4, 1984), pp. 1, 3. Stephen Miller, *Excellence and Equity* (Lexington, Kentucky: University of Kentucky Press, 1984), gives a history of NEH, though his interpretation of that history can be polemical.

9. National Endowment for the Humanities, *Eighteenth Annual Report* (1983), p. 6.

10. For a wonderful discussion, see the Fall and Winter, 1983, issues of *Critical Inquiry*, on the canon. Unfortunately, some people equate a commitment to "greatness" with "disinterestedness," a competence at "objective" thought, and a commitment to anything else with the stain of ideology, a competence at "biased" thought.

11. Mark Lilla, "Art and Anxiety: The Writing on the Museum Wall," *Public Interest*, 66 (Winter 1982), 38. A 1984 poll found that attendance at arts presentations rose between 1980 and 1984; attendance at art museums tended to remain stable, or fall slightly. Douglas C. McGill, "More Americans Attend the Arts," *New York Times* (December 4, 1984), C-17.

12. M. Stevens, *New Yorker* (November 19, 1984), p. 45.

13. The Association of American Colleges did the survey. My figures are from a summary in National Endowment for the Humanities, *Humanities Highlights*, V, 3 (April, 25, 1984).

14. Two helpful introductions to the process of bringing together history and film are "Historians and Filmmakers: Toward Collaboration," ed. Barbara Abrash and Janet Sternburg (New York: Institute for Research on History, Occasional Paper No. 2, 432 Park Avenue South, New York, New York 10016, 1983), and Carlos E. Cortes, "Historians and the Media: Revising the Societal Curriculum of Ethnicity," *Federation Reports*, IV, 1 (January/February 1981), 9–14.

15. Miller, *Excellence and Equity*, has more detail about the founding of the state councils. See, too, NEH annual reports, and issues of *Federation Reports*, once the journal of the National Federation of State Humanities Councils.

16. Daniel Callahan, "The Humanities and Public Policy," *The Public Humanities: An Old Role in Contemporary Perspective*, ed. R.S. French and J.D. Moreno (Washington, D.C.: The George Washington University, 1984), pp. 34–35. The collection of essays as a whole is informative. Callahan's three activities have expanded into a larger field, "applied humanities." See Hastings Center, *On the Uses of the Humanities: Vision and Application* (Hastings-on-Hudson, New York: Hastings Center Institute of Society, Ethics and Life Sciences, 1984).

17. National Endowment for the Humanities, *Eighteenth Annual Report*, pp. 134–35.

18. National Commission on Excellence in Education, *A Nation At Risk: The Imperative for Educational Reform* (1983), p. 13.

19. Doing public programming often teaches the humanists themselves. In July, 1984, John Edgar Tidwell, of the University of Kentucky, spoke at a seminar that the Association of Departments of English sponsored in Park City, Utah. He described a series of programs of black poetry, "Poetry to the People," held in community centers. Because black literature, like Native American literature, brilliantly uses oral materials and street language, it shows everyday life exploding into the text. Tidwell, his Department of English, and the Lexington-Fayette Urban County Government helped to organize the programs with NEH funds. They were to increase university involvement in the community; to show the people of Lexington their own history; and to provoke their ideas about their experience. Unfortunately, attendance at the largely white community center was sparse. When I asked Tidwell if the "academic humanists" had to have special preparation, he said yes. They tended to talk down. He also said that his audiences had changed his mind about the black poet Paul Lawrence Dunbar. For they found Dunbar's dialect poets "entertaining," not "demeaning."

20. The quotes are from Steven Weiland, "Teachers, Truants, and the Humanities," *The Georgia Review*, XXXVII, 3 (Fall 1983), 497–98.

21. Helene Moglen, "Erosion in the Humanities: Blowing the Dust from Our Eyes," *Profession 83* (New York: Modern Language Association, 1983), 1–6 makes a similar point more fully.

22. In the 1980s, powerful voices have begun to argue that the federal government ought not to fund the arts and the humanities at all. See, for example, Edward C. Banfield, *The Democratic Muse: Visual Arts and the Public Interest* (New York: Basic Books, 1984). However strong these voices, they seem not to have yet shaped federal cultural policy.

23. From some parallel comments, see John Churchill, "The Humanities in Public Conversation," *Midwest Quarterly* (Winter 1985), 238–48, and the pamphlet, *Writers on Writers and Social Responsibility* (Amherst, Massachusetts: University of Massachusetts/Amherst, Institute for Advanced Study in the Humanities, 1983). The Massachusetts Foundation for Humanities and Public Policy, a state council, helped to fund the series that ended in this work.

16. NANCY REAGAN WEARS A HAT:
FEMINISM AND ITS CULGURAL CONSENSUS

1. John Berger, *Ways of Seeing* (New York, 1977), p. 46.

2. A irrefutable analysis of the intellectual price feminism has paid for forgetting women of color is Maxine Baca Zinn, Lynn Weber Cannon, Elizabeth Higginbotham, and Bonnie Thornton Dill, "The Costs of Exclusionary Practices in Women's Studies," *Signs: Journal of Women in Culture and Society*, 11 (Winter 1986): 290–303.

3. Nora Dauenhauer, "Genocide," in *That's What She Said: Contemporary Poetry and Fiction by Native American Women*, ed. Rayna Green (Bloomington, Ind., 1984), p. 69.

4. Arlyn Diamond and Lee R. Edwards, eds., *The Authority of Experience: Essays in Feminist Criticism* (Amherst, Mass., 1977). Elaine Marks, "Feminisms (sic) Wake," *Boundary 2*, 12 (Winter 1984): 99–10, offers a similar analysis, but far more subtle and elegant than mine.

5. Miriam Schneir, "The Prisoner of Sexism: Mailer Meets His Match," *Ms.* (Apr. 1986): 82. See, too, PEN American Center, *Newletter*, no. 58 (Spring 1986).

6. Ethel Klein, *Gender Politics: From Consciousness to Mass Politics*, (Cambridge, Mass., 1984), p. 104.

7. Gerald P. Jones and Carol Nagy Jacklin, "Changes in Sexist Attitudes Towards Women During Introductory Women's and Men's Studies Courses (unpublished manuscripts, 1986), p. 13.

8. Agenda items were: arts and humanities; battered women; business; child abuse; child care; credit; disabled women; education; elective and appointive office; employment; Equal Rights Amendment; health; homemakers; insurance; international affairs; media; minority women; offenders; older women; rape; reproductive freedom; rural women; sexual preference; statistics (the need to have information); women, welfare, and poverty. See National Commission on the Observance of International Women's Year, *The Spirit of Houston: The First National Women's Conference. An Official Report to the President, the Congress and the People of the United States* (Washington, D.C., March 1978).

9. See Catherine Reid, "Reweaving the Web of Life," *Reweaving the Web of Life: Feminism and Nonviolence*, ed. Pam McAllister (Philadelphia, 1982), pp. 289–94.

10. See E. Ann Kaplan, *Women and Film: Both Sides of the Camera* (New York, 1983), pp. 125–41. I prefer the term "feminist postmodernism" to "feminist post-structuralism" because the former more capaciously relates feminist thought to late twentieth-century inquiries about origins, hierarchies and power, and "the real" and to late twentieth-century social conditions.

11. Adrienne Rich, "Natural Resources," *The Dream of a Common Language: Poems 1974–1977*, p. 67.

12. Marianne Hirsch, "Review Essay: Mothers and Daughters," *Signs* 7 (Augumn 1981): 200–222, remains a solid survey of this 1970s development. The academic interest in mothering in the 1970s anticipated an increased practice of mothering in the 1980s. In 1976, only 58.3 % of the women in the cohort then in their twenties had at least one child. In 1986, 78.2 % of the women in that same cohort had at least one child. My various writings about women's studies and my essay, "Woolf's Room," cited above, map some of the differences among the theoreticians of women as women. One of the most significant is whether "woman" is social construct or more naturalized being.

13. Midge Decter, *The New Chastity and Other Arguments against Women's Liberation* (New York: Coward, McCann & Geoghegan, Inc. (1972; New York, 1973), p. 142.

14. See Rachel Flick, "The New Feminism and the World of Work," *Public Interest* 71 (Spring 1983): 33–44. See also Rachel Flick, "When Do Parents Grow Up?" *Public Interest* 68 (Summer 1982): 115–120.

15. See Carol Iannone, "Feminism and Literature," review of *The New Feminist Criticism: Essays on Women, Literature and Theory* by Elaine Showalter, *The New Criterion* 4 (Nov. 1985): 83–87. Elizabeth Lilla, "Who's Afraid of Women's Studies?" *Commentary* 81 (Feb. 1986), is more generous. She admits that women's studies comes in many forms, "from serious works of social history to overtly political ideology" (p. 53). But her story about attempts at Kenyon College to incorporate the new scholarship about women's studies into its curriculum tells the familiar N-C story about morally feeble administrators and intellectually feeble feminists who are still tough enough to indoctrinate the academy.

16. See Judith Stacey, "The New Conservative Feminism," *Feminist Studies* 9 (Fall 1983): 559–83. Although I am more sanguine about contemporary feminism than she; although I am more grateful to Jean Elshtain's warnings about the state than she, I am in debt to Stacey. For my own response to Friedan, *The Second Stage*, see my review "From Feminine to Feminist Mystique," *Ms.* Dec. 1981, pp. 16, 18, 21.

17. I owe the phrase "neo-liberal thinking about women" to Sara Lennox, during a seminar I conducted at the University of Massachusetts/Amherst, November 1985. Sylvia Ann Hewlett, *A Lesser Life: The Myth of Women's Liberation in America* (New York, 1986), exemplifies ambitious, somewhat historically suspect, N-L thought. See, too, Jan Rosenberg, "Hard Times for the Women's Movement," *Dissent* 33 (Fall 1986): 401–5.

18. Conference papers are in *The Future of Difference*, ed. Hester Eisenstein and Alice Jardine (1980; New Brunswick, N.J., 1985). Some of feminist postmodernism's most suggestive thinkers were present. In the past decade, inquiries into the meaning of "feminist postmodernism" have grown in several fields: literary theory, e.g., the work of Jane Gallop, Barbara Johnson, Peggy Kamuf, Nancy K. Miller, Naomi Schor; black feminist criticism, e.g., the work of Hortense Spillers; cultural theory and "Third World" studies, e.g., the work of Gayatri C. Spivak; film theory, e.g., the work of Teresa de Lauretis; psychoanalytic theory, e.g., the work of Jane Flax; history of science, e.g., the work of Sandra Harding. Some recent texts include Shari Benstock, "Beyond the Reaches of Feminist Criticism: A Letter from Paris," *Feminist Issues in Literary Scholarship*, ed. Benstock (Bloomington, Ind., 1987), pp. 7–29; Teresa de Lauretis, ed., *Feminist Studies/Critical Studies* (Bloomington, Ind., 1986); Sandra Harding, *The Science Question in Feminism* (Ithaca, N.Y., 1986); Donna Haraway, "A Manifesto for Cyborgs: Science, Technology, and Socialist Feminism in the 1980s," *Socialist Review* 80 (Mar./Apr. 1985): 65–107; the poetry and theory of the HOW(ever) group, 554 Jersey Street, San Francisco, Calif. 94114; Alice A. Jardine, *Gynesis: Configurations of Woman and Modernity* (Ithaca, N.Y., 1985); Kate Linker, guest curator, *Difference: On Representation and Sexuality* (exhibition catalog, New York, New Museum of Contemporary Art, 1984); Elizabeth A. Meese, *Crossing the Double-Cross: The Practice of Feminist Criticism* (Chapel Hill, N.C., 1986). The name Alice returns again and again among the postmodernist feminists—Alice Jardine, Alice in Wonderland, Alice B. Toklas—as if it were a substitute for Adam in the feminist process of beginning, again and again.

19. Lisa Tickner, "Sexuality And/In Representation: Five British Artists," in *Difference: On Representation and Sexuality*, p. 19.

20. *New Yorker* 20 Oct. 1986, p. 20.

21. See Mary Shelley, *The Last Man*, 3 vols. (London, 1826), 1:i–xi.

22. See Sandra M. Gilbert and Susan Gubar, *The Madwoman in the Attic: The Woman Writer and the Nineteenth-Century Literary Imagination* (New Haven, Conn., 1979), pp. 94–99.

23. Toril Moi, *Sexual/Textual Politics* (London and New York: 1985), p. 66.

24. See "Fact-File," *Chronicle of Higher Education*, 5 Feb. 1986, pp. 27–30.

25. No. 84–3147 in the United States Court of Appeals for the Seventh Circuit. On 24 February 1986, the Supreme Court struck down the Indianapolis antipornography legislation, which the "Amici Curiae" brief had opposed.

26. Lisa Duggan and Ann Snitow, "Porn Law Is About Images, Not Power," *Newsday*, 26 Sept. 1984, p. 65.

27. Carole S. Vance, "Pleasure and Danger: Toward a Politics of Sexuality," in *Pleasure and Danger: Exploring Female Sexuality*, ed. Vance (Boston, 1984), p. 23. The book originated in the 1982 Barnard Scholar and the Feminist Conference, as explosive conflict among various theories about the representation of female sexuality. The debate about pornography entered the mainstream feminist press in the April 1985 issue of *Ms.* On a red cover, white letters read, "Is One Woman's Sexuality Another Woman's Pornography?"

28. Nan D. Hunter and Sylvia A. Law, "Brief Amici Curiae of the Feminist Anti-Censorship Taskforce, et al. in the Uited States Court of Appeals for the Seventh Circuit, no. 84–3147, American Booksellers Association, Inc., V. William H. Hudnutt, III, et al., 8 April 1985.

29. See Attorney General's Commission on Pornography, *Final Report*, (Washington, D.C., 1986), 1: 769–72. I am writing a longer paper on the representation of women and gender in the Meese Commission report.

30. "Coming to Grief," review of *Never Guilty, Never Free*, by Ginny Foat with Laura Foreman, *Nation* 12 Oct. 1985, pp. 347–52. Ellen Hawkes, *Feminism on Trial: The Ginny Foat Case and Its Meaning for the Future of the Women's Movement* (New York, 1986), unravels Foat's self-defense persuasively.

31. Hawkes, *Feminism on Trial*, p. 363.

32. See Haraway, "A Manifesto for Cyborgs," p. 73.

33. Ibid., p. 101.

34. Sandra Lipsitz Bem, "Gender Schema Theory and Its Implications for Child Development: Raising Gender-aschematic Children in a Gender-schematic Society," *Signs* 8 (Summer 1983): 598–616, has influenced my thinking here.

35. "See Jim and Pat Cook. Jim Cooks First," *New York Times*, 13 March 1986, sec. A.

36. I wish to thank Marilyn B. Young and Gaye Tuchman for their years of instruction about the meaning of Cagney and Lacey.

37. Leslie W. Rabine, in her fascinating "Romance in the Age of Electronics: Harlequin Enterprises," *Feminist Studies* 11 (Spring 1985): 39–60, suggests that the popularity of Harlequins may lie in their dramatization of the "juncture between . . . [women's] sexual, emotional needs on the one hand and their needs concerning work relations on the other" (p. 39).

Index

Abel, Elizabeth, 127
Abolition movement, 11–30;
    anti-feminists in, 18–20; interracial
    sisterhood and, 20–27; women's
    suffrage and, 20–34; *See also* Slavery
Abortion, 46, 191
Academia, community colleges, 50,
    170; day care and, 46; humanities in,
    167, 170; male sexism in, 41, 46,
    182; NEH and, 175–177; racism in,
    30; women faculty ratios, 44; *See
    also* Women's studies
Adult education programs, 173
Advertising, domesticity in, 90
Ahistoricity, 87, 155
Alcott, Louisa May, 157, 160, 162
American Anti-Slavery Society, 18
American Anti-Slavery Women, 15
American Council for Learned
    Societies, 176
American Literary Anthology, 4
American Woman Suffrage Association,
    25
An American Dilemma (Myrdal), 11
*An Essay on Slavery and Abolitionism,
    with Reference to the Duty of
    American Females* (Beecher), 14
Androgynes, artists as, 93–94; as
    models, 54–61; as psychological
    hermaphrodite, 55–56; patriarchal
    bias and, 59, 61; Rich on, 148
Anger, female insubordination and,
    163; insanity and, 136; letters and,
    133; male outrages and, 94;
    sublimated, 158
Annales school, 168
Anthony, Susan B., 17, 21–23, 28
Anthropolitics, 156
Anti-pornography movement, 147,
    193–94

Antislavery movement. *See* Abolition
    movement
Antiwar politics, 162; *See also* Peace
    movements
Archives, letters as, 130–39
Aristotle, 47
Arnold, June, 99
Art, ahistorical realm of, 87; collapse of
    boundaries in, 168; conceptual, 142;
    degenderized theory of, 117;
    experience and, 182; federal funding
    for, 176; as intellectual alternative,
    75–76; of letter writing, 134; madness
    and, 136; masculinized creativity in,
    158; misconception of, 124; museum
    visits and, 173; performance art, 168;
    prophecy and, 4; romantic myths of,
    85
Association of Southern Women for the
    Prevention of Lynching, 31
Atwood, Margaret, 182
Audiences, chosen, 119–20; female
    reading styles and, 218n.15; literacy
    of, 169–70; as prophets/witnesses,
    151; Woolf on, 137
Aurora Leigh and Other Poems, 85–86
Austen, Jane, 127, 153, 166–67,
    171–72
Auteur epistolaire, 137
Authority, *See* Power; Subordination
*Authority of Experience: Essays in
    Feminist Criticism, The* (Diamond and
    Edwards), 181
Autobiography, biography with, 105,
    142; black, 4, 8; of consciousness,
    130
Autobiography of Alice B. Toklas
    (Stein), 105

Barnes, Djuna, 101, 110

Barthes, Roland, 98, 107, 189, 207n.15, 208n.3
Baym, Nina, 116
Beard, Mary, 185
Beckett, Samuel, 155
Beecher, Catharine A., 14, 17
Behn, Aphra, 67, 157
Bell, Angelica, 135
Bell, Clive, 133–34, 137
Bell, Vanessa Stephen, 134, 139
Berger, John, 180
Bernard, Jessie, 185
Bestiality, 138
Between the Acts (Woolf), 136
Birth control, 44, 98
Bisexuality, androgyny and, 54
Black(s), and black studies, 2, 168–69; castration of, 34–35; families, 16, 113; feminists, 119, 163; lesbians, 210n.27; liberation movement, 11–37; oral tradition of, 3; suffrage and, 20–22; vocabulary of literature, 12; women's studies and, 45; *See also* Abolition movement; Black literature; Slavery
Black Boy (Wright), 6
Black literature, categories in, 6; notions of identity and, 8; white expectations of, 1–2, 5; *See also* specific authors; works
Blackwell, Henry B., 27
Bloomsbury group, 130–37
Body, female language from, 145, 186; *See also* Desire; Pleasure
Bone, Robert, 2
Bontemps, Arna, 5
Bowen, Elizabeth, 138
Bradstreet, Anne, 88
Brenan, Gerald, 131, 138
Brontë, Charlotte, 85–86, 117, 156–58, 161, 189
Brontë, Emily, 85, 174
Brothers Karamazov, The (Dostoevsky), 196
Brown, Rita Mae, 107
Brownmiller, Susan, 114
Buchan, Susie, 135
Burning Questions (Shulman), 160–63

Callahan, Daniel, 174
Castration, of blacks, 34–35
Catt, Carrie Chapman, 29–30

Cave, metaphor of, 190–91
Cecil, Nelly, 135
Censorship, of lesbians, 99
Change, belief in, 148; partisans of, 160; personal vs. political, 61; violence and, 36, 42; *See also* specific movements
Children, abuse of, 111, 114; alternative parenting of, 111, 115 childrearing stereotypes, 32; day care for, 36, 47; guardianship law, 21; socialization of, 67, 144; *See also* Families
Chodorow, Nancy, 114, 185
Churches, *See* Religion
Citizens Organized for Better Schools, 195
Civil rights, 30, 149; Civil Rights Act (1964), 23; Civil War losses of, 21; cooperative goals of, 36; credit access and, 183; Equal Rights movement, 90, 122, 189; humanities and, 172; pornography and, 192; self-determination and, 17; sexual preference and, 57; *See also* specific movement
Civil War, 21, 162
Cixous, Hélène, 94–95, 185–86
Class, abolition movement and, 12, 26–27, 30; advantages of, 149; family form and, 187; women as, 155, 158
Cleaver, Eldridge, 1, 35
Cliff, Michelle, 142, 146
Clitoridectomy, psychic, 12
Coalitions, 168–169, 194; *See also* specific movements
Codes, lesbian, 99–100, 134; representational, 189; Stein's, 209n.10
Colette, 91, 126
Colleges, *See* Academia
Colonialism, 149
Colter, Mary Jane, 149
Commentary, 187
Committee on National Security, 183
Communities, of intimacy, 114; utopian models of, 60, 95, 108, 119, 125, 193; of women, 103, 147, 159, 162
Community colleges, 50, 170
"Compulsory Heterosexuality" (Rich), 146
Congenital invert theory, 101–104

Conrad, Alfred, 150
Consciousness-raising, 36
Conservatism, female, 26–27, 183–90
Continuing education programs, 173
Coriolanus (Shakespeare), 78
Correspondence, *See* Letters
Creativity, *See* Art; Literature
Credit, equal access to, 183
Criticism, *See* Feminist criticism;
    Literary criticism
Cultural feminism, principles of, 147
Culture, deconstruction of, 117,
    168–69; dualistic theory of, 166;
    feminist consensus on, 147, 179–96;
    material, 67–76, 158, 165, 171;
    politics and, 176, 182; preliterate,
    157; of resistance, 149, 182; social
    theory and, 124, 194; supportive
    context of, 162
"Culture and Anarchy" (Rich), 149
Cymbeline (Shakespeare), 81

Daly, Mary, 55
Damnation, narrative of, 98, 100–102
Daughters, Inc., 106
Daughters, mothers and, 108, 144–45
Davis, Rebecca Harding, 68, 71–72,
    74–76
Day care programs, 36, 46
Death, love and, 138; suicide, 139, 150;
    in violent conflict, 156
Death of the Author, The (Barthes), 189
de Beauvoir, Simone, 56, 92, 126
Deconstruction, in feminist criticism,
    117, 168–69; of mass media,
    195–96; *See also* Post-modernism;
    Post-structuralism
Decter, Midge, 186–87
Delaney, Samuel, R., 181
Deming, Barbara, 37
De Pisan, Christine, 160
Desire, defense mechanisms and, 186;
    religious, 161; sexual, 97, 99,
    135–38, 145, 161; in texts, 72, 155;
    See also specific works
Dickinson, Anna E., 26
Dickinson, Emily, 116, 127, 151, 171
Dickinson, Violet, 130, 135–36
Differences, *See* Sex differences
Dinnerstein, Dorothy, 111, 114
Discourse, closed circuit, 119; literal vs.
    literary, 137; modes available to

women, 94; phallocentric, 184; *See
    also* Language
Discrimination, *See* Equality; Racism;
    specific movements
*Diving into the Wreck: Poems
    1971–1972* (Rich), 93–94, 97, 145,
    148, 185,
Divorce, code of inequalities of, 114
Documentaries, as representations, 173,
    184
Domesticity, in advertisements, 90; art
    vs., 69; discontent with, 158;
    humanities and, 165; as middle-class
    ideology, 188; political writing and,
    74; redemptive, 150
Domestic workers, organization of, 36
Domination, 93–94; artist as witness to,
    75; by black men, 26; fear of violence
    and, 155–56, 161, 164; historical
    causes of, 164; identity and, 42, 121,
    155; representations of, 192;
    repudiation of, 162–63; slavery,
    11–30; speech and, 118; universality
    of, 91–94, 217n.1; war and, 156,
    162; by women, 181
Double standard, 158
Douglass, Frederick, 4, 14–15, 20, 23,
    25
Dreams, double meaning of, 71,78
DuBois, W.E.B., 12, 169
Duchene, Roger, 137
Dunbar, Paul Laurence, 5
Dworkin, Andrea, 193

Economic autonomy, 156, 161
Economic discrimination, 12, 36, 68,
    90, 189
Ecriture feminine movement, 152,
    208n.19; *See also* Language
Education, access to, 117, 156; elitism
    in, 39–40; expansion of, 167, 173;
    reform of, 44, 175; *See also*
    Academia
"Education of a Novelist" (Rich), 149
Egalitarian theory, 155
Eliot, George, 47, 85, 169, 191
Elitism, academia and, 39–40; racism
    and, 26–27; women's studies and,
    39–40, 52
Ellis, Havelock, 101, 103
Ellmann, Mary, 189
Elshtain, Jean Bethke, 187

Emerson, Ralph Waldo, 167
Emile (Rosseau), 48–49
Engels, Frederick, 15
Epistolier, 137
Equality, domestic life and, 114; economic, 12, 36, 68, 189; egalitarian theory, 155; Equal Rights Amendment, 122, 189; Equal Rights Association (1866), 24–25; male fear of, 68; of opportunity, 90; sexual discrimination and, 22, 91; See also Civil rights
Eroticism, bestiality and, 138; lesbian, 97, 99, 135–136, 145
Essay-writing, letters as, 134
Existential ethic, identity and, 107

Families, alternative forms of, 114–15; bourgeois forms of, 50, 70–72, 144, 187; limits imposed by, 112; national policy for, 113, 115, 188; patriarchy and, 82; slavery of wife and, 15; support of writers by, 157
Family Protection Act, 113, 188
Fantasies, punitive, 107
Fatalism, in texts, 159
Fathers, blocking force of, 137; power of, 143–44
Female(s), insubordination of, 155; mimetic power of, 184; sociograph of, 130–37; theoreticians of, 185; See also Femininity; Sex differences; Women
Female Anti-Slavery Society, 18, 23
Feminine Mystique, The (Friedan), 186
Femininity, androgynes and, 54–55; dictates of, 64; vs. female term, 84; See also Gender
Feminism, anti-slavery roots of, 15–30; as abstract issue, 182; black-white sisterhood, 27, conservative, 183–90; cultural, 147, 179–96; fragmentation in, 191; herterogeneity in, 195; historical roots of, 13; homosexual label and, 56; neo-liberal, 188–89; polemic, 120, 160, 218n.19; political consensus, 189; as political movement, 51; radical, 185; theological, 180; See also Feminist criticism; New Feminism
Feminist Anti-Censorship Task Force (FACT). 192

Feminist criticism, gynocritical tradition, 128; history and, 123–24; lesbian writers and, 97–110; study of sexual difference in, 118–19; women writers and, 116
Fiction, See Literature; specific works
Films, history and, 173, 184, 220n.14
Flick, Rachel, 187
"Floating Poem, Unnumbered, The" (Rich), 145
Foat, Ginny, 193
"For Ethel Rosenberg" (Rich), 147
"For Judith, Taking Leave" (Rich), 141–42
"For Julia in Nebraska" (Rich), 149
"For L.G.: Unseen for Twenty Years" (Rich), 142
Foucault, Jean Bernard Leon, 123
Foundations, sexism of, 41
Friedan, Betty, 182, 187
"From an Old House in America" (Rich), 149
From Housewife to Heretic (Johnston), 121–22
Fundamentalist theology, 186

Gage, Matilda Joslyn, 26
Garrison, William Lloyd, 19
Gay Liberation movement, 107
Gender, class and, 158; cultural consensus, 179; cultural feminism, 147; demands of, 90; genderlects, 118; language and, 125, 127–29, 189; sexual scripts and, 144–45, 156, 195; studies of, 168; subject's sense of, 189–90; transposition of, 182; See also Femininity; Masculinity; Sex differences
"Genocide" (Lorde), 181
Gilbert, Sandra, M., 191
Gilligan, Carol, 185
Gilman, Charlotte, Perkins, 108
Giovanni, Nikki, 8
Glasgow, Ellen, 149
Golden Notebook, The (Lessing) 91
Goldman, Emma, 161
Gordon, Kate M., 30
Gordon, Linda, 98
Gossip, 120, 137
Government, See Politics
Grahn, Judy, 141
Gramsci, Antonio, 118, 159

Grandmothers, 149
Greer, Germaine, 122
Griffin, Susan, 117, 141
Grimke, Angelina, 13–14, 16–19, 21
Grimke, Sarah, 18–19
Group, The (McCarthy), 105–106
Gubar, Susan, 191
Gynephobia, 146
Gynocritics, 117

Hacker, Marilyn, 141
Hall, Radclyffe, 100–105, 107, 159
Halleck, Sarah M., 20–21
Happiness of Motherhood Eternal
   (HOME), 186
Haraway, Donna, 194
Hardy, Thomas, 191
Harris, Bertha, 108–10
Hastings Center, 174
Hayden, Casey, 32
Heilbrun, Carolyn G., 55, 158
Herland (Gilman), 108, 125
Hermaphrodites, 54–55
Heroine, hybrid, 158–59
Herstory, 108
Heterosexuality, compulsion for, 144,
   146; *See, also* Marriage
"Hey Sailor, What Ship?" (Olsen), 70
Himes, Chester, 6
Historiography, 123
History, ahistoricity, 87, 155; American,
   3–4; construction of, 123–24, 196;
   fidelity to, 116; humanities and, 172;
   kinetic, 122; letters and, 130–37;
   private, 123; social, 168–69;
   women's tradition in, 185
History of Woman Suffrage, The, 13,
   18, 28
Homans, Margaret, 124
Homophobia, 58, 101–102, 159
Homosexuality, defined, 56; as
   deviancy, 97–98, 101; erotic writings,
   106; female, *See* Lesbians; as model,
   54–61, 181; as sickness, 101; threat
   of, 58, 100–102, 159; trade fiction
   and, 106; underworld of, 104
House of Mirth (Wharton), 67, 159
Households, nonfamily, 112
Howells, William Dean, 5
Hughes, Langston, 5
Hull, Helen, R., 105
Humanists, professional, 167, 175

Humanitarians Opposed To Degrading
   Our Girls (HOTDOG), 187
Humanities, adult education programs
   and, 173; applied, 220n.16; duality
   in, 172; purpose of, 176–77; state
   councils, 174–77
Hurston, Zora Neale, 160

Iannone, Carol, 187
Identity, black, 8; characters and, 159;
   denial of, 85; existential ethic, 107;
   female language and, 126; feminist,
   182; lesbian imperative and, 146;
   sexual vs. class, 82; in structuralism,
   189–90; subordination and, 155;
   vision of, 119
Imagery, sexual, 192–93
"Images, The" (Rich), 153
In A Different Voice (Gilligan), 185
Incest, 135; in media, 90; sublimated,
   80
Income, guaranteed annual, 36
Industrialism, Brontë, on, 158; civil
   rights and, 12; Olsen on, 67–76
Infanticide, 27
Insanity, voices in, 139
"In Search of Our Mothers' Gardens"
   (Walker), 169
Insubordination, female, 155, 163; *See
   also* Anger; Feminism
"Integrity" (Rich), 150
Intelligence, bias against women, 47–49
Interpretation, black authority of, 7; in
   modern texts, 155; *See also* Post-
   structuralism
Irigaray, Luce, 185–86
"I Stand Here Ironing" (Olsen), 74

Jacobus, Mary, 127
James, Henry, 88
Jane Eyre (Brontë), 162
Janeway, Elizabeth, 182
Jealousy, 80, 134
Johnston, Jill, 107
Johnston, Sonia, 121, 125
Jones, LeRoi, 7, 35
Jones, Lizzie, 149
Jordan, June, 146
Jung, Carl Gustav, 55
Justice, *See* Civil rights; Equality

Kahn, Coppelia, 82

Kanter, Rosabeth Moss, 114
Keene, Carolyn, 86
Kelly, Mary, 189
King, Mary, 32
Kinsey Report, 105
Kiss, as code, 99–100, 134
Klein, Ethel, 182
Knight, Sonia Sanchez, 35
Kristeva, Julia, 185–86

Labor, See Work
Labyrinth (Hull), 105
Ladies Home Journal, 89–90
Language, corruptness of, 124;
  cryptogramic, 127; of desire, 72;
  evasive, 114; of feminist critic, 116;
  French theory and, 185; genderized,
  125, 127–29; gossip, 120; identity
  and, 122; infidel heteroglossia, 194;
  literacy and, 170; magical power of,
  99; mimetic power of, 155, 184;
  minority, 3, 177–78; moral absolutes
  and, 186; official, 170; oral vs.
  written, 170–71; patterns of
  domination and, 120–21, 212n.19;
  poetic, 151; public histories of, 123;
  reality construction with, 94–95;
  reappropriation of, 152; referential
  power of, 125, 129; sexual
  differentiation and, 86; solitude of,
  119; study of, 95; treachery of, 131;
  vernacular, 170; wise women and,
  48; See also Narratives
Last Man, The (Shelley), 190
Laugh of the Medusa, The (Cixous), 94
Law, sexual difference, See Civil rights
"Leda and the Swan" (Yeats), 121
Leda Reconsidered (Van Duyn), 121
Lee, Don L., 9
Left Hand of Darkness, The (LeGuin),
  60
Legal rights, See Civil rights
LeGuin, Ursula, 60, 95
Lerner, Gerda, 185
Lesbians, black taboo and, 210n.27;
  codes and, 209n.10; congenital invert
  theory, 101–104; credibility of, 143;
  definition of, 97; feminist support of,
  183; informed criticism and, 109;
  legitimizing fiction of, 106–107;
  lesbian rule, 203n.7; masculinized,
  101–102; political, 56; primal female

bond and, 108, 144–45; realism and,
  105; romanticism and, 105;
  separatism issue of, 183–84; stigma
  of, 100, 109–110; Woolf and, 93,
  135–36; writers, 93, 97–110,
  135–36.
Lesbian Nation (Johnston), 107
Les Guèrillères (Wittig), 125
Lessing, Doris, 91, 159
Letters, consciousness and, 130; as
  genre, 133–34; public, 133; as
  sociograph, 130–37; of Woolf,
  130–39
Letter to a Young Poet (Woolf), 133
Levi-Strauss, C., 156
Lewis, Wyndham, 109
Liberals, neo-liberals, 188–89; virility
  cult of, 31–32
Life In the Iron Mills (Davis), 75
Literacy, access to, 117; anthropology
  and, 156; humanities and, 169–70
Literary criticism, anthropology and,
  156; racism and, 6–7; semiotics, 164;
  structure of human nature and, 95;
  See also Feminist criticism
Literature, black, 1–10, 220n.19;
  educational function of, 75–76;
  epistolary, 108, 137, 139; female
  insubordination and, 155; laws of, 6;
  lesbian, 97–110; middle space, 135,
  137, 139; mimesis, 155; political, 67;
  popular culture and, 166–67;
  required reading lists, 171;
  self-revelatory, 95; in social context,
  84–96; See also Feminist criticism;
  Women writers
Literature of Their Own, A (Showalter),
  124
Little Women (Alcott), 160
Llewellyn, Margaret, 135
Lorde, Audre, 141, 146, 180–81
Loss, risk of, 164
Love, charitable, 61; deromanticizing
  of, 141; equation of death and, 138
Lover (Harris), 108–10
Lowell, James Russell, 131
Lowell, Robert, 141, 152
Loyal League, 20–21

McCarthy, Mary, 91, 105–106
Maccoby, Eleanor E., 58
Macdonald, Cynthia, 182

MacKinnon, Catharine A., 193
Madness, as source of art, 136
Mailer, Norman, 49, 181–82
Making of the English Working Class, The (Thompson), 168
Males, control of sex by, 12; dependence of, 161–62; desire for the Female Other, 180; feminist views of, 182; masculinity of, 54, 58, 84; meaning of, xiii rivalry of, 46, 78–79; *See also* Gender; Sex differences
Marcus, Jane, 133
Marriage, code of inequalities of, 114; female sexuality and, 82; stereotypes in, 32; strains of, 141; woman as slave in, 15; *See also* Domesticity; Families, Marshall, Geoffrey, 171–72
Martineau, Harriet, 15
Marx, Karl, 171
Masculinity , vs. male term, 84; stereotypes of, 54, 58
Mass media, depiction of women in, 171, 184, 207n.14; feminist consensus and, 194–96; magazines, 89–90; Rich on, 152; social history and, 173
Masterpiece Theater, 174
Material culture, 67–76, 158, 165, 171
Maternal thinking, 114
Matriarchies, blacks and, 31, 210n.62; myths of, 108
Meaning, para-language, 3; semiotics and, 189–90; *See also* Post-structuralism
Measure for Measure (Shakespeare), 79
"Meditations on History" (Williams), 123
Menopause, 135
Menstruation, 135
Merrick, Carolyn E., 25–26
Metamorphoses (Ovid), 54
Metaphors, 103, 138, 143, 145, 149
Michel, Louise, 161
Milford, Nancy, 145
Mill, John Stuart, 47, 68, 86, 92
Miller, Isabel, 107
Miller, Jean Baker, 185
Millett, Kate, 122
Milton, 159
Minority groups, 177–78; *See also* Blacks
Miscegenation, 36, 79

Mitchell, Juliet, 188
Modern Language Association, 146
Modern Letters (Woolf), 133–34
Moi, Toril, 191
Moore, Honor, 146
Moore, Marianne, 59
Moral imagination, 172
Moral superiority of women theory, 42
Morrell, Ottoline, 133
Mothers, academic interest in, 221n.12; child relationship with, 144; daughters and, 108, 144–45; feminist consensus on motherhood, 184; HOME, 186; representation of, 185
Mott, Lucretia, 17–18, 20, 26
Moynihan Report, 31
Mozert, Robert, B., Jr., 195
Mrs. Dalloway (Woolf), 100, 136
Murry, John Middleton, 133, 138
Muse, women writers and, 88–89
Music, 165–66; black folk, 169; popular culture and, 165–66; *See also* Humanities
Myrdal, Gunnar, 11–12
Myth(s), of female writers, 85; historical, 3–4; of matriarchies, 31, 108; of Muse, 88–89
Mythologies (Barthes), 207n.15

Nachman, Elana, 106
Naming, 99; *See also* Language
Narratives, of damnation, 98, 100–102; of personal event, 182; silence in, 153; slave, 8
National American Woman Suffrage Association, 28
National Association of Colored Women, 28
National Endowment for the Arts (NEA), 176
National Endowment for the Humanities (NEH), 167, 171; funding for, 176; state councils, 174–77
Nationalism, black cultural, 7
National Organization for Women (NOW), 50, 65, 193
National Woman's Rights Convention (1866), 24
National Woman Suffrage Association, 25
National Women's Conferences (1977), 183

Nation At Risk: The Imperative for Educational Reform (NCEE), 175–76
Native Son (Baldwin), 2
"Natural Resources" (Rich), 143, 148, 185
Nature, metaphors and, 103, 145, 149
Neo-conservatives, 186–87
Neo-liberals, 188–89, 222n.17
Never Guilty, Never Free (Foat), 193
New Chastity and Other Arguments Against Women's Liberation, The (Decter), 186–87
New Criterion, The, 187
New Feminism, 65, 161; cultural consensus of, 179–96; divisions in, 147; ideal, 114; moral ecology of, 53; opposition to, 44–45; *See also* Feminism
Nicolson, Nigel, 132
Nightwood (Barnes), 101
Nochlin, Linda, 124
"North American Time" (Rich), 148, 152
Northanger Abbey (Austen), 166
Novels, *See* Literature; specific works

Of Woman Born: Motherhood as Experience and Institution (Rich), 149, 216n.13
O'Hara, Frank, 86
O'Keeffe, Georgia, 189
Olsen, Tillie, 67–76, 157
On Literacy: The Politics of the Word from Homer to the Age of Rock (Pattison), 170
Oppression, *See* Domination; Subordination, of women
Oral tradition, blacks, 3
Orlando (Woolf), 105, 135–36
Osborne, Dorothy, 134
Ostriker, Alicia, 60, 141
"O Yes" (Olsen), 67

Paley, Grace, 182
Paradise Lost (Milton), 48
Para-language, 3
Patience and Sarah (Miller), 107
Patriarchal Poetry (Stein), 117–18
Patriarchy, 93; blacks and, 12; families and, 82; public attacks on, 133; Rich on, 145; time and, 143; white liberals and, 31–32; *See also* Domination
Paul, St., 61, 113

Peace movements, 32, 183
PEN, 181–82
Performance art, 168
Perloff, Marjorie, 141
Phenomenology of Anger, The (Rich), 150
Piercy, Marge, 67, 95, 114
Pinktoes (Hines), 6
Place for Us, A (Miller), 107
Plato, 56, 113, 190
Plays, black, 10; miniature, 138
Pleasure, French theory of, 185; politics of, 192; *See also* Desire
Poe, Edgar Allen, 49
Poetics, female, 207n.12; of lesbian/feminism, 215n.6
Poetry, black, 5, 9–10; classical, 152; cognitive gift of, 144; feminist/lesbian, 141–54; nature metaphors in, 103, 145, 149; politics and, 148; prophecy in, 151
Politics, anthropolitics, 156; black revolutionary, 7; conservative, 183, 186–87; culture and, 182; feminist consensus in, 183, 194; gender and, 182; of humanities, 174–76; lesbian/feminist, 141–54; liberation movements, 11–37; neo-liberals, 188–89, 222n.17; personal reform vs., 61; poetry and, 148; women's studies and, 50
Popular culture, 166; Harlequin Romances, 223n.37; mass media and, 173–74
Pornography, 106; anti-pornography movement, 147, 193–94; civil rights and, 192; meaning of, 147; slavery and, 149
Post-modernism, aesthetic preferences and, 189; deconstructive gestures, 142; feminist, 184, 189
Post-structuralism, 125, 141; feminist, 117, 164, 188, 221n.10; on language, 125; on nature of signs, 141; mass media and, 195–96; vs. post-modernism, 189; wholeness of self and, 189–91
Poverty, women and, 68, 189
Power, distrust of, 39; sources of female, 155–56, 161, 164; victimization, 121
Prison Notes (Deming), 37

Prophecy, art and, 4; false, 152; kinetic history and, 122; letters and, 133; poetry and, 151
Prostitution, 36
Pseudonyms, 85, 158
Psychoanalysis and Feminism (Mitchell), 188
Psychoanalysis, 185; gender positions and, 189–90; revisionary, 188–89
Psychology, female, 127
Public Interest, 187
Public policy, humanities and, 174
Publishing industry, 156

"Queens of the Universe" (Knight), 35

Racism, black literature and, 1; feminist consensus and, 188; in poetry, 149; of white women, 4, 30, 34–35; women's liberation and, 11–12
Radicals, women's studies and, 41–42
Rage, *See* Anger
Ransom, John Crowe, 59
Rape, choice about, 121; feminism and, 128–29; as infidelity, 205n.6; meaning to women, 79–82
"Rape" (Rich), 121
Rape of Lucrece, The (Shakespeare), 77–83
Raverat, Gwen, 136
Raverat, Jacques, 132, 135
Readers, *See* Audiences
Reagan, Nancy, 179–80, 182, 196
Realism, in humanities study, 172–73; representations and, 181, 184
Rebellion, *See* Insubordination, female
Reform, personal vs. political, 61; *See also* specific movements
"Re-forming the Crystal" (Rich), 142
Religion, Conservative Christianity, 186; consolations of, 163; patriarchy and, 121–22, 158; women abolitionists and, 18–19
"Report from Inner Space: Seagoddes, muse" (Ostriker), 60
Representations, 117; cave as, 191; changes in, 181; defined, 179; docudramas and, 173; legal, 192; misogynistic, 180–82; political, 183–84; racial, 1–3; of subordination, 192; *See also* Art; Literature
Republic (Plato), 190

Rich, Adrienne, 93–94, 97, 114, 118, 121, 123, 141–54
Rich, Arnold, 150
Riverfinger Woman (Nachman), 106
Romanticism, lesbian, 105
Room of One's Own, A (Woolf), 55, 82, 92–93, 169
Rose, Ernestine L., 21, 26
Rousseau, Jean Jacques, 48–49, 117
Rossi, Alice, 187
Rubyfruit Jungle (Brown), 107, 109
Ruddick, Sara, 114
Ruffin, Josephine, 30
Rural isolation, 174

Sackville-West, Edward, 133
Sackville-West, Vita, 55–56, 132, 134–35, 138–39
Said, Edward W., 130
Sanday, Peggy Reeves, 155–56, 164
Sapphism, *See* Lesbians
Sarraute, Nathalie, 153
Schlafley, Phyllis, 120, 186
Scholarship, feminism and, 38–53; *See also* Women's studies
Schuster, Marilyn, 126
Science, post-romantic fear of, 49; Women's Studies and, 44
Scott, Ann, 50
Scripts, identity and, 190; sexual, 156
Second Sex, The (de Beauvoir), 126, 180
Segregation, *See* Racism
Self, autonomy of, 161; creation of, 190; post-modernism and, 161, 189–91, 194; *See also* Identity
Semantics, of biology, 128
Semiotics, cultural consensus and, 179; *écriture féminine* movement, 152, 208n.19; literary criticism and, 164; nature of sign, 141; post-modernists and, 189–90; *See also* Post-structuralism
Seneca Falls convention (1848), 13, 20, 23, 167
Separatism, black, 33, 35; lesbian, 184–85, 200n.55
Sex differences, ahistorical strength of, 94; fear of success, 203n.13; feminist post-modernism and, 184, 189, 195; language and, 126; in literature, 86, 91; mass media and, 89; middle-class

roles, 50; naturalness, 189;
neoconservatives and, 187; sexual
discrimination and, 22, 91; study of,
118–19; subjective sense of, 189
Sexology, 106
Sexuality, American, 12; death and,
103; imagery of, 193; inversion
theory of, 101–104; jealousy, 80,
108, 134; male, 142; meaning of, 90;
polymorphous, 114; representation
of female, 103, 192; Rich's theory of,
147; See also Eroticism
Sexual Politics (Millet), 52
Sexual revolution, as heterosexual, 98
Sexual roles, lesbian contempt for, 107;
work and, 63–64; See also Gender
Shakespeare, William, 77–83, 139, 171
Shelley, Mary, 190–91
Shelley, Percy, 190
Sherman, Susan, 141
Shirley (Brontë), 117, 158–59, 217n.5
Showalter, Elaine, 93, 117, 124, 187
Shulman, Alix Kates, 160–63
Sign, See Semiotics
"Silences: When Writers Don't Write"
(Olsen), 69
Sinister Wisdom, 142
Sister Gin (Arnold), 99, 107
Sisterhood, biological, 145; interracial,
27
Slavery, 4; anti-slavery organizations,
15, 18, 31; feminist identification
with, 12–14, 25–26, 33–34; parody
and, 123; pornography and, 149;
slave narratives, 8; See also Abolition
movement
Smith, Lillian, 31
Smyth, Ethyl, 131, 135, 137
Social history, mass media, 173; roots
of, 168; See also Culture
Socialists, feminist, 183
Socialization, 67, 89; See also Gender
Social satire, 139
Sociograph, female, 130–37
"Sonnet to Science" (Poe), 49
Souls of Black Folk, The (DuBois), 169
Sources (Rich), 150
Southern States Woman Suffrage
Conference (1913), 30
Space, female sense of, 135, 137, 139
Speech, male dominance and, 118. See
also Language

Stacey, Judith, 187
Standard English, 170
Stanton, Elizabeth Cady, 13, 15–16, 20,
22–24, 26
Stars in My Pocket Like Grains of Sand
(Delaney), 181
Star system, academic women and, 39,
52; poets and, 141, 151–52
State's rights, 29
Stein, Gertrude, 99, 105, 117, 141, 189
Stephen, Julia, 134
Stephen, Leslie, 137
Stephen, Thoby, 138
Stephen, Vanessa, See Bell, Vanessa
Stephen
Stephen, Virginia, See Woolf, Virginia
Stereotypes, racial, 1–3; See also
Representations
Stone, Lawrence, 82
Stone, Lucy, 27
Stonewall Resistance, 107
STOP-ERA, 186
Strachey, Lytton, 133
Structuralism, See Post-structuralism;
Semiotics; Texts
Styron, William, 4
Subordination, of women, See
Domination
Subversion, humanities and, 175–76;
writing and, 157; See also
Insubordination, female
Suffrage movements, Civil War and,
20–22; history of, 13; militant
feminists and, 20–34; racism in,
26–30
Suicide, 139, 150
"Sweat" (Hurston), 160, 163
Sybil, 190
Symonds, John Addington, 101
Symposium (Plato), 56
Synecdochial voice, 88, 92–93

Taylor, Una, 100
Technology, Women's Studies and, 44;
See also Industrialism
Television, See Mass media
Tell Me a Riddle (Olsen), 69–72, 76
Terrell, Mary Church, 28
Texts, audience of, 87, 92, 119–20;
codes in, 99–100, 134; female
insubordination and, 155; feminine,
85; genetics of, 142; homosexual, 97;

humanistic, 172; ideology in, 159–60; independence of, 124; letters as, 133–34; major historical, 171; mass media and, 89; meaning in, 159; mimetic, 91; realistic, 105, 160; romantic, 105; self-contradictory, 158; sexual differentiation and, 86; study of, 95; *See also* Literature; Post-Structuralism
Thelwell, Mike, 3
Theology, feminist, 55, 186
Thinking About Women (Ellmann), 189
Third World, middle class and, 42
Thompson, E.P., 168
Three Guineas (Woolf), 132–33, 194
Tickner, Lisa, 189
Time, feminizing of, 143; response to, 148
Titus Andronicus (Shakespeare), 78–80
To the Lighthouse (Woolf), 43, 93
"Toward the Solstice"(Rich), 147
"Transcendental Etude" (Rich), 146
Tropes, 138, 143; *See also* Metaphors
Truth, Sojourner, 18, 22–23
"Turning the Wheel" (Rich), 149
Twenty-One Love Poems (Rich), 144, 150

Uncle Tom's Cabin (Stow), 14
Unconscious, 185, 188–90
Universities, *See* Academia
Unlit Lamp, The (Hall), 100–101, 105
Up from Slavery (Washington), 4
U.S. Constitution, 11, 21–22, 25

Van Duyn, Mona, 121
Van Dyne, Susan, 126
Victims, blaming of, 194; of rape, 77–83; women as, 155, 193–94
Vindication of the Rights of Woman, A (Wollstonecraft), 117
Violence, black writers and, 8; domestic, 73, 111, 114, 163; representations of, 192; revolutionary change and, 36, 42; women's insubordination and, 155–56, 161, 164; *See also* Rape
Voice, infidel heteroglossia, 194; of patriarchy, 122; synecdochial, 88, 92–93; *See also* Language

Walker, Alice, 169, 185
Walker, Margaret, 118
Walkowitz, Daniel, 173
War, male dominance and, 156, 162; private, 163–64
Washington, Booker T., 4, 8
Weld, Angelina Grimké, 13–14, 16–19, 21
Weld, Theodore Dwight, 18–19
Well of Loneliness, The (Hall), 100–105, 107, 110, 159
"We Walk the Way of the New World" (Lee), 9
Wharton, Edith, 159
Whitman, Walt, 71, 75, 152
"Who Said It Was Simple" (Lorde), 181
Wife-beating, 114, 163
Wild Patience, A (Rich), 148
Williams, Sherley Anne, 123
Witness, artist as, 76; poet as, 151; as servant, 67–76
Wittig, Monique, 109, 125–26, 146
Wollstonecraft, Mary, 47, 85, 117
Women, average, 188; black analogies of, 33–34; conservative, 26–27, 183–90; cultural consensus of, 179; as focus of women, 185; literature of, *See* Literature; Women writers; movements of, *See* Feminism; neo-liberals on, 188–89, 222n.17; as Other, 192; primal bonds among, 108, 144–45; as readers, 87, 92; studies of, *See* Women's Studies; utopian representations of, 60, 95, 108, 125, 193
"Women" (Rich), 141
Women's Christian Temperance Union, 30
Women's liberation movements, *See* Feminism; New Feminism
Women's Studies, 38–53; categories in, 40–41; common beliefs about, 49–51; educational bias and, 47–49; graduate study in, 191; interdisciplinary, 43–44; internal dissension in, 39; national coalition for, 52–53; opponents of, 45–49; politics of, 39, 50–51; racism in, 221n.2; sexism and, 46, 182; social history and, 168–69; team teaching, 43–44; *See also* Academia
Women writers, 84–96; community of,

87–88, 92, 127; defiance of, 156; economics of, 156–57; female representation and, 117, 173, 179, 181–84, 191–92; feminist criticism of, 67–75, 116; letters, 130–39; models for, 137; personal vs. public lives, 142; postmodern, 192; realism and, 166–67; societal context of, 84–96; support for, 157; *See also* Literature; Texts; specific authors

Woolf, Leonard, 131, 134–35, 138–39

Woolf, Virgina, 43, 47, 55, 82, 88, 92, 99, 118, 130–39, 169, 194

Words, common language, 152; educational differences and, 157; *See also* Language

Work (Alcott), 160–63

Work, demeaning, 160; economic autonomy and, 156–61; equal opportunity and, 12, 36, 68, 90, 189; exploitation in, 73–74; survival and, 62–63

Wright, Richard, 6

Writing, *See* Women writers

Writing Degree Zero (Barthes), 208n.3

Wuthering Heights (Brontë), 174

Yeats, W.B., 120–21, 191

Yonnondio (Olsen), 67–68, 71–72

Young Women's Christian Association, 30